LEGAL RESEARCH AND CITATION STUDENT LIBRARY EXERCISES

Second Edition

To Accompany

PROGRAMMED MATERIALS ON

LEGAL RESEARCH AND CITATION

By

LARRY L. TEPLY

Professor of Law
Creighton University

AMERICAN CASEBOOK SERIES

St. Paul, Minn.
WEST PUBLISHING CO.
1986

COPYRIGHT © 1986

By

WEST PUBLISHING CO.
50 West Kellogg Boulevard
P.O. Box 64526
St. Paul, Minnesota 55164-0526

ALL RIGHTS RESERVED

ISBN 0-314-26685-2

PREFACE

One approach commonly used to teach legal research and writing is to provide students with some type of basic library exercises. Such exercises expose students to the primary research sources in a law library and give students practice in the use of search techniques for those sources. In addition, they are often used to teach students legal citation. Their pedagogical strength lies in their emphasis on learning through the actual use and citation of legal research sources in the law library.

From the point of view of many research and writing instructors, previously available library exercises designed for this purpose have suffered from a number of deficiencies. Those exercises have typically provided only ten or fifteen individual problems for each assignment. If a school's research and writing program were conducted on a large scale, too many students would often be seeking the same library resources, causing bottlenecks and stymieing the students' progress. Another difficulty has been that several students using those exercises have had the same answers for their assignments. As a result, students have been tempted to short-cut the learning process by finding other students who have already prepared their answer sheets. Furthermore, because corrected answer sheets have been readily "transferable," the desirability of re-using the same exercises in subsequent years has been diminished.

The library exercises in these materials differ in two significant ways. First, each of the exercises contains one hundred individual problems that are designed to spread the demand for books over more sources. In most instances, only a few students will be seeking the same volume. Second, the exercises use a problem number system. The students should be assigned an individual problem number that enables them to determine their particular assignment for each exercise. Because the combination of problem numbers shifts with each exercise, the answer sheet overlaps between any two students is minimized. Furthermore, with six hundred individual problem numbers available for assignment, these exercises can be used for three years in a law school with the entering class of two hundred students without assigning the same problem number twice.

These materials are the result of several years of experimentation with various types of exercises. The selection of the forty-six exercises included in this second edition hopefully achieves a balance between the need to provide students with an exposure to the most important and most frequently used research sources and techniques on one hand and the need to limit the exercises to a reasonable number and to avoid unreasonable demands on the library collection on the other. For this reason, I have omitted exercises using the official version of the United States Code, the United States Code Service, the Federal Register, certain Shepard's Citation volumes, loose-leaf services such as United States Law Week, state constitutions, state administrative materials, municipal ordinances, special subject reporters, early treaties in United States Statutes at Large, the Congressional Information Service, certain periodical indexes, Supreme Court briefs and records, presidential documents, microforms, Uniform Laws Annotated, law dictionaries, English statutes, Canadian legal materials, and United Nations and other international organization materials. It should be noted, however, that most of these materials are illustrated and discussed in the Programmed Materials on Legal Research and Citation text.

Library Exercise 45 (WESTLAW) and Library Exercise 46 (LEXIS) provide students preliminary training in the formulation of search requests used in computerized legal research. These exercises, however, do not involve the actual execution of the research requests. For further training, other available training aids, such as WESTLAW for Law Students, are recommended.

Every effort has been made to make these exercises and the instructor's answer manual as accurate as possible. Nevertheless, because of inaccuracies in typing, developments in the law, changes in legal publications, or modifications in A Uniform System of Citation, errors may occur. I sincerely

iii

regret any inconvenience that results from these inaccuracies or changes in the library materials.

I wish to thank Vicki Simants, Carey McBreen, and Karen Duffy of the Creighton Law School secretarial staff for their accurate and cheerful assistance in preparing this second edition. I want to thank Mr. Ed Kovus in the Law School copy center for his untiring assistance in photocopying the material used to check the accuracy of these exercises. I also want to acknowledge the logistical support for this project provided by the Law School administration and library staff.

I am especially indebted to my current student research assistant, Holly Brown (Class of 1986) for her excellent efforts in preparing the final version of these exercises. I am also indebted to Debra Zorn (Class of 1986), Deborah Macdonald (Class of 1980), Bruce Clawson (Class of 1977), Susan Christensen (Class of 1982), and Catherine Dixon (Class of 1980) for their excellent efforts in preparing prior versions of these exercises.

L.L.T.

Omaha, Nebraska
April, 1986

GENERAL INSTRUCTIONS

The students should be assigned an individual problem number (a number from one to six hundred) that will direct them to their particular problem within each library exercise. In order to complete an exercise, the students should examine the instructions at the beginning of the exercise and then find their individual problem number in the six columns of numbers under the heading "Problem #," which identifies the particular problem within each exercise. For example, the instructions to the first exercise require that the students find a volume of the South Western Reporter Second and cite the name of the case that begins on each of the pages designated. For example, if the student was assigned problem number 344, the student would find the following entry:

Problem #   S.W.2d Vol.   Pages

1 170 236 344 485 592   693   (a) 129 (b) 285 (c) 481 (d) 621 (e) 640 (f) 850

This entry directs the student to volume 693 of the South Western Reporter Second. The student would find this volume in the library and would cite the names of the cases that begin on pages 129, 285, 481, 621, 640, and 850. The student would use the same procedure for each subsequent exercise. If a source needed to complete an exercise is unavailable or a change is necessary for some other reason, the student should use a different problem number for that exercise only.

Some of the commonly asked questions about the use of these library exercises include the following:

Do students retain the same problem number throughout the library exercises? Each student uses the same assigned problem number for each of the exercises.

What citation form should a student use? The exercises in most cases do not specify a particular form. Instructors in the course should designate the form they they want the students to use. In absence of specific instructions, the citations should conform to the rules set forth in A Uniform System of Citation. The students should not, however, include the subsequent history of a case in their citations unless they are specifically instructed to do so.

The Uniform System of Citation establishes two basic citation systems: one for memoranda and briefs (M/B) and one for law review footnotes (LR). Unless otherwise instructed, you should use Memo/Brief form as your principal method of citation. In addition, unless otherwise instructed, you should indicate the Law Review form in your answers unless (1) the only difference between the Memo/Brief and Law Review form is the underlining of the entire case name in the Memo/Brief form or (2) when the only difference between the Law Review form and the Memo/Brief form is the use of large and small capitals in the Law Review form (as opposed to ordinary of ordinary roman type).

How should italics be indicated in answers to the exercises? Unless otherwise instructed, italics should be indicated by single underlining.

What does a typical answer sheet look like? A student's answer sheet is simply a listing of the citations or other information required to complete the exercises that a student has been assigned. The student's name and problem number should be listed at the top right-hand corner of the answer sheet. Unless otherwise instructed, the students should not use a cover sheet or folder for their answers:

[Name]
[Problem # 344]

v

[The following case names are not the ones that are assigned and are given for illustrative purposes only.]

1. (a) M/B: Deviney v. State

   (b) M/B: First State Bank v. Gamble

   (c) M/B: Pearson v. Petroleum Equipment Finance Corp.

   LR: Pearson v. Petroleum Equip. Fin. Corp.

   (d) M/B: J.A. Jones Construction Co. v. Carrico

   LR: J.A. Jones Constr. Co. v. Carrico

   (e) M/B: Rosenblum v. Gibbons

   (f) M/B: In re Gwin

   LR: In re Gwin

How are problem numbers reassigned when a student encounters difficulty finding a needed book? The instructor in the course should designate a procedure for a reassignment. One possible procedure is self-reassignment through the addition (or subtraction) of a specified number to (from) your assigned problem number. For example, assume that your instructor states that if you cannot complete your assigned problem in an exercise for some reason, you should add 105 to your problem number and do that problem instead. Assume further that your assigned problem number is 344 and that you are unable to complete one of the exercises because a needed book is unavailable. You would add 105 to 344 and do problem number 449 for this exercise. In this situation you should clearly indicate on your answer sheet which problem number you used and the reason for the change, as shown at the top of the next page.

John Doe
Problem #344

1. (Changed to Problem # 449 - 693 S.W.2d not on the shelf.)

If by adding 105 you still have trouble, you should add 1 more. In the above example, you would do problem number 450. Note that you would use this new problem number only for this exercise.

Do the answers to the exercises have to be typed? In absence of specific permission or instructions from the instructor, the answers should be typewritten. Typewritten answers aid significantly in the speed and accuracy of correction.

Are students permitted to work together on the answers to the exercises? Unless otherwise stated, students should be permitted to discuss the assignments with other students; however, the final written work must reflect the student's own individual work. In any event, students will find that overlap of answer sheets for any given group of students will be minimal.

Should the student keep a copy of his answer sheet? Unless otherwise instructed, students should take care to retain the handwritten answers from which his answers were typed or a photocopy of his answer sheet. In case their answer sheets are misplaced, the student must be able to supply the instructor with copy of their answers.

L.L.T.

Omaha, Nebraska
April, 1986

TABLE OF CONTENTS

	Page
PREFACE	iii
GENERAL INSTRUCTIONS	v
TABLE OF QUICK-REFERENCE ABBREVIATIONS	ix

LIBRARY EXERCISES

1. Citing Case Names: Parties Cited, Omissions, Geographic Terms, Procedural Phrases, Business Firms, and Other Case Name Modifications — 1
2. United States Reports — 3
3. Parallel Citation of United States Reports — 4
4. Supreme Court Reporter — 5
5. Lawyers' Edition of U.S. Supreme Court Reports — 6
6. Early United States Reports — 11
7. Federal Reporter — 12
8. Federal Supplement — 14
9. Federal Rules Decisions — 15
10. Federal Cases — 16
11. Official State Court Reports — 18
12. West's Regional Reporters — 19
13. California Reporter — 20
14. New York Supplement — 22
15. American Law Reports Annotated — 23
16. Annotations in U.S. Supreme Court Reports, Lawyers' Edition — 26
17. English Reports, Full Reprint — 31
18. Law Reports — 32
19. West's Digests: Key Number Digests in West's Reporter Volumes — 34
20. West's Digests: Finding Cases from Known Topics and Key Numbers — 35
21. West's Digests: Descriptive Word Indexes — 37
22. Lawyers Co-operative's Digests — 43
23. Shepard's Case Citations: Subsequent History — 45
24. Shepard's Case Citations: Subsequent Treatment — 47
25. West's Words and Phrases — 49
26. Tables of Cases and Popular Name Tables — 51
27. American Jurisprudence Second — 53

28.	_Corpus Juris Secundum_ -	55
29.	Topic Method of Search in Legal Encyclopedias - - - - - - - - - -	57
30.	Legal Periodicals -	61
31.	_Index to Legal Periodicals_: Articles - - - - - - - - - - - - - -	63
32.	_Index to Legal Periodicals_: Case Notes and Comments - - - - - - -	66
33.	Texts and Treatises -	68
34.	Restatements of the Law -	72
35.	United States Constitution -	76
36.	_United States Treaties and Other International Agreements_ - - - -	78
37.	_United States Statutes at Large_ - - - - - - - - - - - - - - - - -	79
38.	_United States Code Annotated_ - - - - - - - - - - - - - - - - - -	81
39.	State Statutes -	86
40.	_Code of Federal Regulations_ - - - - - - - - - - - - - - - - - - -	88
41.	Federal Administrative Decisions - - - - - - - - - - - - - - - - -	89
42.	Federal Rules of Civil Procedure - - - - - - - - - - - - - - - - -	90
43.	Legislative History of Federal Statutes - - - - - - - - - - - - -	94
44.	_United States Attorney General Opinions_ - - - - - - - - - - - - -	97
45.	Formulating WESTLAW Search Requests - - - - - - - - - - - - - - -	98
46.	Formulating LEXIS Search Requests - - - - - - - - - - - - - - - -	99

TABLE OF QUICK-REFERENCE ABBREVIATIONS

NOTE: Page references below are to discussion or illustrations of reference in the Programmed Text (2d ed. 1986).

AD QUICK REFERENCES:

    ADMINISTRATIVE CITATION 1. CITE THE FEDERAL REGISTER (Fed. Reg.) BY VOLUME, PAGE, AND DATE. [AD 1] - - - - - - - - - - - - 261, 265, 268-70, 274

    ADMINISTRATIVE CITATION 2. CITE THE CODE OF FEDERAL REGULATIONS (C.F.R.) BY TITLE, SECTION, AND YEAR. [AD 2] - - - - 230, 232, 261-62, 264-68, 270-72

    ADMINISTRATIVE CITATION 3. CITE ADMINISTRATIVE CASES TO AN OFFICIAL REPORTER (IF AVAILABLE). [AD 3] - - - - - - - - - - - - - - - - - - - 272-73

    ADMINISTRATIVE CITATION 4. CITE ADMINISTRATIVE CASES BY THE FULL REPORTED NAME OF THE FIRST-LISTED PRIVATE PARTY OR THE OFFICIAL SUBJECT-MATTER TITLE. OMIT ALL PROCEDURAL PHRASES. [AD 4] - - - - - - - - - - - - - 272-73

    ADMINISTRATIVE CITATION 5. CITE EXECUTIVE ORDERS, PRESIDENTIAL PROCLAMATIONS, AND REORGANIZATION PLANS TO THE CODE OF FEDERAL REGULATIONS, IF THEREIN. OTHERWISE, CITE THEM TO THE FEDERAL REGISTER. GIVE A PARALLEL CITATION TO THE UNITED STATES CODE WHENEVER POSSIBLE. [AD 5] - - - - - - 274

    ADMINISTRATIVE CITATION 6. CITE ATTORNEY GENERAL OPINIONS BY VOLUME, PAGE, AND DATE. USE THE ABBREVIATION "Op. Att'y Gen." [AD 6] - - - - 286-87

ANNOT QUICK REFERENCES:

    ANNOTATION CITATION 1. CITE AN ANNOTATION (ABBREVIATED "ANNOT.") BY A.L.R. VOLUME, PAGE, AND A.L.R. PUBLICATION DATE. DO NOT INCLUDE THE NAME OF THE AUTHOR OR THE TITLE. [ANNOT 1] - - - - - - - - - - - - - - - 111-12, 119

    ANNOTATION CITATION 2. DO NOT INCLUDE A PARALLEL REFERENCE TO THE A.L.R. EVEN THOUGH THE CASE IS REPORTED IN THAT SERIES. [ANNOT 2] - - - - - 112, 120

BK QUICK REFERENCES:

    BOOK CITATION 1. IN ABSENCE OF SPECIAL RULES, CITE TEXTS, TREATISES, AND OTHER BOOKS BY THE AUTHOR'S LAST NAME AND AT LEAST THE AUTHOR'S FIRST INITIAL; THE TITLE; THE SERIAL NUMBER (IF ANY); THE PAGE, SECTION, OR PARAGRAPH (IF A SPECIFIC PART OF THE VOLUME IS CITED); THE EDITION (IF MORE THAN ONE); AND THE YEAR OF PUBLICATION. [BK 1] - 192, 195

    BOOK CITATION 2. BEGIN THE CITATION OF A BOOK WITH THE VOLUME NUMBER IF THERE IS MORE THAN ONE, AND INCLUDE THE EDITION IF THERE IS MORE THAN ONE. [BK 2] - 192, 195

    BOOK CITATION 3. USE USOC-REQUIRED SPECIAL FORMS FOR A FEW FREQUENTLY CITED WORKS, ESSAYS IN COLLECTION, INSTITUTIONAL AUTHORS, AND TREATISES PUBLISHED PRIOR TO 1870. [BK 3] - - - - - - - - - - - - - - - - - - - 192-93

    BOOK CITATION 4. IN BRIEFS AND MEMORANDA, UNDERSCORE (ITALICIZE) THE TITLE OF THE BOOK. IN LAW REVIEW FOOTNOTES, PLACE THE AUTHOR'S NAME AND THE TITLE OF THE BOOK IN LARGE AND SMALL CAPITALS. [BK 4] - - - - - - - 193, 195

BRIEF/REC QUICK REFERENCES

    BRIEF AND RECORD CITATION 1. CITE BRIEFS AND RECORDS AS DESIGNATED ON THE DOCUMENT, FOLLOWED BY A CITATION TO THE CASE TO WHICH IT RELATES. [BRIEF/REC 1] - 291-94

    BRIEF AND RECORD CITATION 2. THE CASE NAME MAY BE OMITTED IF THE REFERENCE IS CLEAR OR A SHORT FORM OF THE CASE NAME MAY BE USED. [BRIEF/REC 2] - 292

CH QUICK REFERENCES

CASE HISTORY 1. DO NOT INDICATE THE PRIOR HISTORY OF A CASE UNLESS IT IS SIGNIFICANT TO THE POINT FOR WHICH THE CASE IS CITED OR IT IS NEEDED TO ADD CLARITY TO A CITATION. [CH 1] - 162

CASE HISTORY 2. ALWAYS SHOW THE SUBSEQUENT HISTORY OF A CASE, EXCEPT FOR DENIALS OF REHEARING AND THE HISTORY ON REMAND. [CH 2] - - - - 162, 166, 168

CASE HISTORY 3. USE ITALICIZED EXPLANATORY PHRASES TO APPEND THE PRIOR OR SUBSEQUENT HISTORY TO THE PRIMARY CITATION. [CH 3] - - - - - - - 162, 166

CASE HISTORY 4. THE YEAR OF DECISION SHOULD BE INCLUDED ONLY WITH THE LAST CITED DECISION WHEN SEVERAL DECISIONS WITHIN THE SAME YEAR ARE CITED. IF THE EXACT DATE IS REQUIRED, HOWEVER, BOTH DATES SHOULD BE INCLUDED. [CH 4] - 162-63, 166, 168

CASE HISTORY 5. WHEN THE NAME OF THE CASE DIFFERS IN PRIOR OR SUBSEQUENT HISTORY, USE BOTH NAMES IN THE CITATION UNLESS THE SECOND NAME MERELY REVERSES THE PARTIES' NAMES OR THE DIFFERENCE IN NAMES OCCURS IN A CITATION TO A DENIAL OF A WRIT OF CERTIORARI OR A REHEARING. [CH 5] - - - - - - - - - - - - - 166

CN QUICK REFERENCES

CASE NAME 1. CITE THE FIRST-LISTED ACTION ONLY. [CN 1] - - - - - - 18

CASE NAME 2. CITE THE FIRST-LISTED PARTY ON EACH SIDE OF THE CASE. - 18 [CN 2]

CASE NAME 3. OMIT WORDS INDICATING MULTIPLE PARTIES. [CN 3] - 18, 29-32, 35

CASE NAME 4. OMIT ALTERNATIVE NAMES GIVEN FOR A PARTY. [CN 4] - 18-19, 30, 34

CASE NAME 5. OMIT TERMS THAT DESCRIBE A PARTY THAT HAS BEEN ALREADY NAMED. [CN 5] - 19, 29-30, 33-34

CASE NAME 6. "COMMISSIONER OF INTERNAL REVENUE" SHOULD BE CITED AS "COMMISSIONER." [CN 6] - 19, 30, 34

CASE NAME 7. DO NOT OMIT ANY PORTION OF A PARTNERSHIP NAME. [CN 7] - 19

CASE NAME 8. DO NOT OMIT THE FIRST-LISTED RELATOR. [CN 8] - 19, 23, 31, 35

CASE NAME 9. DO NOT ALTER THE ORDER OF A PARTY'S NAME GIVEN AT THE BEGINNING OF THE OFFICIAL REPORTER. [CN 9] - - - - - - - - - - 19-20, 31, 35

CASE NAME 10. EXCEPT IN CITING CERTAIN FOREIGN NAMES AND BUSINESS FIRMS, GIVEN NAMES AND INITIALS OF INDIVIDUALS ORDINARILY SHOULD BE OMITTED. [CN 10] - 20, 29, 33

CASE NAME 11. SPECIAL RULES APPLY TO FOREIGN NAMES. [CN 11] - - - - 20
  (a) Chinese, Korean, and Similar Names   [CN 11(a)] - - - - - 20, 31, 35
  (b) Spanish and Portuguese Names   [CN 11(b)] - - - - - - - - 20, 31, 35

CASE NAME 12. RETAIN GIVEN NAMES AND INITIALS IN DESIGNATIONS OF BUSINESS FIRMS (CORPORATE OR PARTNERSHIP NAMES). [CN 12] 20, 25, 30-31, 33-34

CASE NAME 13. OMIT "INC," "LTD.," AND SIMILAR TERMS WHEN THE CITED NAME ALSO CONTAINS "CO.," "BROS.," "ASS'N," OR SIMILAR TERMS THAT CLEARLY INDICATE THAT THE PARTY IS A BUSINESS FIRM. [CN 13] - - - - - - - 20-21, 31-32, 34-36

CASE NAME 14. OMIT "CO." WHEN THE CITED PARTY IS A RAILROAD OR RAILWAY COMPANY, EXCEPT WHEN THE FULL NAME IN THE OFFICIAL REPORT IS "RAILROAD CO." OR "RAILWAY CO." [CN 14] - 21, 31, 34

x

CASE NAME 15. SPECIAL RULES APPLY TO GEOGRAPHIC TERMS. [CN 15] - - - 21
   (a) <u>Prepositional Phrases of Location</u>
[CN 15(a)] - 21, 30-31, 33-34, 36, 94
   (b) <u>Geographic Terms Following "Town of," "City of," and Similar Terms</u>
[CN 15(b)] - 21, 31-32, 35, 89
   (c) <u>Geographic Terms Not Introduced by a Preposition</u>
[CN 15(c)] - 21, 31-32, 35, 89
   (d) "Of America" after "United States" [CN 15(d)] - - - - - - - - - 21

CASE NAME 16. OMIT "CITY OF," "TOWN OF," AND LIKE EXPRESSIONS WHEN THEY DO NOT BEGIN A PARTY'S OR RELATOR'S NAME. [CN 16] - 21, 22, 31-32, 34-35, 89

CASE NAME 17. OMIT "STATE OF," "PEOPLE OF," AND "COMMONWEALTH OF" EXCEPT WHEN DECISIONS OF THE COURTS OF THAT STATE ARE CITED, IN WHICH CASE RETAIN ONLY "STATE," "PEOPLE," OR "COMMONWEALTH." [CN 17] - - - - 22, 31, 34-35, 94

CASE NAME 18. SPECIAL RULES APPLY TO LABOR UNIONS. [CN 18] - - - - - 18
   (a) <u>Unit Cited</u> [CN 18(a)] - - - - - - - - - - - - - - - - 22, 32, 35-36
   (b) <u>Craft Designations</u> [CN 18(b)] - - - - - - - - - - - - 22, 32, 35-36
   (c) <u>Prepositional Phrases of Location</u> [CN 18(c)] - - - - 22, 32, 35-36
   (d) <u>Widely Recognized Abbreviations</u> [CN 18(d)] - - - - - 22-23, 35-36
   (e) <u>Other Modifications</u> [CN 18(e)] - - - - - - - - - - - - - - - - - 23

CASE NAME 19. OMIT "THE" WHEN IT IS THE FIRST WORD OF A PARTY'S NAME EXCEPT WHEN CITING A POPULAR NAME, THE NAME OF THE OBJECT OF AN IN REM ACTION, OR "THE KING" OR "THE QUEEN." [CN 19] - - - - - - - - - - - - - - 23, 30, 34

CASE NAME 20. SPECIAL RULES APPLY TO PROCEDURAL PHRASES. [CN 20] - - 23
   (a) <u>Omit Procedural Phrases When Adversary Parties Are Named</u>
[CN 20(a)] - 23, 102
   (b) <u>Omit Procedural Phrases After the First One</u> [CN 20(b)] - - - - 23

CASE NAME 21. IF NO NAME IS GIVEN IN THE OFFICIAL REPORTER, USE A POPULAR NAME OR "JUDGMENT OF [FULL DATE]" IN THE CITATION. [CN 21] - - 23-24

CASE NAME 22. A PARENTHETICAL MAY BE USED TO FURTHER IDENTIFY A CASE NAME WHEN SUCH INFORMATION WOULD BE HELPFUL. [CN 22] - - - - - - - - - - 24

CASE NAME 23. IN LONG CASE NAMES, OMIT WORDS THAT ARE NOT NECESSARY FOR IDENTIFICATION OF THE CASE. [CN 23] - - - - - - - - - - - - - - - - - - - 24

CASE NAME 24. ALWAYS ABBREVIATE "COMPANY," "CORPORATION," "LIMITED," "INCORPORATED," "NUMBER," AND "AND" IN CASE NAMES. - - - [CN 24] 24, 29-34, 36

CASE NAME 25. ALWAYS ABBREVIATE "ON RELATION OF" AND SIMILAR TERMS TO "EX REL." AND "IN THE MATTER OF" AND SIMILAR TERMS TO "<u>IN RE.</u>"
[<u>CN 25</u>] - 24, 31, 34-35

CASE NAME 26. ABBREVIATE A PARTY'S NAME WHEN THE FULL NAME OF THE PARTY CAN BE SHOWN BY WIDELY RECOGNIZED INITIALS (WITHOUT PERIODS).
[CN 26] - 24-25, 28-29, 32-33, 36

CASE NAME 27. DO NOT ABBREVIATE UNITED STATES. [CN 27] - 25, 29, 31-36

CASE NAME 28. WHEN INITIALS OF INDIVIDUALS ARE INCLUDED IN A CASE NAME, THE INITIALS SHOULD BE CLOSED UP. [CN 28] - - - - - - - - - - - - - - - - 25

CASE NAME 29. IN BRIEFS AND MEMORANDA, CASE NAMES SHOULD BE UNDERSCORED OR ITALICIZED, BOTH IN THE TEXT AND IN FOOTNOTES. [CN 29] - - - - 25, 31, 34

CASE NAME 30. IN LAW REVIEW FOOTNOTES, ABBREVIATE "RAILROAD" TO "R.R." AND "RAILWAY" TO "RY." [CN 30] - - - - - - - - - - - - - - - - - 26, 31, 34

CASE NAME 31. IN LAW REVIEW FOOTNOTES, ALL GEOGRAPHIC WORDS IN THE NAMES OF RAILROADS, EXCEPT FOR THE FIRST WORD, SHOULD BE ABBREVIATED TO THE INITIAL LETTER OR TO RECOGNIZED ABBREVIATIONS UNLESS THEY COMPLETE THE NAME OF A

STATE, CITY, OR OTHER ENTITY BEGUN BY THE FIRST WORD. CLOSE UP SINGLE
CAPITALS. [CN 31] - 26, 31, 34

    CASE NAME 32. USE THE <u>USOC</u>-REQUIRED ABBREVIATIONS FOR CASE NAMES IN LAW
REVIEW FOOTNOTES. [CN 32] - - - - - - - - - - - - - - - - 26-28, 29-36, 89

    CASE NAME 33. IN LAW REVIEW FOOTNOTES, FORM PLURALS OF ABBREVIATED WORDS
BY ADDING AN "S" INSIDE THE PERIOD (UNLESS OTHERWISE INDICATED).
[CN 33] - 28, 31, 35

    CASE NAME 34. IN LAW REVIEW FOOTNOTES, DO NOT ABBREVIATE THE FIRST WORD
OF A PARTY'S NAME, INCLUDING A RELATOR. HOWEVER, IT IS PERMISSIBLE TO
ABBREVIATE OTHER WORDS WITH EIGHT OR MORE LETTERS (NOT LISTED ABOVE) IF (1)
SUBSTANTIAL SPACE IS SAVED AND (2) THE RESULT IS UNAMBIGUOUS.
[CN 34] - 28-29, 31-33, 35-36, 89

    CASE NAME 35. IN LAW REVIEW FOOTNOTE CITATIONS, CASES (EXCEPT FOR
PROCEDURAL PHRASES) APPEAR IN ORDINARY ROMAN TYPE. PROCEDURAL PHRASES ALWAYS
APPEAR IN ITALICS (SINGLE UNDERSCORING). [CN 35] - - - - - - 28-29, 31, 33-34

<u>CON QUICK REFERENCES</u>

    CONSTITUTION CITATION 1. CITE THE U.S. CONSTITUTION BY ARTICLE, SECTION,
AND, IF APPROPRIATE, BY CLAUSE. ABBREVIATE "UNITED STATES" TO "U.S." AND
"CONSTITUTION" TO "CONST." [CON 1] - - - - - - - - - - - - - - - - - 202, 205

    CONSTITUTION CITATION 2. CITE AMENDMENTS BY ROMAN NUMBER. ABBREVIATE
"AMENDMENT" TO "AMEND." DO NOT CAPITALIZE "AMEND." [CON 2] - - - - - - - 202

    CONSTITUTION CITATION 3. IN MEMORANDA AND BRIEFS, CITE CONSTITUTIONS IN
ROMAN TYPE. IN LAW REVIEW FOOTNOTES, CITE THE NAME OF CONSTITUTIONS IN LARGE
AND SMALL CAPITALS. [CON 3] - 202, 205

    CONSTITUTION CITATION 4. CITE STATE CONSTITUTIONS IN THE SAME MANNER AS
THE U.S. CONSTITUTION IS CITED. [CON 4] - - - - - - - - - - - - - - - - - 291

<u>DIC QUICK REFERENCES</u>

    LAW DICTIONARY CITATION 1. USE THE <u>USOC</u>'S SPECIAL FORM FOR CITING LAW
DICTIONARIES. [DIC 1] - 291

<u>ENCY QUICK REFERENCES</u>

    LEGAL ENCYCLOPEDIA CITATION 1. CITE <u>AMERICAN JURISPRUDENCE SECOND</u> AND
<u>CORPUS JURIS SECUNDUM</u> BY VOLUME, ABBREVIATED TITLE (Am. Jur. 2d OR C.J.S),
TOPIC, SECTION, AND DATE OF THE PUBLICATION OF THE VOLUME (OR SUPPLEMENT).
[ENCY 1] - 174, 180

    LEGAL ENCYCLOPEDIA CITATION 2. IN CITING A SECTION OF A LEGAL
ENCYCLOPEDIA, ADD A REFERENCE TO THE PAGE NUMBER ONLY WHEN IT IS NECESSARY FOR
FURTHER IDENTIFICATION. [ENCY 2] - - - - - - - - - - - - - - - - - - 174, 180

    LEGAL ENCYCLOPEDIA CITATION 3. IN MEMORANDA AND BRIEFS, UNDERSCORE
(ITALICIZE) THE TOPIC CITED. IN LAW REVIEW FOOTNOTES, ITALICIZE THE TOPIC
CITED AND GIVE THE TITLE OF THE ENCYCLOPEDIA IN LARGE AND SMALL CAPITAL
LETTERS. [ENCY 3] - 174, 180

<u>ENG QUICK REFERENCES</u>

    ENGLISH COURT CITATION 1. EARLY ENGLISH CASES SHOULD BE CITED TO <u>ENGLISH
REPORTS, FULL REPRINT</u> (Eng. Rep.), IF THEY HAVE BEEN REPRINTED THEREIN. A
PARALLEL CITATION TO THE ORIGINAL NOMINATIVE REPORTER MAY BE ADDED.
[ENG 1] - 129, 133

    ENGLISH COURT CITATION 2. INCLUDE A PARENTHETICAL ABBREVIATION OF THE
COURT OF DECISION IN THE CITATION. USE THE YEAR OF THE TERM OF THE COURT IF
THE EXACT DATE OF DECISION IS NOT LISTED. [ENG 2] - - - - - - 129-30, 133

ENGLISH COURT CITATION 3. CITE ENGLISH CASES AFTER 1864 TO LAW REPORTS
IF THEY HAVE BEEN REPORTED THEREIN. OTHERWISE, CITE TO ONE OF THE UNOFFICIAL
REPORTERS AS SPECIFIED BY THE USOC. [ENG 3] - - - - - - - - - - - - - 130, 135

ENGLISH COURT CITATION 4. USE BRACKETS TO ENCLOSE THE YEAR OF A LAW
REPORTS CITATION WHEN SEPARATELY NUMBERED VOLUMES WERE PUBLISHED IN THAT YEAR.
OTHERWISE, DO NOT USE BRACKETS. PLACE THE YEAR OF DECISION, IF IT DIFFERS
FROM THE VOLUME YEAR, IN A PARENTHETICAL AT THE END OF THE CITATION.
[ENG 4] - 130, 135

ENGLISH COURT CITATION 5. INDICATE THE COURT OF DECISION IN CITATIONS OF
K.B., Q.B., CH., P., OR FAM. LAW REPORTS ONLY IF IT IS THE COURT OF APPEAL
(C.A.). FOR A.C. LAW REPORTS, INDICATE THE COURT OF DECISION ONLY IF IT IS
THE PRIVY COUNCIL. [ENG 5] - - - - - - - - - - - - - - - - - - - 130, 135-36

FED QUICK REFERENCES

FEDERAL COURT CITATION 1. CITE U.S. SUPREME COURT OPINIONS ONLY TO
UNITED STATES REPORTS IF THE CASE HAS BEEN REPORTED THEREIN. [FED 1] - - - 48

FEDERAL COURT CITATION 2. IN CITING U.S. SUPREME COURT DECISIONS TO
UNITED STATES REPORTS, OMIT THE ABBREVIATED NAME OF THE COURT, INCLUDING THE
GEOGRAPHIC JURISDICTION, FROM THE PARENTHETICAL CONTAINING THE YEAR OF
DECISION. [FED 2] - 49

FEDERAL COURT CITATION 3. WHEN PARALLEL CITATIONS TO U.S. SUPREME COURT
DECISIONS WOULD BE USEFUL AND A SPECIFIC DIRECTION TO FOLLOW USOC FORM HAS NOT
BEEN GIVEN, INCLUDE PARALLEL CITATIONS IN CITATIONS TO SUPREME COURT CASES.
[FED 3] - 49

FEDERAL COURT CITATION 4. IF PARALLEL CITATIONS TO THE THREE U.S.
SUPREME COURT REPORTERS ARE GIVEN, FOLLOW THE TRADITIONAL PRACTICE OF CITING
UNITED STATES REPORTS FIRST, WEST'S SUPREME COURT REPORTER SECOND, AND THE
LAWYERS' EDITION THIRD. [FED 4] - - - - - - - - - - - - - - - - - - - 49, 53

FEDERAL COURT CITATION 5. ABBREVIATE WEST'S SUPREME COURT REPORTER TO
"S. Ct." AND THE LAWYERS' EDITION TO "L. Ed." OR "L. Ed. 2d." [FED 5] 49, 53

FEDERAL COURT CITATION 6. USE THE STAR PAGING IN THE EARLY UNITED STATES
REPORTS VOLUMES IN THE CITATIONS OF OPINIONS IN THESE VOLUMES. [FED 6] - 53-55

FEDERAL COURT CITATION 7. INCLUDE A PARENTHETICAL INDICATION OF THE
NOMINATIVE REPORTER'S NAME AND THE VOLUME NUMBER OF HIS SERIES IN CITATIONS OF
THE FIRST NINETY VOLUMES OF UNITED STATES REPORTS. PLACE THE PARENTHETICAL
BETWEEN THE "U.S" AND THE CITED PAGE NUMBER AND ABBREVIATE THE NOMINATIVE
REPORTER'S NAME, AS APPROPRIATE. [FED 7] - - - - - - - - - - - - - - - 55, 57

FEDERAL COURT CITATION 8. IF THE YEAR OF DECISION OF AN EARLY SUPREME
COURT DECISION IS UNAVAILABLE, USE THE YEAR OF THE TERM OF THE COURT IN THE
CITATION. [FED 8] - 56

FEDERAL COURT CITATION 9. DECISIONS OF U.S. COURTS OF APPEALS SHOULD BE
CITED TO THE FEDERAL REPORTER. DECISIONS OF THE OLD CIRCUIT COURTS OF APPEALS
SHOULD BE CITED TO THE FEDERAL REPORTER OR FEDERAL CASES. BE SURE TO USE THE
PROPER ABBREVIATION OF THE FEDERAL REPORTER (F., F.2d) AND FEDERAL CASES (F.
Cas.) [FED 9] - 58, 61

FEDERAL COURT CITATION 10. CITE FEDERAL DISTRICT COURT OPINIONS TO THE
FEDERAL REPORTER, THE FEDERAL SUPPLEMENT, FEDERAL RULES DECISIONS, THE
BANKRUPTCY REPORTER, OR THE FEDERAL CASES SET IF THEREIN. BE SURE TO USE THE
PROPER ABBREVIATIONS FOR THESE REPORTERS: F., F.2d, F. Supp., F.R.D., Bankr.,
AND F. Cas. [FED 10] - 58, 61

FEDERAL COURT CITATION 11. CITE THE DECISIONS OF THE VARIOUS SPECIALIZED
FEDERAL COURTS TO THE FEDERAL REPORTER OR THE FEDERAL SUPPLEMENT IF THEY HAVE
BEEN PUBLISHED THEREIN. OTHERWISE, CITE TO THE APPROPRIATE OFFICIAL REPORTER

OR SERVICE. BE SURE TO USE THE PROPER ABBREVIATION OF THE <u>FEDERAL REPORTER</u> (F.2d) OR THE <u>FEDERAL SUPPLEMENT</u> (F. Supp.). [FED 11] - - - - - - - - - 58-59

    FEDERAL COURT CITATION 12. IN CITATIONS OR DECISIONS OF THE U.S. COURTS OF APPEALS AND THE OLD CIRCUIT COURTS OF APPEALS, INCLUDE A PARENTHETICAL INDICATION OF THE CIRCUIT AND DATE. BE SURE TO USE THE PROPER ABBREVIATION OF THE CIRCUIT (E.G., 1st Cir., D.C. Cir., Fed. Cir.). [FED 12] - - - - 59, 61

    FEDERAL COURT CITATION 13. IN CITATIONS OF FEDERAL DISTRICT COURT DECISIONS, INDICATE THE APPROPRIATELY ABBREVIATED DISTRICT AND STATE PARENTHETICALLY. DO NOT INDICATE THE DIVISION WITHIN THE DISTRICT. CLOSE UP ADJOINING CAPITAL LETTERS UNLESS THE SECOND CAPITAL LETTER IS PART OF A LONGER ABBREVIATION. [FED 13] - 59-60, 64

    FEDERAL COURT CITATION 14. INCLUDE THE APPROPRIATELY ABBREVIATED NAME OF A SPECIALIZED FEDERAL COURTS IN THE CITATION IF IT IS NOT INDICATED BY THE NAME OF THE REPORTER CITED. [FED 14] - - - - - - - - - - - - - - - - - 60

    FEDERAL COURT CITATION 15. DO NOT GIVE A PARALLEL CITATION TO THE ORIGINAL REPORT IF AN OPINION HAS BEEN REPRINTED IN WEST'S <u>FEDERAL CASES</u>. [FED 15] - 65, 70

    FEDERAL COURT CITATION 16. ALWAYS INDICATE WEST'S FEDERAL CASE NUMBER PARENTHETICALLY IN A CITATION TO <u>FEDERAL CASES</u>. [FED 16] - - - - - - - 65, 70

    FEDERAL COURT CITATION 17. WHEN CITING OLD CIRCUIT COURT OPINIONS IN THE <u>FEDERAL CASES</u> SET, INDICATE THE COURT (C.C.), THE DISTRICT, AND THE STATE PARENTHETICALLY. CIRCUIT COURT DECISIONS FROM THE DISTRICT OF COLUMBIA SHOULD BE CITED "D.C. CIR.," HOWEVER, NOT "C.C.D.C." [FED 17] - - - - - - 65-66, 168

    FEDERAL COURT CITATION 18. WHEN A SUPREME COURT DECISION HAS NOT YET APPEARED IN <u>UNITED STATES REPORTS</u>, CITE THE CASE TO THE <u>SUPREME COURT REPORTER</u> IF IT HAS APPEARED THEREIN. OTHERWISE, CITE THE CASE TO <u>UNITED STATES LAW WEEK</u>. [FED 18] - 75, 168

    FEDERAL COURT CITATION 19. THE ABBREVIATION OF <u>UNITED STATES LAW WEEK</u> IS "U.S.L.W." IN CITING A SUPREME COURT CASE TO THAT SERVICE, INCLUDE "U.S." AND THE EXACT ABBREVIATED DATE OF DECISION IN THE PARENTHETICAL. [FED 19] - - 75

<u>FS QUICK REFERENCES</u>

    FEDERAL STATUTORY CITATION 1. CITE STATUTES IN THE <u>STATUTES AT LARGE</u> BY NAME, PUBLIC LAW NUMBER OR, PRIOR TO THE 85TH CONGRESS, CHAPTER NUMBER, SECTION (IF APPROPRIATE), VOLUME NUMBER, PAGE, AND YEAR OF ENACTMENT UNLESS IT IS INCLUDED IN THE NAME OF THE STATUTE. [FS 1] - 211, 213-14, 217, 220-21, 229

    FEDERAL STATUTORY CITATION 2. USE THE FULL DATE OF ENACTMENT TO CITE UNNAMED FEDERAL STATUTES IN THE <u>STATUTES AT LARGE</u>. [FS 2] - - - - 211, 213-14

    FEDERAL STATUTORY CITATION 3. CITE THE <u>UNITED STATES CODE</u> BY TITLE, SECTION, AND EDITION OR SUPPLEMENT DATE. INCLUDE THE SUPPLEMENT NUMBER PARENTHETICALLY OF THE OFFICIAL VERSION OF THE <u>CODE</u> IF YOU ARE CITING IT. INCLUDE THE PUBLISHER'S NAME (West or Law. Co-op.) IF YOU ARE CITING AN UNOFFICIAL VERSION. [FS 3] - - - - - - - - - - - - 218, 220-21, 224-26, 233

    FEDERAL STATUTORY CITATION 4. CITE FEDERAL STATUTES NO LONGER IN THE <u>CODE</u> TO THE <u>STATUTES AT LARGE</u>. INDICATE PARENTHETICALLY THAT THEY ARE NO LONGER IN FORCE OR ADD A FULL CITATION TO THE REPEALING STATUTES, INTRODUCED BY "<u>repealed by</u>." [FS 4] - 218, 220

<u>KEY QUICK REFERENCES</u>

    KEY NO. 1. CAREFULLY IDENTIFY THE BASIC PROBLEM[S] BEFORE BEGINNING LIBRARY RESEARCH. [KEY 1] - 10

KEY NO. 2. AFTER IDENTIFYING THE BASIC PROBLEM[S] BUT BEFORE COMMENCING LIBRARY RESEARCH, ANALYZE THE SITUATION FROM A LEGAL VIEWPOINT BASED ON YOUR GENERAL KNOWLEDGE OF THE LAW:

(1) WHAT LEGAL SUBJECT AREA IS INVOLVED?
(2) WHAT SPECIFIC LEGAL TERMS ARE USED TO DESCRIBE THE PARTIES, PLACES, AND THINGS INVOLVED? AND
(3) WHAT SPECIFIC LEGAL ISSUES (IN TERMS OF THEORIES OF RECOVERY, DEFENSES, RELIEF, OR OTHER PROBLEMS) APPEAR TO BE PRESENTED?
[KEY 2] - 10-11, 14

KEY NO. 3. CHECK FOR ANY RESEARCH LEADS BEFORE BEGINNING LIBRARY RESEARCH. [KEY 3] - 11

KEY NO. 4. CHOOSE A LOGICAL STARTING POINT FOR RESEARCH. [KEY 4] - 11-12

KEY NO. 5. BE AWARE OF THE PROCEDURAL CONTEXT OF THE SUBSTANTIVE ISSUES BEING RESEARCHED. [KEY 5] - 12

KEY NO. 6. TAKE FULL NOTES ON EACH RELEVANT SOURCE BEFORE MOVING TO THE NEXT, INCLUDING ALL INFORMATION NEEDED TO CITE THE SOURCE. [KEY 6] - - - 12

KEY NO. 7. DEVELOP THE INITIAL RESEARCH BY CONSULTING CITED AUTHORITIES, OTHER SECONDARY-SEARCH SOURCES, AND PURELY SEARCH SOURCES. BE SURE TO UTILIZE PUBLISHER'S CROSS-REFERENCES TO OTHER MATERIALS. [KEY 7] - - - - - - - 12, 14

KEY NO. 8. DURING THE COURSE OF THE LEGAL RESEARCH, BE ALERT TO MISSING FACTS OR MISFORMULATED ISSUES. [KEY 8] - - - - - - - - - - - - - - - - - 13

KEY NO. 9. ALWAYS UPDATE. [KEY 9] - - - - - - - - - - - - - - - 13-14

KEY NO. 10. ADD SPECIAL REFINEMENTS TO MAJOR RESEARCH PROJECTS.
[KEY 10] - 13

LH QUICK REFERENCES

LEGISLATIVE HISTORY CITATION 1. CITE UNENACTED FEDERAL BILLS BY HOUSE OR SENATE NUMBER, CONGRESS, SESSION, AND DATE. IF POSSIBLE, ADD A CITATION TO THE PRINTING OF THE BILL IN THE CONGRESSIONAL RECORD. [LH 1] - - - - - - 276

LEGISLATIVE HISTORY CITATION 2. CITE THE CONGRESSIONAL RECORD BY VOLUME, PAGE, AND DATE. IF THE DAILY EDITION IS CITED, IDENTIFY THAT FACT.
[LH 2] - 276-77, 286

LEGISLATIVE HISTORY CITATION 3. CITE CONGRESSIONAL RESOLUTIONS ANALOGOUSLY TO UNENACTED FEDERAL BILLS. [LH 3] - - - - - - - - - - - - 277

LEGISLATIVE HISTORY CITATION 4. CITE HEARINGS BY THE ENTIRE SUBJECT MATTER TITLE AS IT APPEARS ON THE COVER, BILL NUMBER (IF ANY), AND SUBCOMMITTEE NAME (IF ANY), COMMITTEE NAME, CONGRESS, SESSION, PAGE, AND DATE.
[LH 4] - 277

LEGISLATIVE HISTORY CITATION 5. CITE CONGRESSIONAL REPORTS AND DOCUMENTS BY NUMBER, CONGRESS, SESSION, PAGE, AND DATE. DO NOT INCLUDE A PART OF THE REPORT OR DOCUMENT NUMBER THAT IDENTIFIES THE CONGRESS. ADD A PARALLEL CITATION TO THE UNITED STATES CODE CONGRESSIONAL AND ADMINISTRATIVE NEWS WHENEVER POSSIBLE. [LH 5] - - - - - - - - - - - - - - - - - - - 278-78, 282

LEGISLATIVE HISTORY CITATION 6. IN MEMORANDA AND BRIEFS, TREAT CONGRESSIONAL HEARINGS, DOCUMENTS, AND COMMITTEE PRINTS AS BOOKS (UNDERSCORE TITLES BUT PRINT AUTHORS' NAME IN ROMAN TYPE); CITE CONGRESSIONAL REPORTS THAT DO NOT HAVE AUTHORS OR TITLES IN ROMAN TYPE. IN LAW REVIEW FOOTNOTES, USE LARGE AND SMALLS CAPITALS FOR CONGRESSIONAL REPORTS DOCUMENT NAMES AND THE ABBREVIATION OF CONGRESSIONAL RECORD. [LH 6] - - - - - - - - - - - - - 277

LL QUICK REFERENCES

LOOSE-LEAF SERVICE CITATION 1. CITE LOOSE-LEAF SERVICES BY VOLUME NUMBER, ABBREVIATED NAME OF THE SERVICE AND PUBLISHER, SUBDIVISION, AND EXACT DATE. [LL 1] - 195

LOOSE-LEAF SERVICE CITATION 2. WHEN CITING A CASE TO A LOOSE-LEAF SERVICE, USE THE EXACT DATE OF DECISION. WHEN CITING UNDATED MATERIAL IN A LOOSE-LEAF SERVICE, USE THE DATE OF THE PAGE ON WHICH THE MATERIAL WAS PRINTED OR THE DATE THE SUBSECTION IN WHICH IT APPEARS WAS PRINTED. [LL 2] - - - 196

PC QUICK REFERENCES

PARENTHETICAL COMMENT 1. USE PARENTHETICAL COMMENTS TO PROVIDE READERS WITH ADDITIONAL INFORMATION. [PC 1] - - - - - - - - - - - - - - - - - - 36-37

PARENTHETICAL COMMENT 2. PARENTHETICALS NOTING THE WEIGHT OF AUTHORITY SHOULD PRECEDE OTHER PARENTHETICALS. [PC 2] - - - - - - - - - - - - - - - 37

PARENTHETICAL COMMENT 3. A PARENTHETICAL COMMENT MUST BE USED WHEN A CASE IS CITED FOR A PROPOSITION THAT IS NOT THE CLEAR, SINGLE HOLDING OF THE MAJORITY OF THE COURT. [PC 3] - 37

PARENTHETICAL COMMENT 4. ONE SPACE SHOULD BE LEFT BETWEEN ADJOINING PARENTHETICALS. [PC 4] - 37

PERIOD QUICK REFERENCES

PERIODICAL CITATION 1. CITE LEAD ARTICLES BY THE LAST NAME OF THE AUTHOR, TITLE, VOLUME, ABBREVIATED NAME OF THE PERIODICAL, PAGE, AND DATE. [PERIOD 1] - 181, 185, 190

PERIODICAL CITATION 2. CITE LONG STUDENT WORKS BY THE TITLE OF THE NOTE OR COMMENT WITHOUT GIVING THE STUDENT'S NAME. [PERIOD 2] - - - - - - 181, 186

PERIODICAL CITATION 3. SHORT STUDENT COMMENTARY ON RECENT DEVELOPMENTS MAY BE CITED WITHOUT DESIGNATION OR TITLE. [PERIOD 3] - - - - - - - - - - 181

PERIODICAL CITATION 4. CITE BOOK REVIEWS BY THE NAME OF THE REVIEWER. [PERIOD 4] - 181, 188

PERIODICAL CITATION 5. USE THE USOC ABBREVIATION OF THE PERIODICAL TITLE IN THE CITATION. FOLLOW THE GENERAL SPACING RULES IN USOC RULE 6.1(a). [PERIOD 5] - 181-82, 185-86, 190

PERIODICAL CITATION 6. IF A PERIODICAL DOES NOT HAVE A VOLUME NUMBER BUT IS PAGINATED CONSECUTIVELY THROUGHOUT THE ENTIRE VOLUME, USE THE YEAR OF PUBLICATION AS THE VOLUME NUMBER. OMIT THE YEAR DESIGNATION AT THE END OF THE CITATION. [PERIOD 6] - 182

PERIODICAL CITATION 7. IF EACH ISSUE OF A PERIODICAL IS PAGINATED SEPARATELY, CITE THE PERIODICAL BY THE DATE OR PERIOD OF PUBLICATION. OMIT THE YEAR DESIGNATION AT THE END OF THE CITATION. [PERIOD 7] - - - - - - 182

PERIODICAL CITATION 8. IN MEMORANDA AND BRIEFS, UNDERSCORE (ITALICIZE) THE TITLE OF THE ARTICLE. IN LAW REVIEW FOOTNOTES, ITALICIZE THE TITLE OF THE ARTICLE, AND CITE THE NAME OF THE PERIODICAL IN LARGE AND SMALL CAPITALS. [PERIOD 8] - 182, 185

PERIODICAL CITATION 9. ALWAYS CITE THE PAGE ON WHICH AN ARTICLE BEGINS AND OTHER PAGES TO REFER TO MATERIAL ON THOSE PAGES. WHEN YOU WANT TO REFER TO THE FIRST PAGE, REPEAT THE PAGE NUMBER. [PERIOD 9] - - - - - - - - - - 185

RESTAT QUICK REFERENCES

RESTATEMENT CITATION 1. FOLLOW THE SPECIAL USOC FORM FOR CITING RESTATEMENTS OF THE LAW. [RESTAT 1] - - - - - - - - - - - - - - - - 196, 199

RESTATEMENT CITATION 2. CITE RESTATEMENTS BY SECTION OR OTHER RELEVANT SUBDIVISION (E.G., COMMENT, ILLUSTRATION, ETC.). DO NOT CAPITALIZE "COMMENT" OR "ILLUSTRATION." [RESTAT 2] - - - - - - - - - - - - - - - - - - - 196, 199

RESTATEMENT CITATION 3. IN MEMORANDA AND BRIEFS, CITE RESTATEMENTS IN ORDINARY ROMAN TYPE. IN LAW REVIEW FOOTNOTES, CITE THE NAME OF THE RESTATEMENT IN LARGE AND SMALL CAPITALS. [RESTAT 3] - - - - - - - - 197, 199

RUL QUICK REFERENCES

RULE CITATION 1. CITE CURRENT RULES OF PROCEDURE OR EVIDENCE WITHOUT DATE. ABBREVIATE "FEDERAL" TO "FED.," RULES TO "R.," "PROCEDURE" TO "P.," "CIVIL" TO "CIV.," "CRIMINAL" TO "CRIM.," "EVIDENCE" TO "EVID.," AND "APPELLATE" TO "APP." [RUL 1] - 275

RULE CITATION 2. IN MEMORANDA AND BRIEFS, CITE RULES OF PROCEDURE AND EVIDENCE IN ORDINARY ROMAN TYPE. IN LAW REVIEW FOOTNOTES, CITE THEM IN LARGE AND SMALL CAPITALS. [RUL 2] - 275

SIG QUICK REFERENCES

CITATION SIGNAL 1. IN LEGAL WRITING, USE THE PROPER CITATION SIGNAL TO INDICATE THE PURPOSE FOR WHICH AN AUTHORITY IS CITED OR THE DEGREE OF SUPPORT THE CITED AUTHORITY GIVES TO A PROPOSITION. [SIG 1] - - - - - - - - - - 37-39

CITATION SIGNAL 2. PLACE THE CITATION INTRODUCED BY CITATION SIGNALS IN THE REQUIRED PROPER ORDER. [SIG 2] - - - - - - - - - - - - - - - - - - - 40

CITATION SIGNAL 3. CITATION STRINGS MAY CONTAIN MORE THAN ONE TYPE OF SIGNAL IN APPOSITIVE CITATION CLAUSES BUT NOT IN CITATION SENTENCES (START A NEW SENTENCE WHEN A SIGNAL OF A DIFFERENT TYPE IS USED). [SIG 3] - - - - 40

CITATION SIGNAL 4. SIGNALS OF THE SAME BASIC TYPE MUST BE STRUNG TOGETHER WITHIN A SINGLE CITATION SENTENCE. [SIG 4] - - - - - - - - - - - 40

CITATION SIGNAL 5. USE SHORT CITATION FORMS IN SUBSEQUENT CITATION OF CASES. [SIG 5] - 40

CITATION SIGNAL 6. IN BRIEFS AND MEMORANDA, USE ID. TO REFER TO THE IMMEDIATELY PRECEDING CITED CASE WHEN THAT CASE WAS THE SOLE ITEM IN THE PRIOR CITATION SENTENCE OR APPOSITIVE CITATION CLAUSE. [SIG 6] - - - - - - - - 41

CITATION SIGNAL 7. IN LAW REVIEW FOOTNOTES, USE ID. ONLY IN CITATIONS OF THE SAME CASE APPEARING IN THE IMMEDIATELY PRECEDING CITATION WITH THE SAME FOOTNOTE OR IN THE IMMEDIATELY PRECEDING FOOTNOTE IF THE PRECEDING FOOTNOTE CONTAINS ONLY A CITATION TO THAT CASE. [SIG 7] - - - - - - - - - - - - - - 41

CITATION SIGNAL 8. DO NOT USE SUPRA TO REFER TO PREVIOUSLY CITED CASES WHEN ID. WOULD BE INAPPROPRIATE. INSTEAD, ONCE A CASE HAS BEEN TEXTUALLY NAMED AND FULLY CITED, IT MAY BE REFERRED TO BY ONE OF THE PARTIES' NAMES (OTHER THAN THE NAME OF A GOVERNMENTAL LITIGANT) OR BY AN ESTABLISHED POPULAR NAME. A SHORTENED CITATION REFERENCE WITH THE RELEVANT PAGE NUMBER MAY BE USED. [SIG 8] - 41

SS QUICK REFERENCES

STATE STATUTORY CITATION 1. CITE STATE STATUTES TO THE CURRENT OFFICIAL CODE (IF AVAILABLE) OR TO A CURRENT UNOFFICIAL CODE, SESSION LAWS, ADVANCE SHEETS, OR OTHER SOURCE. CITE THE TITLE OR SECTION (AS APPROPRIATE) AND THE PROPER DATE. [SS 1] - 241, 250-51

STATE STATUTORY CITATION 2. USE THE PROPER ABBREVIATION OF STATE STATUTES AND INCLUDE AN INDICATION OF THE PUBLISHER WHEN APPROPRIATE. [SS 2] - 241-43, 254

STATE STATUTORY CITATION 3. INCLUDE THE APPROPRIATE SUBJECT-MATTER CODE WHEN RELEVANT. [SS 3] - 243, 253-54

STATE STATUTORY CITATION 4. FOR CODIFIED STATUTES, USE (IN ORDER OF
PREFERENCE) (1) THE YEAR ON THE SPINE OF THE VOLUME, (2) THE YEAR ON THE TITLE
PAGE, OR (3) THE LATEST COPYRIGHT YEAR. [SS 4] - - - - - - - - - 243, 250-51

STATE STATUTORY CITATION 5. IF THE STATUTE IS CITED TO A LOOSE-LEAF
SERVICE, USE (IN ORDER OF PREFERENCE) (1) THE YEAR ON THE PAGE OF THE CITED
SUBDIVISION IS PRINTED OR (2) THE YEAR ON THE FIRST PAGE OF THE SUBDIVISION
CONTAINING THE CITED PROVISION. [SS 5] - - - - - - - - - - - - - - - - 243-44

STATE STATUTORY CITATION 6. IF YOU CITE A SUPPLEMENT TO A COMPILATION,
YOU MUST INDICATE THAT FACT. [SS 6] - - - - - - - - - - - - - - - - 244, 254

STATE STATUTORY CITATION 7. IF YOU CITE A SESSION LAW, INCLUDE THE YEAR
IN THE NAME OF THE SESSION LAWS AND THE NAME OF THE STATUTE OR THE "ACT OF"
FORM. [SS 7] - 244

STATE STATUTORY CITATION 8. IN MEMORANDA AND BRIEFS, CITE STATE STATUTES
IN ORDINARY ROMAN TYPE. IN LAW REVIEW FOOTNOTES, SHOW THE NAME OF THE
STATUTORY CODES IN LARGE AND SMALL CAPITALS. [SS 8] - - - - - - - - 244, 254

STATE STATUTORY CITATION 9. GENERALLY, CITE UNIFORM ACTS AS SEPARATE
CODES. A CITATION TO WEST'S UNIFORM LAWS ANNOTATED MAY BE ADDED. WHEN A
UNIFORM ACT IS CITED AS THE LAW OF A PARTICULAR STATE, HOWEVER, CITE IT AS A
STATE STATUTE. [SS 9] - 254-55

ST QUICK REFERENCES

STATE COURT CITATION 1. CITE STATE COURT DECISIONS TO THE OFFICIAL
REPORTER FIRST (IF IT IS STILL PUBLISHED) AND THEN TO THE PREFERRED UNOFFICIAL
REPORTER OR REPORTERS. ALWAYS CITE THE OFFICIAL REPORTER FIRST.
[ST 1] - 77, 85-86, 88-90

STATE COURT CITATION 2. IF A RECENT DECISION HAS NOT YET BEEN PUBLISHED
IN THE OFFICIAL REPORTER, CITE THE CASE INSTEAD TO A CONTINUOUSLY PAGINATED
ADVANCE SHEET SERVICE (IF AVAILABLE). [ST 2] - - - - - - - - - - - - - - - 77

STATE COURT CITATION 3. IN REPORTER ABBREVIATIONS, CLOSE UP ADJACENT
SINGLE CAPITALS. TREAT NUMERALS AND ORDINALS AS SINGLE CAPITALS. HOWEVER, DO
NOT CLOSE UP SINGLE CAPITALS WITH LONGER ABBREVIATIONS. [ST 3] - 83, 94, 104

STATE COURT CITATION 4. IN CITING LOWER AND INTERMEDIATE APPELLATE STATE
COURT DECISIONS, A PARENTHETICAL INDICATION OF THE FULL ABBREVIATED NAME OF
THE COURT, INCLUDING ITS GEOGRAPHIC JURISDICTION, SHOULD BE INCLUDED IN THE
CITATION. HOWEVER, ELIMINATE FROM THE PARENTHETICAL ANY INFORMATION THAT THE
REPORTER TITLE UNAMBIGUOUSLY CONVEYS. [ST 4] - - - - - - - 84, 86-87, 89, 98

STATE COURT CITATION 5. DO NOT INCLUDE AN INDICATION OF THE SPECIFIC
DEPARTMENT, DIVISION, CIRCUIT, OR DISTRICT IN THE PARENTHETICAL UNLESS IT IS
OF PARTICULAR RELEVANCE. [ST 5] - - - - - - - - - - 84, 86-87, 89, 94, 96-98

STATE COURT CITATION 6. WHEN THE HIGHEST STATE COURT IS CITED, INDICATE
ONLY THE ABBREVIATED NAME OF THE JURISDICTION IN THE PARENTHETICAL. WHEN THE
NAME OF THE REPORT IS THE SAME AS THE NAME OF THE JURISDICTION, ELIMINATE THE
THE INDICATION OF THE JURISDICTION AS WELL. [ST 6] - 84, 86-87, 89, 96-97, 102

STATE COURT CITATION 7. FOR EARLY STATE COURT DECISION, CITE THE EARLY
NOMINATIVE REPORT AS REQUIRED BY THE USOC. [ST 7] - - - - - - - - - - 104-05

TREAT QUICK REFERENCES

TREATY CITATION 1. ORDINARILY, CITE TREATIES AND OTHER INTERNATIONAL
AGREEMENTS BY NAME, THE DATE OF SIGNING (UNLESS THE DATE OR YEAR IS INCLUDED
IN THE NAME OF THE AGREEMENT), THE PARTIES, AND THE SOURCES IN WHICH IT CAN BE
FOUND. [TREAT 1] - 205, 208-09, 210

TREATY CITATION 2. FOR THE CITED NAME, USE THE POPULAR NAME OF THE TREATY. OTHERWISE, USE A SHORTENED VERSION OF ITS NAME AND SUBJECT MATTER. USE ONLY THE FIRST FORM THAT APPEARS ON THE TITLE PAGE. [TREAT 2] - 205-06, 208-09

TREATY CITATION 3. IF THE TREATY WAS SIGNED ON A SINGLE DATE, USE THAT DATE. WHEN IT WAS SIGNED BY THREE OR FEWER PARTIES ON DIFFERENT DATES, CITE THE FIRST AND LAST DATES OF SIGNING. TREATIES WITH MORE THAN THREE SIGNATORIES SHOULD BE CITED TO THE DATE ON WHICH THE TREATY WAS OPENED FOR SIGNATURE, APPROVED, OR ADOPTED. [TREAT 3] - - - - - - - - - - - 206, 209-10

TREATY CITATION 4. INDICATE THE NAMES OF THE PARTIES WHEN THERE ARE LESS THAN FOUR. OTHERWISE, THE PARTIES' NAMES NEED NOT BE GIVEN. THE NAMES OF THE SIGNATORIES MAY BE SHORTENED. [TREAT 4] - - - - - - - - - - - - - 206, 208-09

TREATY CITATION 5. TREATIES TO WHICH THE UNITED STATES IS A PARTY SHOULD BE CITED EITHER THE STATUTES AT LARGE (PRIOR TO 1950) OR U.S. TREATIES AND OTHER INTERNATIONAL AGREEMENTS (SINCE 1950) AND ONE STATE DEPARTMENT SOURCE. A PARALLEL CITATION TO AN INTERNATIONAL TREATY SERIES SHOULD BE ADDED WHEN THE UNITED STATES IS A PARTY TO A MULTILATERAL AGREEMENT. [TREAT 5] - - - 206-210

LIBRARY EXERCISE 1. CITING CASE NAMES: PARTIES CITED, OMISSIONS, GEOGRAPHIC
TERMS, PROCEDURAL PHRASES, BUSINESS FIRMS, AND OTHER CASE NAME MODIFICATIONS.
The purpose of this exercise is to give you practice in citing case names in
proper form. To complete this exercise, you must find in the library the
volume of the South Western Reporter Second listed for your problem number
below. Note that all the volumes listed are from second series (S.W.2d). For
your answer, cite the name of the case that begins on each of the listed pages
((a)-(f)) in that volume in proper form. Do not rely on the form of citation
used by the publisher in running head for your answer.

```
       Problem #          S.W.2d Vol.                    Pages

 1  170 236 344 485 592    693   (a) 129 (b) 285 (c) 481 (d) 621 (e) 640 (f) 850
 2  171 237 345 486 593    692   (a) 209 (b) 420 (c) 470 (d) 525 (e) 803 (f) 926
 3  172 238 346 487 594    691   (a) 423 (b) 485 (c) 498 (d) 717 (e) 784 (f) 857
 4  173 239 347 488 595    690   (a) 358 (b) 465 (c) 473 (d) 517 (e) 672 (f) 897
 5  174 240 348 489 596    689   (a)  45 (b)  78 (c) 399 (d) 599 (e) 647 (f) 830
 6  175 241 349 490 597    688   (a) 182 (b) 198 (c) 307 (d) 446 (e) 757 (f) 827
 7  176 242 350 491 598    687   (a) 268 (b) 374 (c) 410 (d) 444 (e) 560 (f) 713
 8  177 243 351 492 599    686   (a)  87 (b) 101 (c) 226 (d) 469 (e) 543 (f) 799
 9  178 244 352 493 600    586   (a)  24 (b)  40 (c) 137 (d) 229 (e) 429 (f) 934
10  179 245 353 494 501    684   (a) 252 (b) 440 (c) 624 (d) 876 (e) 903 (f) 929
11  180 246 354 495 502    683   (a) 173 (b) 180 (c) 318 (d) 741 (e) 763 (f)  28
12  181 247 355 496 503    682   (a) 236 (b) 366 (c) 567 (d) 634 (e) 803 (f) 5'6
13  182 248 356 497 504    680   (a) 153 (b) 362 (c) 365 (d) 420 (e) 709 (f) 9L'
14  183 249 357 498 505    679   (a)  15 (b) 370 (c) 416 (d) 544 (e) 740 (f) 77'
←15 184 250 358 499 506    678   (a)  61 (b) 205 (c) 225 (d) 443 (e) 661 (f) 800
16  185 251 359 500 507    677   (a) 147 (b) 293 (c) 449 (d) 669 (e) 781 (f) 881
17  186 252 360 401 508    676   (a)   1 (b) 159 (c) 231 (d) 375 (e) 448 (f) 693
18  187 253 361 402 509    675   (a)  92 (b) 245 (c) 293 (d) 376 (e) 481 (f) 845
19  188 254 362 403 510    674   (a) 139 (b) 293 (c) 437 (d) 737 (e) 781 (f) 953
20  189 255 363 404 511    673   (a) 218 (b) 236 (c) 291 (d) 334 (e) 512 (f) 858
21  190 256 364 405 512    672   (a) 349 (b) 394 (c) 470 (d) 769 (e) 852 (f) 922
22  191 257 365 406 513    671   (a) 591 (b) 644 (c) 757 (d) 801 (e) 812 (f) 941
23  192 258 366 407 514    670   (a) 319 (b) 494 (c) 828 (d) 857 (e) 882 (f) 954
24  193 259 367 408 515    669   (a)   3 (b) 251 (c) 519 (d) 736 (e) 779 (f) 878
25  194 260 368 409 516    668   (a)   1 (b)  37 (c) 252 (d) 533 (e) 569 (f) 641
26  195 261 369 410 517    667   (a) 250 (b) 299 (c) 347 (d) 743 (e) 773 (f) 885
27  196 262 370 411 518    666   (a)  11 (b)  48 (c)  61 (d) 213 (e) 416 (f) 613
28  197 263 371 412 519    665   (a)  87 (b) 132 (c) 133 (d) 208 (e) 278 (f) 324
29  198 264 372 413 520    664   (a) 625 (b) 698 (c) 734 (d) 805 (e) 830 (f) 851
30  199 265 373 414 521    663   (a)  37 (b) 196 (c) 420 (d) 685 (e) 761 (f) 776
31  200 266 374 415 522    662   (a) 129 (b) 141 (c) 396 (d) 693 (e) 709 (f) 928
32  101 267 375 416 523    661   (a)   2 (b) 285 (c) 433 (d) 567 (e) 657 (f) 740
33  102 268 376 417 524    660   (a)  58 (b) 144 (c) 265 (d) 404 (e) 471 (f) 584
34  103 269 377 418 525    659   (a) 201 (b) 227 (c) 714 (d) 775 (e) 827 (f) 869
35  104 270 378 419 526    658   (a)  17 (b)  70 (c) 186 (d) 218 (e) 323 (f) 665
36  105 271 379 420 527    657   (a) 207 (b) 425 (c) 494 (d) 583 (e) 636 (f) 824
37  106 272 380 421 528    656   (a) 107 (b) 470 (c) 589 (d) 612 (e) 740 (f) 836
38  107 273 381 422 529    655   (a) 110 (b) 327 (c) 506 (d) 515 (e) 638 (f) 845
39  108 274 382 423 530    653   (a)  35 (b)  93 (c) 377 (d) 436 (e) 539 (f) 703
40  109 275 383 424 531    652   (a) 202 (b) 252 (c) 515 (d) 655 (e) 851 (f) 856
41  110 276 384 425 532    651   (a)  31 (b) 232 (c) 525 (d) 613 (e) 616 (f) 851
42  111 277 385 426 533    650   (a)  68 (b) 312 (c) 467 (d) 623 (e) 879 (f) 938
43  112 278 386 427 534    649   (a) 198 (b) 456 (c) 524 (d) 561 (e) 791 (f) 812
44  113 279 387 428 535    648   (a) 351 (b) 542 (c) 568 (d) 763 (e) 800 (f) 858
45  114 280 388 429 536    646   (a)  17 (b) 177 (c) 246 (d) 347 (e) 717 (f) 765
46  115 281 389 430 537    645   (a)  70 (b)  91 (c) 149 (d) 204 (e) 310 (f) 346
47  116 282 390 431 538    640   (a) 137 (b) 222 (c) 343 (d) 362 (e) 619 (f) 781
48  117 283 391 432 539    641   (a) 108 (b) 193 (c) 451 (d) 477 (e) 780 (f) 927
49  118 284 392 433 540    642   (a)   1 (b) 160 (c) 336 (d) 504 (e) 820 (f) 907
50  119 285 393 434 541    643   (a)  46 (b) 195 (c) 222 (d) 526 (e) 592 (f) 737
51  120 286 394 435 542    644   (a) 148 (b) 292 (c) 355 (d) 533 (e) 615 (f) 815
52  121 287 395 436 543    647   (a)   5 (b)   8 (c) 477 (d) 539 (e) 625 (f) 866
53  122 288 396 437 544    654   (a)  31 (b)  68 (c) 367 (d) 376 (e) 835 (f) 889
54  123 289 397 438 545    639   (a)  86 (b) 286 (c) 545 (d) 700 (e) 786 (f) 825
55  124 290 398 439 546    638   (a) 108 (b) 218 (c) 272 (d) 557 (e) 905 (f) 908
```

1

Problem #					S.W.2d Vol.		Pages										
56	125	291	399	440	547	637	(a)	84	(b)	94	(c)	251	(d)	373	(e)	903	(f)	943
57	126	292	400	441	548	636	(a)	484	(b)	530	(c)	648	(d)	706	(e)	828	(f)	896
58	127	293	301	442	549	635	(a)	51	(b)	98	(c)	268	(d)	554	(e)	615	(f)	658
59	128	294	302	443	550	634	(a)	2	(b)	153	(c)	234	(d)	249	(e)	286	(f)	815
60	129	295	303	444	551	633	(a)	73	(b)	161	(c)	366	(d)	488	(e)	733	(f)	761
61	130	296	304	445	552	632	(a)	6	(b)	227	(c)	323	(d)	621	(e)	885	(f)	950
62	131	297	305	446	553	631	(a)	1	(b)	73	(c)	103	(d)	410	(e)	825	(f)	893
63	132	298	306	447	554	629	(a)	201	(b)	324	(c)	524	(d)	645	(e)	816	(f)	943
64	133	299	307	448	555	628	(a)	329	(b)	497	(c)	582	(d)	637	(e)	887	(f)	941
65	134	300	308	449	556	627	(a)	166	(b)	382	(c)	567	(d)	741	(e)	868	(f)	882
66	135	201	309	450	557	626	(a)	30	(b)	422	(c)	478	(d)	817	(e)	850	(f)	912
67	136	202	310	451	558	625	(a)	1	(b)	151	(c)	192	(d)	581	(e)	731	(f)	874
68	137	203	311	452	559	624	(a)	11	(b)	453	(c)	474	(d)	573	(e)	886	(f)	933
69	138	204	312	453	560	623	(a)	448	(b)	699	(c)	745	(d)	797	(e)	843	(f)	895
70	139	205	313	454	561	622	(a)	36	(b)	319	(c)	482	(d)	535	(e)	736	(f)	844
71	140	206	314	455	562	620	(a)	5	(b)	157	(c)	181	(d)	362	(e)	648	(f)	732
72	141	207	315	456	563	619	(a)	199	(b)	725	(c)	814	(d)	873	(e)	904	(f)	910
73	142	208	316	457	564	618	(a)	229	(b)	280	(c)	288	(d)	502	(e)	543	(f)	591
74	143	209	317	458	565	617	(a)	61	(b)	262	(c)	329	(d)	479	(e)	731	(f)	767
75	144	210	318	459	566	616	(a)	39	(b)	373	(c)	452	(d)	587	(e)	600	(f)	679
76	145	211	319	460	567	615	(a)	1	(b)	164	(c)	293	(d)	309	(e)	574	(f)	869
77	146	212	320	461	568	621	(a)	12	(b)	22	(c)	451	(d)	539	(e)	731	(f)	889
78	147	213	321	462	569	614	(a)	227	(b)	429	(c)	563	(d)	695	(e)	701	(f)	903
79	148	214	322	463	570	613	(a)	431	(b)	440	(c)	716	(d)	793	(e)	800	(f)	833
80	149	215	323	464	571	612	(a)	257	(b)	503	(c)	766	(d)	799	(e)	866	(f)	935
81	150	216	324	465	572	611	(a)	1	(b)	860	(c)	869	(d)	897	(e)	911	(f)	928
82	151	217	325	466	573	610	(a)	217	(b)	681	(c)	744	(d)	807	(e)	922	(f)	935
83	152	218	326	467	574	608	(a)	51	(b)	374	(c)	405	(d)	576	(e)	722	(f)	819
84	153	219	327	468	575	607	(a)	421	(b)	507	(c)	677	(d)	832	(e)	856	(f)	857
85	154	220	328	469	576	606	(a)	169	(b)	578	(c)	696	(d)	725	(e)	732	(f)	792
86	155	221	329	470	577	605	(a)	43	(b)	501	(c)	506	(d)	749	(e)	800	(f)	955
87	156	222	330	471	578	604	(a)	221	(b)	396	(c)	415	(d)	511	(e)	623	(f)	791
88	157	223	331	472	579	603	(a)	37	(b)	335	(c)	793	(d)	829	(e)	930	(f)	931
89	158	224	332	473	580	602	(a)	118	(b)	150	(c)	327	(d)	400	(e)	609	(f)	874
90	159	225	333	474	581	601	(a)	186	(b)	191	(c)	280	(d)	717	(e)	766	(f)	923
91	160	226	334	475	582	600	(a)	358	(b)	457	(c)	601	(d)	660	(e)	695	(f)	850
92	161	227	335	476	583	599	(a)	121	(b)	427	(c)	545	(d)	655	(e)	841	(f)	900
93	162	228	336	477	584	598	(a)	11	(b)	503	(c)	528	(d)	640	(e)	660	(f)	783
94	163	229	337	478	585	597	(a)	434	(b)	510	(c)	724	(d)	783	(e)	861	(f)	871
95	164	230	338	479	586	596	(a)	150	(b)	240	(c)	397	(d)	716	(e)	796	(f)	824
96	165	231	339	480	587	594	(a)	163	(b)	449	(c)	545	(d)	723	(e)	898	(f)	908
97	166	232	340	481	588	593	(a)	84	(b)	193	(c)	731	(d)	749	(e)	869	(f)	923
98	167	233	341	482	589	592	(a)	35	(b)	38	(c)	134	(d)	285	(e)	432	(f)	670
99	168	234	342	483	590	590	(a)	173	(b)	241	(c)	563	(d)	783	(e)	878	(f)	946
100	169	235	343	484	591	588	(a)	46	(b)	50	(c)	199	(d)	489	(e)	602	(f)	877

LIBRARY EXERCISE 2. UNITED STATES REPORTS. This exercise teaches you how to find a case in the official reporter of U.S. Supreme Court decisions from a known citation and gives you practice in citing that case in proper form. To complete this exercise, find the case that begins on the page listed with your problem below in the designated volume of United States Reports. Cite the case to United States Reports only. Do not rely on the running head for your answer. Note that the volume of United States Reports used to complete this exercise is also used to complete Exercise 3.

Problem #					Citation	Problem #					Citation
1	131	201	305	404	503	135 U.S. 342	51	181	251	355	454	553	272 U.S. 321
2	132	202	306	405	504	343 U.S. 214	52	182	252	356	455	554	362 U.S. 458
3	133	203	307	406	505	333 U.S. 591	53	183	253	357	456	555	257 U.S. 85
4	134	204	308	407	506	346 U.S. 119	54	184	254	358	457	556	359 U.S. 231
5	135	205	309	408	507	434 U.S. 159	55	185	255	359	458	557	250 U.S. 153
6	136	206	310	409	508	322 U.S. 238	56	186	256	360	459	558	252 U.S. 538
7	137	207	311	410	509	252 U.S. 308	57	187	257	361	460	559	256 U.S. 170
8	138	208	312	411	510	379 U.S. 378	58	188	258	362	461	560	220 U.S. 428
9	139	209	313	412	511	336 U.S. 176	59	189	259	363	462	561	334 U.S. 624
10	140	210	314	413	512	334 U.S. 219	60	190	260	364	463	562	175 U.S. 178
11	141	211	315	414	513	378 U.S. 1	61	191	261	365	464	563	303 U.S. 283
12	142	212	316	415	514	257 U.S. 308	62	192	262	366	465	564	244 U.S. 332
13	143	213	317	416	515	297 U.S. 288	63	193	263	367	466	565	336 U.S. 220
14	144	214	318	417	516	317 U.S. 217	64	194	264	368	467	566	383 U.S. 715
15	~~145~~	~~215~~	~~319~~	~~418~~	~~517~~	328 U.S. 293	65	195	265	369	468	567	343 U.S. 90
16	146	216	320	419	518	247 U.S. 231	66	196	266	370	469	568	262 U.S. 361
17	147	217	321	420	519	219 U.S. 121	67	197	267	371	470	569	321 U.S. 126
18	148	218	322	421	520	299 U.S. 248	68	198	268	372	471	570	339 U.S. 186
19	149	219	323	422	521	332 U.S. 407	69	199	269	373	472	571	310 U.S. 354
20	150	220	324	423	522	146 U.S. 338	70	200	270	374	473	572	288 U.S. 152
21	151	221	325	424	523	251 U.S. 146	71	101	271	375	474	573	273 U.S. 83
22	152	222	326	425	524	351 U.S. 105	72	102	272	376	475	574	263 U.S. 1
23	153	223	327	426	525	385 U.S. 276	73	103	273	377	476	575	270 U.S. 59
24	154	224	328	427	526	149 U.S. 273	74	104	274	378	477	576	332 U.S. 194
25	155	225	329	428	527	301 U.S. 402	75	105	275	379	478	577	171 U.S. 220
26	156	226	330	429	528	312 U.S. 410	76	106	276	380	479	578	133 U.S. 67
27	157	227	331	430	529	258 U.S. 483	77	107	277	381	480	579	322 U.S. 31
28	158	228	332	431	530	297 U.S. 500	78	108	278	382	481	580	308 U.S. 256
29	159	229	333	432	531	411 U.S. 182	79	109	279	383	482	581	263 U.S. 103
30	160	230	334	433	532	349 U.S. 1	80	110	280	384	483	582	342 U.S. 437
31	161	231	335	434	533	118 U.S. 271	81	111	281	385	484	583	258 U.S. 365
32	162	232	336	435	534	282 U.S. 481	82	112	282	386	485	584	166 U.S. 601
33	163	233	337	436	535	314 U.S. 212	83	113	283	387	486	585	330 U.S. 545
34	164	234	338	437	536	243 U.S. 210	84	114	284	388	487	586	276 U.S. 467
35	165	235	339	438	537	367 U.S. 687	85	115	285	389	488	587	266 U.S. 503
36	166	236	340	439	538	333 U.S. 683	86	116	286	390	489	588	312 U.S. 195
37	167	237	341	440	539	380 U.S. 300	87	117	287	391	490	589	253 U.S. 300
38	168	238	342	441	540	369 U.S. 404	88	118	288	392	491	590	261 U.S. 140
39	169	239	343	442	541	206 U.S. 158	89	119	289	393	492	591	295 U.S. 295
40	170	240	344	443	542	210 U.S. 339	90	120	290	394	493	592	291 U.S. 227
41	171	241	345	444	543	382 U.S. 323	91	121	291	395	494	593	316 U.S. 4
42	172	242	346	445	544	373 U.S. 221	92	122	292	396	495	594	302 U.S. 556
43	173	243	347	446	545	365 U.S. 624	93	123	293	397	496	595	355 U.S. 587
44	174	244	348	447	546	317 U.S. 217	94	124	294	398	497	596	308 U.S. 241
45	175	245	349	448	547	296 U.S. 459	95	125	295	399	498	597	277 U.S. 258
46	176	246	350	449	548	345 U.S. 427	96	126	296	400	499	598	251 U.S. 108
47	177	247	351	450	549	340 U.S. 474	97	127	297	301	500	599	201 U.S. 344
48	178	248	352	451	550	358 U.S. 242	98	128	298	302	401	600	267 U.S. 233
49	179	249	353	452	551	359 U.S. 500	99	129	299	303	402	501	408 U.S. 204
50	180	250	354	453	552	234 U.S. 245	100	130	300	304	403	502	376 U.S. 86

LIBRARY EXERCISE 3. PARALLEL CITATION OF UNITED STATES REPORTS. This exercise teaches you how to find parallel citations for U.S. Supreme Court decisions when the official citation is known. It also gives you practice in citing Supreme Court cases using parallel citations. To complete this exercise, find the case that begins on the page listed below in the designated volume of <u>United States Reports</u>. Cite that case using parallel citations to all three Supreme Court reporters. Use the appropriate volume of <u>Shepard's Citations</u> to find the parallel citations. If the appropriate <u>Shepard's</u> volume is unavailable, use the "Table of Cases" in one of the Supreme Court digests to find the parallel citations. Note that the citation below is to a <u>different</u> page in the same volume used to complete Exercise 2.

Problem #					Citation	Problem #					Citation
1	131	201	305	404	503	135 U.S. 100	51	181	251	355	454	553	272 U.S. 476
2	132	202	306	405	504	343 U.S. 579	52	182	252	356	455	554	362 U.S. 29
3	133	203	307	406	505	333 U.S. 364	53	183	253	357	456	555	257 U.S. 441
4	134	204	308	407	506	346 U.S. 537	54	184	254	358	457	556	359 U.S. 520
5	135	205	309	408	507	434 U.S. 246	55	185	255	359	458	557	250 U.S. 300
6	136	206	310	409	508	322 U.S. 137	56	186	256	360	459	558	252 U.S. 85
7	137	207	311	410	509	252 U.S. 416	57	187	257	361	460	559	256 U.S. 208
8	138	208	312	411	510	379 U.S. 294	58	188	258	362	461	560	220 U.S. 373
9	139	209	313	412	511	336 U.S. 525	59	189	259	363	462	561	334 U.S. 495
10	140	210	314	413	512	334 U.S. 653	60	190	260	364	463	562	175 U.S. 211
11	141	211	315	414	513	378 U.S. 158	61	191	261	365	464	563	303 U.S. 177
12	142	212	316	415	514	257 U.S. 377	62	192	262	366	465	564	244 U.S. 310
13	143	213	317	416	515	297 U.S. 537	63	193	263	367	466	565	336 U.S. 460
14	144	214	318	417	516	317 U.S. 341	64	194	264	368	467	566	383 U.S. 190
15	~~145~~	~~215~~	~~319~~	~~418~~	~~517~~	328 U.S. 408	65	195	265	369	468	567	343 U.S. 306
16	146	216	320	419	518	247 U.S. 251	66	196	266	370	469	568	262 U.S. 390
17	147	217	321	420	519	219 U.S. 346	67	197	267	371	470	569	321 U.S. 573
18	148	218	322	421	520	299 U.S. 304	68	198	268	372	471	570	339 U.S. 485
19	149	219	323	422	521	332 U.S. 689	69	199	269	373	472	571	310 U.S. 150
20	150	220	324	423	522	146 U.S. 183	70	200	270	374	473	572	288 U.S. 344
21	151	221	325	424	523	251 U.S. 417	71	101	271	375	474	573	273 U.S. 392
22	152	222	326	425	524	351 U.S. 345	72	102	272	376	475	574	263 U.S. 255
23	153	223	327	426	525	385 U.S. 493	73	103	273	377	476	575	270 U.S. 593
24	154	224	328	427	526	149 U.S. 481	74	104	274	378	477	576	332 U.S. 392
25	155	225	329	428	527	301 U.S. 548	75	105	275	379	478	577	171 U.S. 604
26	156	226	330	429	528	312 U.S. 100	76	106	276	380	479	578	133 U.S. 375
27	157	227	331	430	529	258 U.S. 495	77	107	277	381	480	579	322 U.S. 607
28	158	228	332	431	530	297 U.S. 1	78	108	278	382	481	580	308 U.S. 188
29	159	229	333	432	531	411 U.S. 677	79	109	279	383	482	581	263 U.S. 444
30	160	230	334	433	532	349 U.S. 294	80	110	280	384	483	582	342 U.S. 371
31	161	231	335	434	533	118 U.S. 356	81	111	281	385	484	583	258 U.S. 451
32	162	232	336	435	534	282 U.S. 555	82	112	282	386	485	584	166 U.S. 489
33	163	233	337	436	535	314 U.S. 488	83	113	283	387	486	585	330 U.S. 743
34	164	234	338	437	536	243 U.S. 502	84	114	284	388	487	586	276 U.S. 311
35	165	235	339	438	537	367 U.S. 497	85	115	285	389	488	587	266 U.S. 17
36	166	236	340	439	538	333 U.S. 287	86	116	286	390	489	588	312 U.S. 600
37	167	237	341	440	539	380 U.S. 479	87	117	287	391	490	589	253 U.S. 421
38	168	238	342	441	540	369 U.S. 186	88	118	288	392	491	590	261 U.S. 463
39	169	239	343	442	541	206 U.S. 46	89	119	289	393	492	591	295 U.S. 555
40	170	240	344	443	542	210 U.S. 405	90	120	290	394	493	592	291 U.S. 304
41	171	241	345	444	543	382 U.S. 172	91	121	291	395	494	593	316 U.S. 114
42	172	242	346	445	544	373 U.S. 341	92	122	292	396	495	594	302 U.S. 379
43	173	243	347	446	545	365 U.S. 320	93	123	293	397	496	595	355 U.S. 96
44	174	244	348	447	546	317 U.S. 111	94	124	294	398	497	596	308 U.S. 321
45	175	245	349	448	547	296 U.S. 287	95	125	295	399	498	597	277 U.S. 438
46	176	246	350	449	548	345 U.S. 22	96	126	296	400	499	598	251 U.S. 385
47	177	247	351	450	549	340 U.S. 349	97	127	297	301	500	599	201 U.S. 43
48	178	248	352	451	550	358 U.S. 534	98	128	298	302	401	600	267 U.S. 132
49	179	249	353	452	551	359 U.S. 207	99	129	299	303	402	501	408 U.S. 169
50	180	250	354	453	552	234 U.S. 600	100	130	300	304	403	502	376 U.S. 254

LIBRARY EXERCISE 4. SUPREME COURT REPORTER. Sometimes you will know the United States Reports citation of a Supreme Court decision, but only West's Supreme Court Reporter will be available. This exercise teaches you a simple way of handling this situation. To complete this exercise, locate in the library the Supreme Court Reporter volume that covers the volume of United States Reports listed for your problem number. The volumes of United States Reports covered by a given Supreme Court Reporter volume are printed on the outside binding. Find the Table of "Supreme Court Reporter References" in the front part (or sometimes at the end) of the volume, and locate the page at which the case is reported. If the table has been deleted during the binding process, use the appropriate volume of Shepard's Citations to find the Supreme Court Reporter citation. This latter approach is the other common way of handling this situation. For purposes of this exercise, cite the case to the Supreme Court Reporter without parallel citations.

Problem #					Citation	Problem #					Citation
1	128	210	322	411	590	106 U.S. 95	51	178	260	372	461	540	269 U.S. 328
2	129	211	323	412	591	454 U.S. 290	52	179	261	373	462	541	430 U.S. 349
3	130	212	324	413	592	107 U.S. 265	53	180	262	374	463	542	276 U.S. 358
4	131	213	325	414	593	449 U.S. 456	54	181	263	375	464	543	278 U.S. 300
5	132	214	326	415	594	109 U.S. 336	55	182	264	376	465	544	280 U.S. 218
6	133	215	327	416	595	444 U.S. 460	56	183	265	377	466	545	284 U.S. 263
7	134	216	328	417	596	111 U.S. 43	57	184	266	378	467	546	288 U.S. 436
8	135	217	329	418	597	440 U.S. 59	58	185	267	379	468	547	291 U.S. 610
9	136	218	330	419	598	112 U.S. 150	59	186	268	380	469	548	293 U.S. 322
10	137	219	331	420	599	114 U.S. 417	60	187	269	381	470	549	282 U.S. 379
11	138	220	332	421	600	115 U.S. 683	61	188	270	382	471	550	297 U.S. 227
12	139	221	333	422	501	119 U.S. 513	62	189	271	383	472	551	300 U.S. 414
13	140	222	334	423	502	435 U.S. 6	63	190	272	384	473	552	304 U.S. 126
14	141	223	335	424	503	128 U.S. 129	64	191	273	385	474	553	306 U.S. 346
15	142	224	336	425	504	132 U.S. 131	65	192	274	386	475	554	309 U.S. 94
16	143	225	337	426	505	137 U.S. 62	66	193	275	387	476	555	311 U.S. 570
17	144	226	338	427	506	143 U.S. 621	67	194	276	388	477	556	316 U.S. 174
18	145	227	339	428	507	147 U.S. 486	68	195	277	389	478	557	319 U.S. 598
19	146	228	340	429	508	151 U.S. 303	69	196	278	390	479	558	321 U.S. 158
20	147	229	341	430	509	156 U.S. 1	70	197	279	391	480	559	324 U.S. 401
21	148	230	342	431	510	162 U.S. 1	71	198	280	392	481	560	328 U.S. 331
22	149	231	343	432	511	166 U.S. 150	72	199	281	393	482	561	331 U.S. 752
23	150	232	344	433	512	168 U.S. 90	73	200	282	394	483	562	335 U.S. 106
24	151	233	345	434	513	460 U.S. 370	74	101	283	395	484	563	336 U.S. 422
25	152	234	346	435	514	178 U.S. 327	75	102	284	396	485	564	339 U.S. 707
26	153	235	347	436	515	180 U.S. 471	76	103	285	397	486	565	340 U.S. 602
27	154	236	348	437	516	183 U.S. 191	77	104	286	398	487	566	343 U.S. 99
28	155	237	349	438	517	187 U.S. 553	78	105	287	399	488	567	345 U.S. 981
29	156	238	350	439	518	192 U.S. 243	79	106	288	400	489	568	347 U.S. 128
30	157	239	351	440	519	197 U.S. 394	80	107	289	301	490	569	349 U.S. 435
31	158	240	352	441	520	202 U.S. 1	81	108	290	302	491	570	351 U.S. 79
32	159	241	353	442	521	204 U.S. 522	82	109	291	303	492	571	354 U.S. 234
33	160	242	354	443	522	209 U.S. 211	83	110	292	304	493	572	357 U.S. 63
34	161	243	355	444	523	212 U.S. 354	84	111	293	305	494	573	359 U.S. 171
35	162	244	356	445	524	216 U.S. 531	85	112	294	306	495	574	361 U.S. 147
36	163	245	357	446	525	220 U.S. 462	86	113	295	307	496	575	363 U.S. 278
37	164	246	358	447	526	224 U.S. 1	87	114	296	308	497	576	430 U.S. 564
38	165	247	359	448	527	229 U.S. 523	88	115	297	309	498	577	368 U.S. 157
39	166	248	360	449	528	231 U.S. 222	89	116	298	310	499	578	370 U.S. 626
40	167	249	361	450	529	236 U.S. 247	90	117	299	311	500	579	371 U.S. 132
41	168	250	362	451	530	241 U.S. 22	91	118	300	312	401	580	374 U.S. 174
42	169	251	363	452	531	242 U.S. 568	92	119	201	313	402	581	378 U.S. 478
43	170	252	364	453	532	245 U.S. 603	93	120	202	314	403	582	379 U.S. 241
44	171	253	365	454	533	249 U.S. 454	94	121	203	315	404	583	390 U.S. 341
45	172	254	366	455	534	252 U.S. 465	95	122	204	316	405	584	393 U.S. 297
46	173	255	367	456	535	256 U.S. 296	96	123	205	317	406	585	395 U.S. 352
47	174	256	368	457	536	423 U.S. 336	97	124	206	318	407	586	404 U.S. 528
48	175	257	369	458	537	261 U.S. 428	98	125	207	319	408	587	416 U.S. 21
49	176	258	370	459	538	265 U.S. 269	99	126	208	320	409	588	418 U.S. 656
50	177	259	371	460	539	268 U.S. 295	100	127	209	321	410	589	420 U.S. 395

(33 L. Ed 287)

10 S. CT 47

5

LIBRARY EXERCISE 5. LAWYERS' EDITION OF U.S. SUPREME COURT REPORTS. This exercise familiarizes you with Lawyers' Edition of U.S. Supreme Court Reports and gives you practice in using star paging to cite quoted material within a source. It also teaches you the USOC rule on how to cite multiple pages from a source. To complete this exercise, find the page[s] listed below in the designated volume of Lawyers' Edition of United States Reports. Assume you have quoted the language on the page[s] given with your problem below. Cite the case and the quotation in proper form to United States Reports using the star paging in the Lawyers' Edition. Do not give parallel citations.

For example, if your problem read as follows, "6 L. Ed. 2d 525 'The position adopted by the Court of Appeals would mean that two subcontractors who committed similar acts and caused similar damage could be subjected to widely disparate penalties,'" your answer would be: United States v. Bornstein, 423 U.S. 303, 315-16 (1976) (memo/brief form) or United States v. Bornstein, 423 U.S. 303, 315-16 (1976) (law review form). Note that when the quoted portion of the case extends over more than one page in United States Reports (as above), use inclusive page numbers covering the quotation, separated by a hyphen. In doing so, retain the last two digits and delete other repetitious digits. See USOC, at 17-18 (Rules 3.3(a) and (c)).

1 142 220 365 409 517   1 L. Ed. 2d 489   "In short, Congress in § 2 was referring to a group of unions already defined and constituted under the § 3 procedures."
2 143 221 366 410 518   1 L. Ed. 2d 742   "No special threat to appellees arises from the ... assertion of Commission jurisdiction to regulate Alleghany."
3 144 222 367 411 519   2 L. Ed. 2d 477   "There the question, much mooted, was whether the federal policy conflicted with the state policy fixing the price of milk which the United States purchased."
4 145 223 368 412 520   2 L. Ed. 2d 1129   "[W]e find it unnecessary to decide whether the respondent was a transferee within the meaning of § 311 because we hold that the Kentucky statutes govern the question of the beneficiary's liability."
5 146 224 369 413 521   3 L. Ed. 2d 32   "[T]he taxpayers in this case have met those conditions and should be allowed the claimed deductions. The meaning of 'home' was expressly left undecided in Flowers."
6 147 225 370 414 522   3 L. Ed. 2d 999   "Clearly these conspiracy allegations stated a cause of action triable as of right by a jury."
7 148 226 371 415 523   4 L. Ed. 2d 8   "The equipment then had to be moved for a similar operation on the second car."
8 149 227 372 416 524   4 L. Ed. 2d 725   "The State in which the respondent is incorporated prohibits unfair or deceptive practices in the insurance business there or 'in any other state.'"
9 150 228 373 417 525   5 L. Ed. 2d 4   "[T]he United States instituted proceedings to redeem the property pursuant to . . . 28 U.S.C. § 2410(c)."
10 151 229 374 418 526   5 L. Ed. 2d 600-01 "Congress did not want patentees to be barred from prosecuting their claims for direct infringement."
11 152 230 375 419 527   6 L. Ed. 2d 53   "The highest court of Delaware has thus construed this legislative enactment as authorizing discriminatory classifications based exclusively on color."
12 153 231 376 420 528   6 L. Ed. 2d 1115   "To interpret its careful consideration of the problem otherwise is to accuse the Congress of engaging in sciamachy."
13 154 232 377 421 529   7 L. Ed. 2d 631   "[T]he Court issued a writ of mandamus ordering a district judge to issue a bench warrant which he had refused to do, in the purported exercise of his discretion, for a person under an indictment returned by a properly constituted grand jury."
14 155 233 378 422 530   7 L. Ed. 2d 329   "[T]he term 'reorganization' means 'the acquisition by one corporation, in exchange solely for all or a part of its voting stock, of at least 80[%] of the . . . stock of another corporation.'"
15 156 234 379 423 531   8 L. Ed. 2d 190   "The Court of Appeals for the Second Circuit affirmed the Tax Court's orders sustaining the Commissioner's deficiency determination."

16 157 235 380 424 532   8 L. Ed. 2d 740   "Petitioner voluntarily chose this attorney as his representative in the action, and he cannot now avoid the consequences of the acts or omissions of this freely selected agent."
17 158 236 381 425 533   9 L. Ed. 2d 567   "The charge in the indictment was in the exact language of the statute, and, in specifying the conduct covered by the charge, the indictment did nothing more than state the price the defendant was alleged to have collected."
18 159 237 382 426 534   9 L. Ed. 2d 640   "The Government's theories would force upon an accrual-basis taxpayer a cash basis for advance payments in disregard of the federal statute which explicitly authorizes income tax returns to be based upon sound accrual accounting methods."
19 160 238 383 427 535   10 L. Ed. 2d 293   "Congress restricted the full deduction under § 23(k) to bad debts incurred in the taxpayer's trade or business and provided that 'nonbusiness' bad debts were to be deducted as short- term capital losses."
20 161 239 384 428 536   10 L. Ed. 2d 775   "[T]he state law creditor, asserting that the assignment under which he claimed was a mortgage within the predecessor to § 6323, insisted upon priority over the federal lien."
21 162 240 385 429 537   11 L. Ed. 2d 593   "Under the labor agreement, however, the 'upgraded' helper does not immediately acquire permanent seniority as a journeyman."
22 163 241 386 430 538   11 L. Ed. 2d 358   "New York law . . . does not require any such express promise by the agent in order to create a valid agency for receipt of process."
23 164 242 387 431 539   12 L. Ed. 2d 694   "We hold that the constitutional privilege against self-incrimination protects a state witness against incrimination under federal as well as state law."
24 165 243 388 432 540   12 L. Ed. 2d 784   "This is the first case reaching this Court . . . that directly involves the validity under § 7 of the joint
participation of two corporations in the creation of a third as a new domestic producing organization."
25 166 244 389 433 541   13 L. Ed. 2d 861   "No one would deny that an employer is free to shut down his enterprise temporarily for reasons of renovation or lack of profitable work unrelated to his collective bargaining situation."
26 167 245 390 434 542   13 L. Ed. 2d 915   "The Commission, on the other hand, submits that the misrepresentation of any fact so long as it materially induces a purchaser's decision to buy is a deception prohibited by § 5."
27 168 246 391 435 543   14 L. Ed. 2d 245   "[T]he more compelling inference is that Congress intended the inquiry into the project's effect on commerce to include, but not be limited to, effect on downstream navigability."
28 169 247 392 436 544   14 L. Ed. 2d 129   "The regulation thus indicates that the question to be asked is whether the mine operators have a significant investment in the coal in place."
29 170 248 393 437 545   15 L. Ed. 2d 298   "It established that the term 'connecting lines' extends beyond physical connection to encompass lines participating in a through route."
30 171 249 394 438 546   15 L. Ed. 2d 224   "[T]he Commission's analysis of the merger was fatally defective because the Commission had not determined whether the merger violated § 7 of the Clayton Act."
31 172 250 395 439 547   16 L. Ed. 2d 243-44   "The defendants moved to dismiss the indictment on the ground it did not charge an offense under the laws of the United States."
32 173 251 396 440 548   16 L. Ed. 2d 344   "[Section] 9 appears firmly anchored to the assumption that the Sherman Act will deter any attempts . . . to preserve [the] price level by conspiring to raise prices at which liquor is sold elsewhere in the country."
33 174 252 397 441 549   17 L. Ed. 2d 255   "This unreliability in turn undermines the security of the prime contractor's performance."
34 175 253 398 442 550   17 L. Ed. 2d 379   "He was also under a federal indictment for embezzling union funds."
35 176 254 399 443 551   55 L. Ed. 2d 237   "After a jury of 5 persons had been selected and sworn, petitioner moved that the court impanel a jury of 12 persons."

36 177 255 400 444 552   18 L. Ed. 2d 857   "There is no Commission power to compel the railroads to do so, and it is argued that from this we should derive a congressional intent that the ICC may not compel the railroads to furnish services to motor carriers in any circumstances."
37 178 256 301 445 553   19 L. Ed. 2d 443   "In holding that this Florida law . . . conflicts with the Supremacy Clause of the Constitution we but follow the unbroken rule that has come down through the years."
38 179 257 302 446 554   19 L. Ed. 2d 793   "Several bills were then introduced combining the grant of borrowing power with various provisions to prohibit territorial expansion, and one of these bills was eventually enacted as the TVA amendments of 1959."
39 180 258 303 447 555   20 L. Ed. 2d 584   "[C]ounsel's affidavit pointed to the following evidence as tending to show a participation by Cities in the alleged conspiracy to boycott his attempts to resell the Iranian oil to which he allegedly had access under his contract."
40 181 259 304 448 556   20 L. Ed. 2d 453   "[T]he Internal Revenue Service had ruled that shareholders who sold rights would realize ordinary income in the amount of the sales price."
41 182 260 305 449 557   21 L. Ed. 2d 352   "Since in all relevant aspects the transactions here were American, not Korean, we hold that they are not 'export trade' within the meaning of the Webb-Pomerene Act."
42 183 261 306 450 558   21 L. Ed. 2d 482   "If HUD's power is not so limited, the Authority argues, HUD would be free to impair its contractual obligations to the Authority through unilateral action."
43 184 262 307 451 559   22 L. Ed. 2d 375-76   "[A]n employer who pays compensation benefits to the representative of a deceased employee may be subrogated to the rights of the representative against third persons."
44 185 263 308 452 560   22 L. Ed. 2d 715   "They generally provide a guide to action that the agency may be expected to take in future cases."
45 186 264 309 453 561   23 L. Ed. 2d 76   "The text and legislative history of the Marihuana Tax Act plainly disclose a similar congressional purpose."
46 187 265 310 454 562   23 L. Ed. 2d 363   "The state statute would have allowed recovery for additional elements of damage."
47 188 266 311 455 563   24 L. Ed. 2d 261   "The experts . . . testified that they had been doubtful that radiant heat would solve the problem of the cold joint."
48 189 267 312 456 564   24 L. Ed. 2d 727   "[T]he provisions of the charter of Northern Pacific Railroad Company which are urged to bar this merger were directed only to the operations of the federal corporation, not to the operation of the railroad."
49 190 268 313 457 565   25 L. Ed. 2d 583   "This is not such a borderline case."
50 191 269 314 458 566   25 L. Ed. 2d 376   "[C]ivil labels and good intentions do not themselves obviate the need for criminal due process safeguards in juvenile courts."
51 192 270 315 459 567   26 L. Ed. 2d 305   "The Brantley case presented a situation where a defendant's appeal from a conviction for a lesser included offense ultimately led to retrial and conviction on the greater offense."
52 193 271 316 460 568   26 L. Ed. 2d 590   "[T]he effect of the sentence imposed here required appellant to be confined for 101 days beyond the maximum period of confinement fixed by the statute."
53 194 272 317 461 569   27 L. Ed. 2d 663   "Nor may the State penalize petitioner solely because he personally, as the committee suggests, 'espouses illegal aims.'"
54 195 273 318 462 570   27 L. Ed. 2d 747   "The principle of prudent restraint we invoke today is nothing new."
55 196 274 319 463 571   28 L. Ed. 2d 376   "It is settled that courts should give great weight to any reasonable construction of a regulatory statute adopted by the agency charged with the enforcement of that statute."
56 197 275 320 464 572   28 L. Ed. 2d 262   "[I] is a time-honored maxim of the Anglo-American common-law tradition that a court possessed of jurisdiction generally must exercise it."
57 198 276 321 465 573   29 L. Ed. 2d 527   "The payment was made during the taxable year."

58	199	277	322	466	574	29 L. Ed. 2d 82	"[T]he Commission concluded that no standby charge should be imposed on either party to the interconnection."
59	200	278	323	467	575	30 L. Ed. 2d 719	"The court did not . . . consider the constitutionality of § 501(c)(3) 'as a whole.'"
60	101	279	324	468	576	30 L. Ed. 2d 580	"'[O]wnership of this quantity of stock suffices to provide access to inside information.'"
61	102	280	325	469	577	31 L. Ed. 2d 619	"Petitioner . . . asserted a claim against an additional party that had virtually no relationship to the claim or relief sought."
62	103	281	326	470	578	31 L. Ed. 2d 779	"Courts are powerless to prevent the social opprobrium suffered by these hapless children, but the Equal Protection Clause does enable us to strike down discriminatory laws relating to status of birth."
63	104	282	327	471	579	32 L. Ed. 2d 701	"[T]he cause is remanded to the Special Master for further proceedings."
64	105	283	328	472	580	32 L. Ed. 2d 264	"They also contend that the Michigan statute conflicts with or is pre-empted by federal law."
65	106	284	329	473	581	33 L. Ed. 2d 127	"The Board ordered the company to rescind its no-distribution rule."
66	107	285	330	474	582	33 L. Ed. 2d 353	"The words 'cruel and unusual' certainly include penalties that are barbaric."
67	108	286	331	475	583	34 L. Ed. 2d 429	"[T]he policy of § 7 would not be frustrated by a holding that an employee could . . . knowingly waive his § 7 right to resign from the union and to return to work without sanction."
68	109	287	332	476	584	34 L. Ed. 2d 535	"We declined to hold that Congress intended to oust completely the antitrust laws and supplant them with the self-regulatory scheme authorized by the Exchange Act."
69	110	288	333	477	585	35 L. Ed. 2d 305	"At trial, he endeavored to develop two grounds of defense."
70	111	289	334	478	586	35 L. Ed. 2d 240	"Charges are fixed that nonowning railroads must pay owning railroads for boxcars of the latter that are on the tracks of the former."
71	112	290	335	479	587	61 L. Ed. 2d 421	"The court concluded that the investigations and the speech were clearly within the ambit of the Clause."
72	113	291	336	480	588	36 L. Ed. 2d 573	"'Congress did not, however, intend criminal penalties for people who failed to comply with a non-existent regulatory program.'"
73	114	292	337	481	589	37 L. Ed. 2d 453	"The two films in question, 'Magic Mirror' and 'It All Comes Out in the End,' depict sexual conduct characterized by the Georgia Supreme Court as 'hard core pornography' leaving 'little to the imagination.'"
74	115	293	338	482	590	37 L. Ed. 2d 41	"The judgment of the Court of Claims on this issue is reversed and the case is remanded for further proceedings."
75	116	294	339	483	591	38 L. Ed. 2d 383	"[E]ver since 1789, Congress has granted this Court the power to intervene in State litigation only after 'the highest court of a State in which a decision in the suit could be had' has rendered a 'final judgment or decree.'"
76	117	295	340	484	592	38 L. Ed. 2d 514	"From the outset, Congress has provided that suits between citizens of different States are maintainable in the district courts only if the 'matter in controversy' exceeds the statutory minimum, now set at $10,000."
77	118	296	341	485	593	54 L. Ed. 2d 264	"However, the House and Senate initially differed on the significance that should be given the convenience-of-the employer doctrine for purposes of § 119."
78	119	297	342	486	594	39 L. Ed. 2d 23	"Objection to permitting recovery for loss of society often centers upon the fear that such damages are somewhat speculative and that factfinders will return excessive verdicts."
79	120	298	343	487	595	40 L. Ed. 2d 220	"We do not suggest that where there is doubt as to local law and where the certification procedure is available, resort to it is obligatory."
80	121	299	344	488	596	53 L. Ed. 2d 413	"Indeed, the one-year statute of limitations . . . could under some circumstances directly conflict with the timetable for administrative action expressly established in the 1972 Act."
81	122	300	345	489	597	41 L. Ed. 2d 543	"There is no disagreement as to the allocation of depreciation between construction and maintenance."

82 123 201 346 490 598   41 L. Ed. 2d 248   "In furtherance of its long-range responsibilities the Reorganization Court enjoined secured creditors from selling collateral to reduce their claims."
83 124 202 347 491 599   42 L. Ed. 2d 405   "Petitioners therefore are able to state that the requirements . . . are satisfied."
84 125 203 348 492 600   42 L. Ed. 2d 460   "The testimony thus presented the carriers' maximum potential exposure, leaving considerable leeway for predicting what was likely if applications were granted."
85 126 204 349 493 501   43 L. Ed. 2d 181   "A single employee confronted by an employer investigating whether certain conduct deserves discipline may be too fearful or inarticulate to relate accurately the incident being investigated, or too ignorant to raise extenuating factors."
86 127 205 350 494 502   43 L. Ed. 2d 126   "Suspending or changing demurrage charges may increase the transportation charges."
87 128 206 351 495 503   44 L. Ed. 2d 649   "This phrase might also merely mean . . . that the time limit established by this provision . . . runs from the date of the last voluntary payment."
88 129 207 352 496 504   44 L. Ed. 2d 271   "Even failing those alternatives, a firm may be able to liquidate under supervision of one of the self-regulatory organizations, or the district court, without danger of loss to customers."
89 130 208 353 497 505   45 L. Ed. 2d 494   "This case focuses . . . on the potential secondary market in mutual-fund shares."
90 131 209 354 498 506   45 L. Ed. 2d 189   "The District Court, therefore, properly concluded that the acquisition and merger in this case were not within the coverage of § 7 of the Clayton Act."
91 132 210 355 499 507   46 L. Ed. 2d 176   "Under the Motor Carrier Act [of] 1935, . . . only a properly certificated carrier may haul freight in interstate or foreign commerce."
92 133 211 356 500 508   46 L. Ed. 2d 550   "Neither the propriety of the removal nor the jurisdiction of the court was questioned by respondent in the slightest."
93 134 212 357 401 509   47 L. Ed. 2d 456   "'Embodied in the words 'cases' and 'controversies' are two complementary but somewhat different limitations.'"
94 135 213 358 402 510   47 L. Ed. 2d 291   "Here the Government seized respondent's property and contends that it has absolutely no obligation to prove that the seizure has any basis in fact no matter how severe or irreparable the injury."
95 136 214 359 403 511   71 L. Ed. 2d 415   "[T]he court [of appeals] correctly noted that the certificate of deposit is not expressly excluded from the definition since it is not currency and it has a maturity exceeding nine months."
96 137 215 360 404 512   72 L. Ed. 2d 801   "These arguments do not apply with the same force to classifications imposing disabilities on the minor children of such illegal entrants."
97 138 216 361 405 513   73 L. Ed. 2d 847   "[T]he fact that the prohibitions of § 1981 encompass private as well as governmental action does not suggest that the statute reaches more than purposeful discrimination, whether public or private."
98 139 217 362 406 514   74 L. Ed. 2d 304   "Given the broad powers of states under the [t]wenty-first [a]mendment, judicial deference to the legislative exercise of zoning powers by a city council or other legislative zoning body is especially appropriate in the area of liquor regulation."
99 140 218 363 407 515   75 L. Ed. 2d 153   "As long as the payment itself was not negated by a refund to the corporation, the change in character of the funds in the hands of the State does not require the corporation to recognize income."
100 141 219 364 408 516   76 L. Ed. 2d 289   "States have only a negligible interest, if any, in having insubstantial claims adjudicated by their courts, particularly in the face of the strong federal interest in vindicating the rights protected by the national labor laws."

LIBRARY EXERCISE 6. EARLY UNITED STATES REPORTS. This exercise familiarizes you with the publication of early Supreme Court decisions in nominative reporters (which now have been incorporated in the first ninety volumes of United States Reports). It requires you to cite an early Supreme Court case using the special USOC form and gives you further practice in using star paging. To complete this exercise, find and cite the case that begins on the page listed below in the designated volume of United States Reports. Note that the page listed below, which is the page that should be used in the citation of the case, is the star page when the pagination in United States Reports differs from that of the original nominative report. For purposes of this exercise, use the year of the term of the court if the date of decision is not given with the opinion in United States Reports.

Problem #	Citation	Problem #	Citation
1 199 232 316 493 589	50 U.S. 356	51 149 282 366 443 539	62 U.S. 248
2 200 233 317 494 590	73 U.S. 719	52 150 283 367 444 540	11 U.S. 339
3 101 234 318 495 591	65 U.S. 553	53 151 284 368 445 541	58 U.S. 478
4 102 235 319 496 592	7 U.S. 337	54 152 285 369 446 542	7 U.S. 268
5 103 236 320 497 593	37 U.S. 264	55 153 286 370 447 543	76 U.S. 203
6 104 237 321 498 594	85 U.S. 350	56 154 287 371 448 544	83 U.S. 314
7 105 238 322 499 595	29 U.S. 332	57 155 288 372 449 545	28 U.S. 33
8 106 239 323 500 596	51 U.S. 270	58 156 289 373 450 546	69 U.S. 591
9 107 240 324 401 597	57 U.S. 451	59 157 290 374 451 547	40 U.S. 284
10 108 241 325 402 598	74 U.S. 506	60 158 291 375 452 548	82 U.S. 187
11 109 242 326 403 599	44 U.S. 707	61 159 292 376 453 549	73 U.S. 441
12 110 243 327 404 600	88 U.S. 36	62 160 293 377 454 550	21 U.S. 642
13 111 244 328 405 501	27 U.S. 58	63 161 294 378 455 551	12 U.S. 462
14 112 245 329 406 502	45 U.S. 131	64 162 295 379 456 552	60 U.S. 126
15 ~~113 246 330 407 503~~	61 U.S. 6	65 163 296 380 457 553	85 U.S. 623
16 114 247 331 408 504	33 U.S. 75	66 164 297 381 458 554	2 U.S. 419
17 115 248 332 409 505	36 U.S. 226	67 165 298 382 459 555	23 U.S. 473
18 116 249 333 410 506	56 U.S. 272	68 166 299 383 460 556	42 U.S. 169
19 117 250 335 411 507	31 U.S. 761	69 167 300 384 461 557	26 U.S. 351
20 118 251 335 412 508	89 U.S. 308	70 168 201 385 462 558	38 U.S. 263
21 119 252 336 413 509	80 U.S. 434	71 169 202 386 463 559	19 U.S. 204
22 120 253 337 414 510	68 U.S. 81	72 170 203 387 464 560	47 U.S. 279
23 121 254 338 415 511	16 U.S. 246	73 171 204 388 465 561	62 U.S. 394
24 122 255 339 416 512	25 U.S. 408	74 172 205 389 466 562	60 U.S. 252
25 123 256 340 417 513	90 U.S. 150	75 173 206 390 467 563	4 U.S. 14
26 124 257 341 418 514	53 U.S. 407	76 174 207 391 468 564	8 U.S. 384
27 125 258 342 419 515	74 U.S. 564	77 175 208 392 469 565	61 U.S. 162
28 126 259 343 420 516	78 U.S. 193	78 176 209 393 470 566	88 U.S. 354
29 127 260 344 421 517	14 U.S. 408	79 177 210 394 471 567	3 U.S. 305
30 128 261 345 422 518	15 U.S. 290	80 178 211 395 472 568	5 U.S. 137
31 129 262 346 423 519	79 U.S. 259	81 179 212 396 473 569	6 U.S. 187
32 130 263 347 424 520	73 U.S. 231	82 180 213 397 474 570	9 U.S. 173
33 131 264 348 425 521	87 U.S. 201	83 181 214 398 475 571	10 U.S. 53
34 132 265 349 426 522	77 U.S. 304	84 182 215 399 476 572	13 U.S. 456
35 133 266 350 427 523	19 U.S. 453	85 183 216 400 477 573	18 U.S. 116
36 134 267 351 428 524	22 U.S. 1	86 184 217 301 478 574	24 U.S. 78
37 135 268 352 429 525	41 U.S. 315	87 185 218 302 479 575	30 U.S. 248
38 136 269 353 430 526	75 U.S. 314	88 186 219 303 480 576	32 U.S. 171
39 139 270 354 431 527	49 U.S. 402	89 187 220 304 481 577	34 U.S. 86
40 138 271 355 432 528	81 U.S. 244	90 188 221 305 482 578	39 U.S. 77
41 139 272 356 433 529	87 U.S. 571	91 189 222 306 483 579	43 U.S. 65
42 140 273 357 434 530	70 U.S. 713	92 190 223 307 484 580	52 U.S. 232
43 141 274 358 435 531	67 U.S. 510	93 191 224 308 485 581	54 U.S. 115
44 142 275 359 436 532	71 U.S. 409	94 192 225 309 486 582	55 U.S. 79
45 143 276 360 437 533	35 U.S. 298	95 193 226 310 487 583	63 U.S. 144
46 144 277 361 438 534	72 U.S. 545	96 194 227 311 488 584	74 U.S. 32
47 145 278 362 439 535	66 U.S. 595	97 195 228 312 489 585	61 U.S. 372
48 146 279 363 440 536	86 U.S. 41	98 196 229 313 490 586	51 U.S. 627
49 147 280 364 441 537	84 U.S. 123	99 197 230 314 491 587	45 U.S. 336
50 148 281 365 442 538	37 U.S. 178	100 198 231 315 492 588	37 U.S. 511

LIBRARY EXERCISE 7. FEDERAL REPORTER. This exercise familiarizes you with the Federal Reporter and gives you practice in citing opinions published in that reporter. To complete this exercise, find and cite the following cases that begin on the pages listed below in the designated volumes of the Federal Reporter Second. Note that the second series of the Federal Reporter is to be consulted and that two separate citations [(a) and (b)] are required for your answer to this exercise.

Problem #					(a)	(b)
1	150	235	311	460	525	277 F.2d 177	116 F.2d 273
2	151	236	312	461	526	421 F.2d 602	65 F.2d 191
3	152	237	313	462	527	151 F.2d 392	262 F.2d 19
4	153	238	314	463	528	205 F.2d 13	413 F.2d 381
5	154	239	315	464	529	176 F.2d 498	169 F.2d 965
6	155	240	316	465	530	304 F.2d 623	176 F.2d 449
7	156	241	317	466	531	261 F.2d 631	127 F.2d 13
8	157	242	318	467	532	322 F.2d 397	91 F.2d 860
9	158	243	319	468	533	81 F.2d 198	184 F.2d 245
10	159	244	320	469	534	149 F.2d 770	154 F.2d 307
11	160	245	321	470	535	164 F.2d 481	130 F.2d 860
12	161	246	322	471	536	110 F.2d 566	323 F.2d 882
13	162	247	323	472	537	416 F.2d 949	321 F.2d 463
14	163	248	324	473	538	208 F.2d 457	114 F.2d 91
15	~~164 249 325 474 539~~					~~118 F.2d 7~~	~~49 F.2d 849~~
16	165	250	326	475	540	275 F.2d 166	232 F.2d 112
17	166	251	327	476	541	427 F.2d 131	422 F.2d 831
18	167	252	328	477	542	241 F.2d 661	342 F.2d 219
19	168	253	329	478	543	170 F.2d 606	426 F.2d 800
20	169	254	330	479	544	421 F.2d 1065	320 F.2d 24
21	170	255	331	480	545	402 F.2d 62	323 F.2d 850
22	171	256	332	481	546	379 F.2d 329	194 F.2d 164
23	172	257	333	482	547	347 F.2d 96	775 F.2d 1349
24	173	258	334	483	548	361 F.2d 903	180 F.2d 1019
25	174	259	335	484	549	222 F.2d 508	154 F.2d 38
26	175	260	336	485	550	336 F.2d 425	123 F.2d 215
27	176	261	337	486	551	333 F.2d 363	190 F.2d 409
28	177	262	338	487	552	106 F.2d 598	232 F.2d 185
29	178	263	339	488	553	91 F.2d 12	328 F.2d 817
30	179	264	340	489	554	374 F.2d 550	168 F.2d 229
31	180	265	341	490	555	403 F.2d 687	285 F.2d 714
32	181	266	342	491	556	119 F.2d 204	326 F.2d 941
33	182	267	343	492	557	427 F.2d 1322	195 F.2d 764
34	183	268	344	493	558	584 F.2d 48	369 F.2d 505
35	184	269	345	494	559	174 F.2d 89	170 F.2d 721
36	185	270	346	495	560	236 F.2d 412	295 F.2d 496
37	186	271	347	496	561	61 F.2d 889	355 F.2d 488
38	187	272	348	497	562	375 F.2d 889	430 F.2d 558
39	188	273	349	498	563	413 F.2d 256	414 F.2d 1168
40	189	274	350	499	564	396 F.2d 438	180 F.2d 45
41	190	275	351	500	565	282 F.2d 913	245 F.2d 201
42	191	276	352	401	566	235 F.2d 860	373 F.2d 619
43	192	277	353	402	567	19 F.2d 357	148 F.2d 857
44	193	278	354	403	568	202 F.2d 180	254 F.2d 373
45	194	279	355	404	569	181 F.2d 1008	195 F.2d 567
46	195	280	356	405	570	268 F.2d 391	57 F.2d 407
47	196	281	357	406	571	346 F.2d 82	173 F.2d 405
48	197	282	358	407	572	199 F.2d 460	294 F.2d 678
49	198	283	359	408	573	112 F.2d 119	195 F.2d 69
50	199	284	360	409	574	355 F.2d 849	161 F.2d 839
51	200	285	361	410	575	290 F.2d 666	430 F.2d 1299
52	101	286	362	411	576	82 F.2d 427	318 F.2d 453
53	102	287	363	412	577	132 F.2d 790	394 F.2d 178
54	103	288	364	413	578	295 F.2d 698	583 F.2d 19
55	104	289	365	414	579	159 F.2d 330	328 F.2d 97
56	105	290	366	415	580	180 F.2d 220	362 F.2d 263
57	106	291	367	416	581	426 F.2d 1388	194 F.2d 834

12

Problem #						(a)			(b)		
58	107	292	368	417	582	317	F.2d	47	405	F.2d	867
59	108	293	369	418	583	351	F.2d	905	115	F.2d	479
60	109	294	370	419	584	341	F.2d	908	396	F.2d	128
61	110	295	371	420	585	340	F.2d	227	358	F.2d	711
62	111	296	372	421	586	261	F.2d	952	110	F.2d	911
63	112	297	373	422	587	384	F.2d	886	357	F.2d	320
64	113	298	374	423	588	257	F.2d	22	386	F.2d	684
65	114	299	375	424	589	175	F.2d	626	311	F.2d	182
66	115	300	376	425	590	115	F.2d	873	353	F.2d	30
67	116	201	377	426	591	406	F.2d	1035	287	F.2d	500
68	117	202	378	427	592	261	F.2d	233	282	F.2d	256
69	118	203	379	428	593	245	F.2d	317	343	F.2d	210
70	119	204	380	429	594	168	F.2d	305	389	F.2d	882
71	120	205	381	430	595	171	F.2d	696	139	F.2d	42
72	121	206	382	431	596	219	F.2d	271	197	F.2d	807
73	122	207	383	432	597	225	F.2d	235	337	F.2d	93
74	123	208	384	433	598	200	F.2d	614	189	F.2d	637
75	124	209	385	434	599	198	F.2d	550	386	F.2d	809
76	125	210	386	435	600	342	F.2d	754	166	F.2d	214
77	126	211	387	436	501	375	F.2d	742	265	F.2d	521
78	127	212	388	437	502	582	F.2d	604	238	F.2d	633
79	128	213	389	438	503	188	F.2d	177	313	F.2d	596
80	129	214	390	439	504	377	F.2d	864	329	F.2d	684
81	130	215	391	440	505	143	F.2d	907	327	F.2d	660
82	131	216	392	441	506	122	F.2d	852	408	F.2d	343
83	132	217	393	442	507	152	F.2d	422	193	F.2d	760
84	133	218	394	443	508	186	F.2d	297	162	F.2d	654
85	134	219	395	444	509	107	F.2d	26	234	F.2d	830
86	135	220	396	445	510	423	F.2d	32	107	F.2d	337
87	136	221	397	446	511	123	F.2d	962	112	F.2d	155
88	137	222	398	447	512	287	F.2d	687	209	F.2d	26
89	138	223	399	448	513	242	F.2d	828	309	F.2d	161
90	139	224	400	449	514	247	F.2d	604	411	F.2d	1142
91	140	225	301	450	515	627	F.2d	1032	475	F.2d	918
92	141	226	302	451	516	411	F.2d	565	428	F.2d	693
93	142	227	303	452	517	221	F.2d	264	446	F.2d	649
94	143	228	304	453	518	13	F.2d	588	444	F.2d	113
95	144	229	305	454	519	255	F.2d	246	445	F.2d	1163
96	145	230	306	455	520	355	F.2d	485	441	F.2d	495
97	146	231	307	456	521	102	F.2d	703	396	F.2d	432
98	147	232	308	457	522	266	F.2d	52	442	F.2d	393
99	148	233	309	458	523	255	F.2d	118	434	F.2d	1009
100	149	234	310	459	524	625	F.2d	1291	360	F.2d	118

LIBRARY EXERCISE 8. FEDERAL SUPPLEMENT. Sometimes you will know that a case is reported in a particular reporter volume, but you will not know the exact page on which it begins. This exercise teaches you how to find the case using the "Table of Cases Reported" in the front of the volume. This exercise also familiarizes you with West's *Federal Supplement*. To complete this exercise, find and cite the case in the *Federal Supplement* volume listed below.

	Problem #				Vol.	Plaintiff's Name		Problem #				Vol.	Plaintiff's Name
1	116	211	335	450	555	210	Allen	51	166	261	385	500	505	81 Loroco Indus.
2	117	212	336	451	556	208	Titcomb	52	167	262	386	401	506	80 Zalkind
3	118	213	337	452	557	207	Randall	53	168	263	387	402	507	79 O'Connor
4	119	214	338	453	558	204	Becken Co.	54	169	264	388	403	508	78 Lo Bue
5	120	215	339	454	559	490	Hanson	55	170	265	389	404	509	77 Wright
6	121	216	340	455	560	202	Nickel Rim Mines	56	171	266	390	405	510	474 Mardirosian
7	122	217	341	456	561	470	Anderson	57	172	267	391	406	511	75 Mahon
8	123	218	342	457	562	200	Stancil	58	173	268	392	407	512	613 Warren
9	124	219	343	458	563	199	Falcon Sales Co.	59	174	269	393	408	513	3 Monamotor Oil
10	125	220	344	459	564	198	Wiley	60	175	270	394	409	514	72 Worel
11	126	221	345	460	565	197	Rota-Carb	61	176	271	395	410	515	71 Alley
12	127	222	346	461	566	471	Pharmaceutical Manufacturers Ass'n	62	177	272	396	411	516	614 Stokes
13	128	223	347	462	567	195	Miller	63	178	273	397	412	517	1 Flynn
14	129	224	348	463	568	493	Parker	64	179	274	398	413	518	2 Harp
15	130	225	349	464	569	205	Lipp	65	180	275	399	414	519	73 Weaver
16	131	226	350	465	570	258	Denton	66	181	276	400	415	520	615 Texasgulf
17	132	227	351	466	571	259	Silver	67	182	277	301	416	521	135 Mitchell
18	133	228	352	467	572	260	McDonald	68	183	278	302	417	522	136 Mattheis
19	134	229	353	468	573	261	Stockwell	69	184	279	303	418	523	495 Ward
20	135	230	354	469	574	262	Paley	70	185	280	304	419	524	138 Ferenz
21	136	231	355	470	575	263	Wagner	71	186	281	305	420	525	139 Vanderveer
22	137	232	356	471	576	264	Crowder	72	187	282	306	421	526	140 Bierman
23	138	233	357	472	577	265	Weaver	73	188	283	307	422	527	141 Buffa
24	139	234	358	473	578	266	Sanders	74	189	284	308	423	528	142 Garden Homes
25	140	235	359	474	579	267	Sugarman	75	190	285	309	424	529	143 Harrison
26	141	236	360	475	580	494	Moore	76	191	286	310	425	530	144 Muller
27	142	237	361	476	581	269	Unruh	77	192	287	311	426	531	145 Stookey
28	143	238	362	477	582	472	Leon Industries	78	193	288	312	427	532	6 Century Indemnity
29	144	239	363	478	583	271	Kapral	79	194	289	313	428	533	147 Wilt
30	145	240	364	479	584	272	Abee	80	195	290	314	429	534	148 Whittenberg
31	146	241	365	480	585	312	Abramson	81	196	291	315	430	535	85 Russick
32	147	242	366	481	586	313	Scott	82	197	292	316	431	536	84 In re Bush
33	148	243	367	482	587	314	Zanoviak	83	198	293	317	432	537	83 Lowe
34	149	244	368	483	588	315	Lovan	84	199	294	318	433	538	475 Sexe
35	150	245	369	484	589	316	Runyon	85	200	295	319	434	539	146 Tague
36	151	246	370	485	590	317	Ross	86	101	296	320	435	540	7 Rosenstadt
37	152	247	371	486	591	318	Stone	87	102	297	321	436	541	8 Utah Radio
38	153	248	372	487	592	319	Tucker	88	103	298	322	437	542	9 Whitehall Lunch Club
39	154	249	373	488	593	320	Callaway	89	104	299	323	438	543	10 Acme, Inc.
40	155	250	374	489	594	321	Pitts	90	105	300	324	439	544	19 In re Beachley
41	156	251	375	490	595	322	Walsh	91	106	201	325	440	545	20 Apex Hosiery
42	157	252	376	491	596	323	Clark	92	107	202	326	441	546	21 Edison Light
43	158	253	377	492	597	360	Schonfeld	93	108	203	327	442	547	22 Evale
44	159	254	378	493	598	362	Von Brimer	94	109	204	328	443	548	23 Sampson
45	160	255	379	494	599	363	Garrett	95	110	205	329	444	549	29 Heal
46	161	256	380	495	600	364	Wuillamey	96	111	206	330	445	550	28 Gray
47	162	257	381	496	501	365	Sims	97	112	207	331	446	551	27 Standard Rice
48	163	258	382	497	502	366	Newhall	98	113	208	332	447	552	26 Shields
49	164	259	383	498	503	134	Woodard	99	114	209	333	448	553	25 Ripperger
50	165	260	384	499	504	82	Sutherland Paper Co.	100	115	210	334	449	554	24 Bahr Starting Gate Corp.

14

LIBRARY EXERCISE 9. FEDERAL RULES DECISIONS. This exercise familiarizes you with West's Federal Rules Decisions reporter and gives you further practice in citing cases in proper form. To complete this exercise, find and cite the case that begins on the page listed below in the designated volume of Federal Rules Decisions.

Problem #					Vol.	Page	Problem #					Vol.	Page
1	112	225	304	488	519	1	679	51	162	275	354	438	569	45	375
2	113	226	305	489	520	102	172	52	163	276	355	439	570	46	465
3	114	227	306	490	521	2	405	53	164	277	356	440	571	47	278
4	115	228	307	491	522	80	449	54	165	278	357	441	572	48	404
5	116	229	308	492	523	81	490	55	166	279	358	442	573	83	556
6	117	230	309	493	524	4	325	56	167	280	359	443	574	49	271
7	118	231	310	494	525	5	126	57	168	281	360	444	575	50	179
8	119	232	311	495	526	6	340	58	169	282	361	445	576	51	512
9	120	233	312	496	527	7	239	59	170	283	362	446	577	52	139
10	121	234	313	497	528	8	99	60	171	284	363	447	578	53	531
11	122	235	314	498	529	9	590	61	172	285	364	448	579	84	46
12	123	236	315	499	530	10	381	62	173	286	365	449	580	85	597
13	124	237	316	500	531	105	83	63	174	287	366	450	581	54	524
14	125	238	317	401	532	11	553	64	175	288	367	451	582	55	475
15	~~126~~	~~239~~	~~318~~	~~402~~	~~533~~	12	346	65	176	289	368	452	583	89	346
16	127	240	319	403	534	13	96	66	177	290	369	453	584	56	21
17	128	241	320	404	535	14	351	67	178	291	370	454	585	57	503
18	129	242	321	405	536	15	385	68	179	292	371	455	586	90	589
19	130	243	322	406	537	16	472	69	180	293	372	456	587	58	570
20	131	244	323	407	538	107	215	70	181	294	373	457	588	91	267
21	132	245	324	408	539	17	277	71	182	295	374	458	589	59	577
22	133	246	325	409	540	18	347	72	183	296	375	459	590	92	375
23	134	247	326	410	541	19	115	73	184	297	376	460	591	60	671
24	135	248	327	411	542	20	228	74	185	298	377	461	592	94	672
25	136	249	328	412	543	21	372	75	186	299	378	462	593	86	145
26	137	250	329	413	544	22	238	76	187	300	379	463	594	61	427
27	138	251	330	414	545	23	281	77	188	201	380	464	595	62	480
28	139	252	331	415	546	24	205	78	189	202	381	465	596	98	569
29	140	253	332	416	547	79	98	79	190	203	382	466	597	100	255
30	141	254	333	417	548	26	113	80	191	204	383	467	598	63	662
31	142	255	334	418	549	106	1	81	192	205	384	468	599	99	279
32	143	256	335	419	550	27	243	82	193	206	385	469	600	101	405
33	144	257	336	420	551	28	368	83	194	207	386	470	501	64	690
34	145	258	337	421	552	29	138	84	195	208	387	471	502	65	375
35	146	259	338	422	553	82	122	85	196	209	388	472	503	75	511
36	147	260	339	423	554	31	256	86	197	210	389	473	504	76	192
37	148	261	340	424	555	32	365	87	198	211	390	474	505	66	105
38	149	262	341	425	556	87	642	88	199	212	391	475	506	97	427
39	150	263	342	426	557	33	335	89	200	213	392	476	507	78	190
40	151	264	343	427	558	35	373	90	101	214	393	477	508	79	671
41	152	265	344	428	559	36	434	91	102	215	394	478	509	69	69
42	153	266	345	429	560	37	51	92	103	216	395	479	510	104	42
43	154	267	346	430	561	38	482	93	104	217	396	480	511	103	421
44	155	268	347	431	562	39	309	94	105	218	397	481	512	68	583
45	156	269	348	432	563	40	8	95	106	219	398	482	513	96	227
46	157	270	349	433	564	41	279	96	107	220	399	483	514	72	564
47	158	271	350	434	565	42	398	97	108	221	400	484	515	95	391
48	159	272	351	435	566	88	44	98	109	222	301	485	516	71	652
49	160	273	352	436	567	43	374	99	110	223	302	486	517	93	512
50	161	274	353	437	568	44	453	100	111	224	303	487	518	77	430

LIBRARY EXERCISE 10. FEDERAL CASES. This exercise familiarizes you with West's <u>Federal Cases</u> set and gives you practice in citing cases therein. This set is the one that you will use to find early lower federal court opinions. It makes available in thirty volumes over 18,000 lower federal court opinions that had been published by over 230 different nominative reporters prior to 1882. To complete this exercise, find and cite the following early federal decision published in <u>Federal Cases</u>. Note carefully the Federal Case Number because there are sometimes two different cases with the same name. If the exact date of decision is not given in <u>Federal Cases</u>, use the year of the term of the court. <u>See</u> Rule 10.5(a).

Problem #	Case	Federal Case No.
1 161 300 310 420 530	Abbe	6
2 162 201 311 421 531	Acker	26
3 163 202 312 422 532	Ada	38
4 164 203 313 423 533	Babbitt	695
5 165 204 314 424 534	Backus	713
6 166 205 315 425 535	Bates	1102
7 167 206 316 426 536	Bishop	1439
8 168 207 317 427 537	B.J. Willard	1454
9 169 208 318 428 538	Berry	1358a
10 170 209 319 429 539	Brown	2026
11 171 210 320 430 540	Brown	2033
12 172 211 321 431 541	Burke	2157
13 173 212 322 432 542	Catlin	2522
14 174 213 323 433 543	Clover	2908
15 ~~175 214 324 434 544~~	~~Chacon~~	~~2568~~
16 176 215 325 435 545	Cooke	3170
17 177 216 326 436 546	Cooke	3181
18 178 217 327 437 547	Corcoran	3227
19 179 218 328 438 548	Delhi	3770
20 180 219 329 439 549	Delight	3772
21 181 220 330 440 550	Delta	3778
22 182 221 331 441 551	Evans	4571
23 183 222 332 442 552	Fagan	4605
24 184 223 333 443 553	Fairchild	4610
25 185 224 334 444 554	Flower	4891
26 186 225 335 445 555	Focke	4894
27 187 226 336 446 556	Fowler	4997
28 188 227 337 447 557	Geib	5297
29 189 228 338 448 558	Gay	5281
30 190 229 339 449 559	Georgetown	5342
31 191 230 340 450 560	Hall	5919
32 192 231 341 451 561	Green	5761
33 193 232 342 452 562	Greene	5765
34 194 233 343 453 563	Henry	6384
35 195 234 344 454 564	Hill	6498
36 196 235 345 455 565	Hinds	6516
37 197 236 346 456 566	Jewett	7307
38 198 237 347 457 567	Janeway	7208
39 199 238 348 458 568	Johnson	7416
40 200 239 349 459 569	Kennedy	7708
41 101 240 350 460 570	Keys	7747
42 102 241 351 461 571	Kingston	7822
43 103 242 352 462 572	Laski	8098
44 104 243 353 463 573	Kohlsaat	7918
45 105 244 354 464 574	Lowerre	8577
46 106 245 355 465 575	Maud Webster	9302
47 107 246 356 466 576	Marsh	9120
48 108 247 357 467 577	Marsh	9117
49 109 248 358 468 578	Napoleon	10,011
50 110 249 359 469 579	Narragansett	10,020
51 111 250 360 470 580	Neidlinger	10,086
52 112 251 361 471 581	Parker	10,733
53 113 252 362 472 582	Osprey	10,606
54 114 253 363 473 583	Odorless Rubber Co.	10,438

16

		Problem #			Case	Federal Case No.
55	115	254	364	474	584	Phelps	11,073
56	116	255	365	475	585	Philips	11,092
57	117	256	366	476	586	Plastic Slate-Roofing	11,209
58	118	257	367	477	587	Pusey	11,477
59	119	258	368	478	588	Richmond	11,796
60	120	259	369	479	589	Ready Roofing	11,613
61	121	260	370	480	590	Silver Moon	12,856
62	122	261	371	481	591	Stansfield	13,294
63	123	262	372	482	592	Smythe	13,134
64	124	263	373	483	593	Taylor	13,803
65	125	264	374	484	594	Swearinger	13,683
66	126	265	375	485	595	Thorp	14,003
67	127	266	376	486	596	Tong Duck Chung	14,093
68	128	267	377	487	597	Trigg	14,173
69	129	268	378	488	598	Towanda	14,109
70	130	269	379	489	599	U.S. (v. Faw)	15,077
71	131	270	380	490	600	U.S. (v. Fossat)	15,137
72	132	271	381	491	501	U.S. (v. Gadsby)	15,180
73	133	272	382	492	502	U.S. (v. Keen)	15,511
74	134	273	383	493	503	U.S. (v. Hare)	15,304
75	135	274	384	494	504	U.S. (v. Horn)	15,389
76	136	275	385	495	505	U.S. (v. Queen)	16,109
77	137	276	386	496	506	U.S. (v. Reagan)	16,128
78	138	277	387	497	507	U.S. (v. Ringgold)	16,167
79	139	278	388	498	508	U.S. (v. Thompkins)	16,483
80	140	279	389	499	509	U.S. (v. Two Horses)	16,578
81	141	280	390	500	510	U.S. (v. Whiskey)	16,671
82	142	281	391	401	511	Wall	17,093
83	143	282	392	402	512	Warren	17,194
84	144	283	393	403	513	Watson	17,286
85	145	284	394	404	514	Winans	17,861
86	146	285	395	405	515	Works	18,046
87	147	286	396	406	516	Winthrop	17,900
88	148	288	397	407	517	Einstein	4320
89	149	288	398	408	518	Hattie	6216
90	150	289	399	409	519	Lowe	8565
91	151	290	400	410	520	Parker	10,751
92	152	291	301	411	521	Russell	12,165
93	153	292	302	412	522	Tallman	13,739
94	154	293	303	413	523	U.S. (v. The Good Friends)	15,227
95	155	294	304	414	524	U.S. (v. Stott)	16,408
96	156	295	305	415	525	Whitcomb	17,529
97	157	296	306	416	526	Whipple	17,513
98	158	297	307	417	527	Zenobia	18,209
99	159	298	308	418	528	Thompson	13,938
100	160	299	309	419	529	Steam Stone Cutter	13,334

LIBRARY EXERCISE 11. OFFICIAL STATE COURT REPORTS. This exercise is designed to familiarize you with official state court reporters and gives you further practice in the use of parallel citations. To complete this exercise, find and cite the case that begins on the page listed below in the designated official state court reporter volume. Use the National Reporter Blue Book to find the parallel West regional reporter citation when necessary. If the National Reporter Blue Book is unavailable, use the Table of Cases volume in the appropriate West state or regional digest or the appropriate state edition of Shepard's Citations to find the parallel citation. If the library does not have the state reporter designated for your problem number, note in your answer "official report not available" and state the parallel West reporter citation (e.g., "158 N.W. 202") based upon the appropriate entry in the National Reporter Blue Book.

Problem #	Citation	Problem #	Citation
1 200 222 394 417 576	102 Neb. 361	51 150 272 344 467 526	112 Ohio St. 284
2 101 223 395 418 577	103 Neb. 111	52 151 273 345 468 527	113 Ohio St. 377
3 102 224 396 419 578	104 Neb. 465	53 152 274 346 469 528	123 Ohio St. 378
4 103 225 397 420 579	119 Neb. 153	54 153 275 347 470 529	124 Ohio St. 39
5 104 226 398 421 580	120 Neb. 525	55 154 276 348 471 530	125 Ohio St. 291
6 105 227 399 422 581	121 Neb. 488	56 155 277 349 472 531	126 Ohio St. 251
7 106 228 400 423 582	141 Neb. 538	57 156 278 350 473 532	144 Ohio St. 443
8 107 229 301 424 583	142 Neb. 736	58 157 279 351 474 533	145 Ohio St. 198
9 108 230 302 425 584	161 Neb. 404	59 158 280 352 475 534	146 Ohio St. 288
10 109 231 303 426 585	179 Neb. 817	60 159 281 353 476 535	147 Ohio St. 263
11 110 232 304 427 586	111 Kan. 577	61 160 282 354 477 536	109 Or. 254
12 111 233 305 428 587	112 Kan. 708	62 161 283 355 478 537	110 Okla. 57
13 112 234 306 429 588	113 Kan. 513	63 162 284 356 479 538	111 Okla. 282
14 113 235 307 430 589	134 Kan. 149	64 163 285 357 480 539	114 Okla. 103
15 114 236 308 431 590	135 Kan. 100	65 164 286 358 481 540	116 Okla. 50
16 115 237 309 432 591	136 Kan. 591	66 165 287 359 482 541	169 Okla. 336
17 116 238 310 433 592	159 Kan. 520	67 166 288 360 483 542	170 Okla. 349
18 117 239 311 434 593	160 Kan. 258	68 167 289 361 484 543	171 Okla. 337
19 118 240 312 435 594	288 Mo. 482	69 168 290 362 485 544	172 Okla. 221
20 119 241 313 436 595	289 Mo. 506	70 169 291 363 486 545	180 Iowa 833
21 120 242 314 437 596	290 Mo. 143	71 170 292 364 487 546	181 Iowa 1081
22 121 243 315 438 597	161 Minn. 269	72 171 293 365 488 547	182 Iowa 973
23 122 244 316 439 598	162 Minn. 410	73 172 294 366 489 548	183 Iowa 956
24 123 245 317 440 599	163 Minn. 389	74 173 295 367 490 549	213 Iowa 800
25 124 246 318 441 600	184 Minn. 309	75 174 296 368 491 550	214 Iowa 825
26 125 247 319 442 501	287 Ill. 182	76 175 297 369 492 551	215 Iowa 600
27 126 248 320 443 502	288 Ill. 304	77 176 298 370 493 552	216 Iowa 688
28 127 249 321 444 503	289 Ill. 315	78 177 299 371 494 553	223 Iowa 780
29 128 250 322 445 504	348 Ill. 441	79 178 300 372 495 554	224 Iowa 439
30 129 251 323 446 505	349 Ill. 436	80 179 201 373 496 555	225 Iowa 809
31 130 252 324 447 506	350 Ill. 200	81 180 202 374 497 556	226 Iowa 712
32 131 253 325 448 507	395 Ill. 348	82 181 203 375 498 557	136 Md. 334
33 132 254 326 449 508	382 Ill. 218	83 182 204 376 499 558	137 Md. 349
34 133 255 327 450 509	396 Ill. 404	84 183 205 377 500 559	138 Md. 446
35 134 256 328 451 510	275 Pa. 542	85 184 206 378 401 560	139 Md. 450
36 135 257 329 452 511	276 Pa. 212	86 185 207 379 402 561	140 Md. 45
37 136 258 330 453 512	277 Pa. 184	87 186 208 380 403 562	159 Md. 370
38 137 259 331 454 513	302 Pa. 254	88 187 209 381 404 563	160 Md. 407
39 138 260 332 455 514	303 Pa. 156	89 188 210 382 405 564	161 Md. 375
40 139 261 333 456 515	304 Pa. 221	90 189 211 383 406 565	162 Md. 419
41 140 262 334 457 516	346 Pa. 584	91 190 212 384 407 566	163 Md. 353
42 141 263 335 458 517	347 Pa. 510	92 191 213 385 408 567	164 Md. 381
43 142 264 336 459 518	348 Pa. 409	93 192 214 386 409 568	71 Colo. 410
44 143 265 337 460 519	22 Fla. 627	94 193 215 387 410 569	72 Colo. 42
45 144 266 338 461 520	127 Va. 563	95 194 216 388 411 570	73 Colo. 356
46 145 267 339 462 521	128 Va. 517	96 195 217 389 412 571	74 Colo. 268
47 146 268 340 463 522	129 Va. 297	97 196 218 390 413 572	126 Wis. 216
48 147 269 341 464 523	130 Va. 584	98 197 219 391 414 573	127 Wis. 451
49 148 270 342 465 524	129 Wis. 245	99 198 220 392 415 574	110 Ohio St. 636
50 149 271 343 466 525	130 Wis. 560	100 199 221 393 416 575	111 Ohio St. 448

18

LIBRARY EXERCISE 12. WEST'S REGIONAL REPORTERS. This exercise familiarizes you with some of the special characteristics of West's regional reporter series and gives you practice in citing cases therein. To complete this exercise, (a) find the case listed for your problem number in the appropriate West regional reporter. Cite the case using Shepard's Citations or the appropriate state or regional digest to find parallel citations when necessary. Do not include the subsequent history of the case on remand. (b) Give the name of the law firm(s) and the last name of the individual attorney(s) who presented the case for the parties, as listed by West Publishing Company. No special format is required for stating these names. (c) List the Digest Topics and Key Numbers for the first two headnotes. (d) Give the page number in the text of the opinion where the point of law identified by the second headnote number is discussed in the opinion.

Problem #	Citation	Problem #	Citation
1 121 241 331 421 521	11 S.E.2d 631	51 171 291 381 471 571	237 A.2d 320
2 122 242 332 422 522	10 S.E.2d 506	52 172 292 382 472 572	239 A.2d 640
3 123 243 333 423 523	7 S.E.2d 394	53 173 293 383 473 573	240 A.2d 60
4 124 244 334 424 524	99 A.2d 860	54 175 294 384 474 574	146 A.2d 281
5 125 245 335 425 525	146 S.E.2d 257	55 175 295 385 475 575	92 A.2d 222
6 126 246 336 426 526	148 S.E.2d 149	56 176 296 386 476 576	93 A.2d 349
7 127 247 337 427 527	188 S.W.2d 564	57 177 297 387 477 577	94 A.2d 385
8 128 248 338 428 528	100 A.2d 630	58 178 298 388 478 578	95 A.2d 689
9 129 249 339 429 529	190 S.W.2d 450	59 179 299 389 479 579	96 A.2d 246
10 130 250 340 430 530	252 S.W.2d 809	60 180 300 390 480 580	97 A.2d 540
11 131 251 341 431 531	255 S.W.2d 961	61 181 201 391 481 581	36 N.W.2d 507
12 132 252 342 432 532	250 S.W.2d 549	62 182 202 392 482 582	37 N.W.2d 473
13 133 253 343 433 533	168 N.W.2d 710	63 183 203 393 483 583	38 N.W.2d 863
14 134 254 344 434 534	167 N.W.2d 587	64 184 204 394 484 584	39 N.W.2d 468
15 135 255 345 435 535	179 N.W.2d 641	65 185 205 395 485 585	40 N.W.2d 252
16 136 256 346 436 536	388 P.2d 637	66 186 206 396 486 586	201 P. 1029
17 137 257 347 437 537	387 P.2d 319	67 187 207 397 487 587	202 P. 316
18 138 258 348 438 538	386 P.2d 249	68 188 208 398 488 588	203 P. 920
19 139 259 349 439 539	98 A.2d 55	69 189 209 399 489 589	204 P. 754
20 140 260 350 440 540	384 P.2d 256	70 190 210 400 490 590	206 P. 587
21 141 261 351 441 541	91 N.E.2d 401	71 191 211 301 491 591	103 N.E.2d 527
22 142 262 352 442 542	93 N.E.2d 5	72 192 212 302 492 592	104 N.E.2d 669
23 143 263 353 443 543	90 N.E.2d 908	73 193 213 303 493 593	105 N.E.2d 99
24 144 264 354 444 544	96 N.E.2d 739	74 194 214 304 494 594	106 N.E.2d 350
25 145 265 355 445 545	95 N.E.2d 685	75 195 215 305 495 595	107 N.E.2d 3
26 146 266 356 446 546	190 So. 2d 334	76 196 216 306 496 596	21 So. 2d 418
27 147 267 357 447 547	179 So. 2d 324	77 197 217 307 497 597	22 So. 2d 417
28 148 268 358 448 548	44 So. 2d 748	78 198 218 308 498 598	8 So. 2d 689
29 149 269 359 449 549	43 So. 2d 763	79 199 219 309 499 599	24 So. 2d 525
30 150 270 360 450 550	30 N.W.2d 484	80 200 220 310 500 600	25 So. 2d 625
31 151 271 361 451 551	29 N.W.2d 704	81 101 221 311 401 501	343 S.W.2d 869
32 152 272 362 452 552	28 N.W.2d 363	82 102 222 312 402 502	344 S.W.2d 153
33 153 273 363 453 553	31 N.W.2d 170	83 103 223 313 403 503	345 S.W.2d 170
34 154 274 364 454 554	63 P.2d 693	84 104 224 314 404 504	346 S.W.2d 3
35 155 275 365 455 555	62 P.2d 445	85 105 225 315 405 505	347 S.W.2d 233
36 156 276 366 456 556	61 P.2d 559	86 106 226 316 406 506	348 S.W.2d 930
37 157 277 367 457 557	59 P.2d 771	87 107 227 317 407 507	349 S.W.2d 416
38 158 278 368 458 558	131 P. 843	88 108 228 318 408 508	350 S.W.2d 446
39 159 279 369 459 559	132 P. 1170	89 109 229 319 409 509	132 S.E.2d 263
40 160 280 370 460 560	133 P. 118	90 110 230 320 410 510	133 S.E.2d 122
41 161 281 371 461 561	134 P. 807	91 111 231 321 411 511	134 S.E.2d 889
42 162 282 372 462 562	45 N.E.2d 280	92 112 232 322 412 512	135 S.E.2d 205
43 163 283 373 463 563	42 N.E.2d 627	93 113 233 323 413 513	137 S.E.2d 319
44 164 284 374 464 564	39 N.E.2d 734	94 114 234 324 414 514	136 S.E.2d 404
45 165 285 375 465 565	33 N.E.2d 282	95 115 235 325 415 515	160 A.2d 694
46 166 286 376 466 566	36 N.E.2d 760	96 116 236 326 416 516	161 A.2d 843
47 167 287 377 467 567	236 A.2d 737	97 117 237 327 417 517	162 A.2d 854
48 168 288 378 468 568	234 A.2d 334	98 118 238 328 418 518	83 A.2d 355
49 169 289 379 469 569	233 A.2d 828	99 119 239 329 419 519	84 A.2d 511
50 170 290 380 470 570	231 A.2d 740	100 120 240 330 420 520	85 A.2d 102

LIBRARY EXERCISE 13. CALIFORNIA REPORTER. This exercise familiarizes you with West's special reporter for California appellate state court opinions and also teaches you how to find the latest cases construing a particular statute or rule. To complete this exercise, find the volume of the California Reporter given for your problem number. Using the "Table of Statutes Construed," which lists all statutes interpreted by cases reported in the volume, find the case in that volume which construes the California Code provision listed below. Cite the case using the Table of Cases volumes accompanying West's California Digest or Pacific Digest to find parallel citations when necessary. If the appropriate Table of Cases volume is unavailable, use Shepard's California Reporter Citations. If the California Reporter volume was bound without including the "Table of Statutes Construed," check a duplicate copy. If the Table cannot be located, complete a different problem for this exercise.

Problem #	Cal. Rptr. Volume #	California Code Provision
1 157 240 329 411 516	1	Bus. & Prof. § 24200(e)
2 158 241 330 412 517	2	Civ. Proc. § 32
3 159 242 331 413 518	3	Civ. Proc. § 614
4 160 243 332 414 519	4	Civ. § 2982(d)
5 161 244 333 415 520	5	Welf. & Inst. § 2004
6 162 245 334 416 521	6	Pub. Util. § 1002
7 163 246 335 417 522	7	Welf. & Inst. § 2353
8 164 247 336 418 523	8	Pub. Res. § 4010
9 165 248 337 419 524	9	Health & Safety § 11503
10 166 249 338 420 525	10	Civ. Proc. § 657(4)
11 167 250 339 421 526	11	Penal § 261(1)
12 168 251 340 422 527	12	Civ. §§ 1734-1736
13 169 252 341 423 528	13	Bus. & Prof. § 23090
14 170 253 342 424 529	14	Penal § 647(4)
15 171 254 343 425 530	15	Penal § 825
16 172 255 344 426 531	16	Lab. § 4750
17 173 256 345 427 532	17	Bus. & Prof. § 2392
18 174 257 346 428 533	18	Bus. & Prof. § 2552(b)
19 175 258 347 429 534	19	Pub. Util. § 1007
20 176 259 348 430 535	20	Water § 31084
21 177 260 349 431 536	21	Penal § 1368
22 178 261 350 432 537	22	Civ. Proc. § 2042
23 179 262 351 433 538	23	Veh. § 10851
24 180 263 352 434 539	24	Civ. Proc. § 348
25 181 264 353 435 540	25	Gov't § 1090
26 182 265 354 436 541	26	Prob. § 202
27 183 266 355 437 542	27	Ins. § 530
28 184 267 356 438 543	28	Penal § 1026
29 185 268 357 439 544	29	Penal § 1239(b)
30 186 269 358 440 545	30	Penal § 189
31 187 270 359 441 546	31	Educ. § 984(a)
32 188 271 360 442 547	32	Penal § 1382
33 189 272 361 443 548	33	Civ. Proc. § 681
34 190 273 362 444 549	34	Rev. & Tax. § 6204
35 191 274 363 445 550	35	Civ. § 3399
36 192 275 364 446 551	36	Civ. Proc. § 1845
37 193 276 365 447 552	37	Rev. & Tax. § 17745
38 194 277 366 448 553	38	Lab. § 3202
39 195 278 367 449 554	39	Veh. § 22850
40 196 279 368 450 555	40	Civ. Proc. § 1190.1(h)
41 197 280 369 451 556	41	Penal § 1367
42 198 281 370 452 557	42	Penal § 1043
43 199 282 371 453 558	43	Civ. § 140.5
44 200 283 372 454 559	44	Penal § 203
45 101 284 373 455 560	45	Civ. § 1732
46 102 285 374 456 561	46	Penal § 203
47 103 286 375 457 562	47	Bus. & Prof. § 7071.5
48 104 287 376 458 563	48	Lab. § 4600

Problem #	Cal. Rptr. Volume #	California Code Provision
49 105 288 377 459 564	49	Penal § 1555.2
50 106 289 378 460 565	50	Penal § 1555.1
51 107 290 379 461 566	51	Penal §§ 4852.01-.17
52 108 291 380 462 567	52	Civ. Proc. § 1870(15)
53 109 292 381 463 568	53	Welf. & Inst. § 5501
54 110 293 382 464 569	54	Penal § 3047.5
55 111 294 383 465 570	55	Veh. § 23102
56 112 295 384 466 571	56	Penal § 816
57 113 296 385 467 572	57	Evid. 623
58 114 297 386 468 573	58	Ins. § 700
59 115 298 387 469 574	59	Civ. § 1710(4)
60 116 299 388 470 575	60	Penal § 288
61 117 300 389 471 576	61	Evid. § 1105
62 118 201 390 472 577	62	Corp. § 9300
63 119 202 391 473 578	63	Rev. & Tax. § 4151
64 120 203 392 474 579	64	Welf. & Inst. § 707
65 121 204 393 475 580	65	Streets & Highways § 102
66 122 205 394 476 581	66	Rev. & Tax. § 987
67 123 206 395 477 582	67	Pub. Util. § 1757
68 124 207 396 478 583	68	Civ. Proc. § 335
69 125 208 397 479 584	69	Civ. Proc. § 170(4)
70 126 209 398 480 585	70	Penal § 285
71 127 210 399 481 586	71	Lab. § 6407
72 128 211 400 482 587	72	Evid. § 621
73 129 212 301 483 588	73	Welf. & Inst. § 1176
74 130 213 302 484 589	74	Ins. § 10115
75 131 214 303 485 590	110	Civ. Proc. § 259a(4)
76 132 215 304 486 591	76	Evid. § 1235
77 133 216 305 487 592	77	Agric. § 52256-52258
78 134 217 306 488 593	78	Civ. Proc. § 544
79 135 218 307 489 594	79	Penal § 188
80 136 219 308 490 595	80	Penal § 1086
81 137 220 309 491 596	81	Civ. Proc. § 631.8
82 138 221 310 492 597	82	Evid. § 12(b)
83 139 222 311 493 598	83	Penal § 1239(b)
84 140 223 312 494 599	84	Penal § 1096
85 141 224 313 495 600	85	Civ. Proc. § 1211
86 142 225 314 496 501	86	Civ. Proc. § 1048
87 143 226 315 497 502	87	Penal § 1474
88 144 227 316 498 503	88	Penal § 187
89 145 228 317 499 504	89	Evid. § 1200
90 146 229 318 500 505	90	Bus. & Prof. § 6083(c)
91 147 230 319 401 506	91	Health & Safety § 24101.4
92 148 231 320 402 507	92	Educ. § 925
93 149 232 321 403 508	93	Corp. § 25510
94 150 233 322 404 509	94	Evid. § 351
95 151 234 323 405 510	95	Gov't §§ 17300-17302
96 152 235 324 406 511	96	Evid. § 1103
97 153 236 325 407 512	97	Bus. & Prof. § 6101
98 154 237 326 408 513	98	Welf. & Inst. § 11450
99 155 238 327 409 514	99	Gov't § 75070
100 156 239 328 410 515	100	Civ. Proc. § 284

LIBRARY EXERCISE 14. NEW YORK SUPPLEMENT. This exercise familiarizes you with West's special reporter for New York state court opinions and gives you practice in citing opinions in that reporter. To complete this exercise, find the case listed with your problem number below, and cite it in proper form. Be sure to find the correct series of West's New York Supplement. Use the appropriate volume of Shepard's New York Supplement Citations when necessary to find parallel citations. If the relevant Shepard's volume is unavailable, use the Table of Cases volumes accompanying West's New York Digest to find parallel citations. For purposes of this exercise, do not include the subsequent history of the case in your citation.

Problem #	Citation	Problem #	Citation
1 155 219 383 448 596	32 N.Y.S.2d 59	51 105 269 333 498 546	206 N.Y.S. 391
2 156 220 384 449 597	33 N.Y.S.2d 673	52 106 270 334 499 547	207 N.Y.S. 721
3 157 221 385 450 598	34 N.Y.S.2d 556	53 107 271 335 500 548	209 N.Y.S. 759
4 158 222 386 451 599	35 N.Y.S.2d 221	54 108 272 336 401 549	210 N.Y.S. 737
5 159 223 387 452 600	36 N.Y.S.2d 786	55 109 273 337 402 550	211 N.Y.S. 858
6 160 224 388 453 501	37 N.Y.S.2d 511	56 110 274 338 403 551	212 N.Y.S. 189
7 161 225 389 454 502	38 N.Y.S.2d 619	57 111 275 339 404 552	300 N.Y.S. 932
8 162 226 390 455 503	179 N.Y.S.2d 393	58 112 276 340 405 553	299 N.Y.S. 593
9 163 227 391 456 504	180 N.Y.S.2d 287	59 113 277 341 406 554	298 N.Y.S. 433
10 164 228 392 457 505	181 N.Y.S.2d 633	60 114 278 342 407 555	297 N.Y.S. 827
11 165 229 393 458 506	183 N.Y.S.2d 605	61 115 279 343 408 556	296 N.Y.S. 649
12 166 230 394 459 507	182 N.Y.S.2d 411	62 116 280 344 409 557	295 N.Y.S. 360
13 167 231 395 460 508	184 N.Y.S.2d 613	63 117 281 345 410 558	294 N.Y.S. 381
14 168 232 396 461 509	185 N.Y.S.2d 538	64 118 282 346 411 559	293 N.Y.S. 85
15 169 233 397 462 510	186 N.Y.S.2d 73	65 119 283 347 412 560	292 N.Y.S. 502
16 170 234 398 463 511	178 N.Y.S.2d 270	66 120 284 348 413 561	291 N.Y.S. 314
17 171 235 399 464 512	194 N.Y.S.2d 695	67 121 285 349 414 562	290 N.Y.S. 726
18 172 236 400 465 513	415 N.Y.S.2d 529	68 122 286 350 415 563	289 N.Y.S. 687
19 173 237 301 466 514	187 N.Y.S.2d 737	69 123 287 351 416 564	288 N.Y.S. 500
20 174 238 302 467 515	188 N.Y.S.2d 295	70 124 288 352 417 565	287 N.Y.S. 396
21 175 239 303 468 516	189 N.Y.S.2d 194	71 125 289 353 418 566	286 N.Y.S 208
22 176 240 304 469 517	190 N.Y.S.2d 656	72 126 290 354 419 567	285 N.Y.S. 548
23 177 241 305 470 518	191 N.Y.S.2d 673	73 127 291 355 420 568	284 N.Y.S. 409
24 178 242 306 471 519	192 N.Y.S.2d 797	74 128 292 356 421 569	283 N.Y.S. 681
25 179 243 307 472 520	193 N.Y.S.2d 166	75 129 293 357 422 570	282 N.Y.S. 593
26 180 244 308 473 521	303 N.Y.S.2d 245	76 130 294 358 423 571	106 N.Y.S. 330
27 181 245 309 474 522	304 N.Y.S.2d 810	77 131 295 359 424 572	75 N.Y.S. 209
28 182 246 310 475 523	305 N.Y.S.2d 477	78 132 296 360 425 573	76 N.Y.S. 293
29 183 247 311 476 524	306 N.Y.S.2d 789	79 133 297 361 426 574	39 N.Y.S. 744
30 184 248 312 477 525	416 N.Y.S.2d 573	80 134 298 362 427 575	42 N.Y.S. 576
31 185 249 313 478 526	308 N.Y.S.2d 385	81 135 299 363 428 576	94 N.Y.S. 178
32 186 250 314 479 527	309 N.Y.S.2d 145	82 136 300 364 429 577	93 N.Y.S. 283
33 187 251 315 480 528	310 N.Y.S.2d 500	83 137 201 365 430 578	92 N.Y.S. 163
34 188 252 316 481 529	311 N.Y.S.2d 481	84 138 202 366 431 579	91 N.Y.S. 503
35 189 253 317 482 530	312 N.Y.S.2d 317	85 139 203 367 432 580	88 N.Y.S. 52
36 190 254 318 483 531	313 N.Y.S.2d 97	86 140 204 368 433 581	126 N.Y.S. 880
37 191 255 319 484 532	314 N.Y.S.2d 638	87 141 205 369 434 582	125 N.Y.S. 613
38 192 256 320 485 533	315 N.Y.S.2d 353	88 142 206 370 435 583	124 N.Y.S. 406
39 193 257 321 486 534	316 N.Y.S.2d 221	89 143 207 371 436 584	123 N.Y.S. 301
40 194 258 322 487 535	317 N.Y.S.2d 73	90 144 208 372 437 585	122 N.Y.S. 793
41 195 259 323 488 536	318 N.Y.S.2d 467	91 145 209 373 438 586	121 N.Y.S. 11
42 196 260 324 489 537	319 N.Y.S.2d 89	92 146 210 374 439 587	120 N.Y.S. 580
43 197 261 325 490 538	320 N.Y.S.2d 433	93 147 211 375 440 588	119 N.Y.S. 751
44 198 262 326 491 539	321 N.Y.S.2d 239	94 148 212 376 441 589	118 N.Y.S. 591
45 199 263 327 492 540	322 N.Y.S.2d 238	95 149 213 377 442 590	141 N.Y.S. 868
46 200 264 328 493 541	323 N.Y.S.2d 440	96 150 214 378 443 591	140 N.Y.S. 916
47 101 265 329 494 542	330 N.Y.S.2d 336	97 151 215 379 444 592	139 N.Y.S. 6
48 102 266 330 495 543	331 N.Y.S.2d 377	98 152 216 380 445 593	138 N.Y.S. 456
49 103 267 331 496 544	332 N.Y.S.2d 552	99 153 217 381 446 594	137 N.Y.S. 466
50 104 268 332 497 545	333 N.Y.S.2d 410	100 154 218 382 447 595	136 N.Y.S. 688

LIBRARY EXERCISE 15. AMERICAN LAW REPORTS ANNOTATED. This exercise is
designed to familiarize you with several of the basic features of Lawyers
Co-operative's American Law Report Annotated series. To complete this
exercise, (a) find and cite the A.L.R. annotation that is listed below in
proper USOC form. See Rule 16.1.4. (b) Cite the case accompanying
(preceding) the annotation in proper USOC form. Do not include a reference to
the A.L.R. citation the case nor a notation of the subsequent history of the
case (e.g., certiorari denied, rehearing denied) in your citation. Use
Shepard's Citations to find any missing parallel citations. (c) Using the
"Index" to the annotation, determine in what section or sections of the
annotation deal with the topic listed with your problem number below? For
your answer, simply state the sections (e.g., §§ 3[b], 5, 6). No special form
is required for this answer. (d) Find the "Total Client-Service Library
References" listing at the beginning of the annotation. This list provides
references to several other related (and very useful) research sources.
Examine this list, and determine what topic(s) and section(s) of American
Jurisprudence (a legal encyclopedia) that you could look to find a textual
discussion of the topic covered by the annotation. For purposes of this
exercise, simply state the reference to American Jurisprudence in the manner
that it is given in the "Total Client-Service Library References." USOC form
need not be used. If your typewriter does not have section signs, write them
in with a pen or pencil.

Problem #	A.L.R. Citation	(c) Topic
1 146 230 308 427 529	39 A.L.R.3d 719	Improper grading of bar examination
2 147 231 309 428 530	14 A.L.R. Fed. 806	General discussion of the "Scope-of-the-Project" test
3 148 232 310 429 531	13 A.L.R. Fed. 416	Use of school records to meet age requirement
4 149 233 311 430 532	9 A.L.R. Fed. 533	Review of arbitrary decisions
5 150 234 312 431 533	8 A.L.R. Fed. 180	Value of a coal interest for eminent domain purposes
6 151 235 313 432 534	7 A.L.R. Fed. 876	Scope of review of decisions relying on an exemption of material by the Freedom of Information Act
7 152 236 314 433 535	5 A.L.R. Fed. 566	The probative value of expert testimony about claims of mineral interests on public lands
8 153 237 315 434 536	2 A.L.R. Fed. 691	Requirement of pleading substantial evidence in a "dispute clause" case
9 154 238 316 435 537	11 A.L.R. Fed. 368	Improper composition of a draft board as a denial of due process
10 155 239 317 436 538	38 A.L.R.3d 452	Loss of driving privileges because of advance age
11 156 240 318 437 539	6 A.L.R. Fed. 988	Safety standards for car windows
12 157 241 319 438 540	98 A.L.R.3d 453	Effect of subsequent illegitimate children on a divorce decree
13 158 242 320 439 541	27 A.L.R.3d 1254	Wearing dress of the opposite sex in a bar
14 159 243 321 440 542	17 A.L.R.3d 1408	Entrapment of a pharmacist
15 ~~160 244 322 441 543~~	22 A.L.R.3d 749	Effect on an alien's return after an unintentional or involuntary departure from the United States
16 161 245 323 442 544	47 A.L.R.3d 822	Best evidence objection to radar devices
17 162 246 324 443 545	28 A.L.R.3d 788	Acceptance of the work by the owner
18 163 247 325 444 546	15 A.L.R.3d 847	Assessments for turnpikes
19 164 248 326 445 547	33 A.L.R.3d 229	Assistance of counsel in labor relations hearings
20 165 249 327 446 548	32 A.L.R.3d 1151	Effect of reciprocity between states
21 166 250 328 447 549	20 A.L.R.3d 599	Requirements as to written contracts
22 167 251 329 448 550	1 A.L.R. Fed. 838	Gambling conducted on vessels
23 168 252 330 449 551	1 A.L.R.4th 411	Absence of a "kill switch"
24 169 253 331 450 552	8 A.L.R.3d 749	Impeachment of a witness based on intoxication in a conversion action
25 170 254 332 451 553	3 A.L.R.3d 1082	Warranty of fitness for duty
26 171 255 333 452 554	1 A.L.R.3d 642	Death on the High Seas Act

23

Problem #	A.L.R. Citation	(c) Topic
27 172 256 334 453 555	50 A.L.R. Fed. 420	Failure to publish an allowance in a tariff schedule
28 173 257 335 454 556	3 A.L.R. Fed. 203	Necessity of signals
29 174 258 336 455 557	9 A.L.R. Fed. 768	Contributory negligence
30 175 259 337 456 558	35 A.L.R.3d 907	Election of remedies in unauthorized policy cases
31 176 260 338 457 559	6 A.L.R.3d 519	Waiver of the right to object
32 177 261 339 458 560	4 A.L.R.3d 224	Teller of a bank as a dual agent
33 178 262 340 459 561	42 A.L.R.3d 1099	Block-busting rule
34 179 263 341 460 562	30 A.L.R.3d 1395	Privity of contract as a factor
35 180 264 342 461 563	45 A.L.R.3d 1181	Liability of attorneys for negligent drafting or execution of wills
36 181 265 343 462 564	40 A.L.R.3d 1158	Effect of residency on the power to confess judgments
37 182 266 344 463 565	31 A.L.R.3d 953	Disqualification in quo warranto proceedings
38 183 267 345 464 566	50 A.L.R. Fed. 661	Validity of "Bad Boy" clauses
39 184 268 346 465 567	21 A.L.R.3d 483	The English common-law rule and exception to taking a client's oath
40 185 269 347 466 568	97 A.L.R.3d 989	Resentment of wife working as a ground for divorce
41 186 270 348 467 569	17 A.L.R.3d 743	Validity of minimum area restrictions
42 187 271 349 468 570	2 A.L.R.4th 859	Sales and use taxes on leased roadside advertising signs
43 188 272 350 469 571	12 A.L.R. Fed. 638	Traditional authority of military commanders to exclude civilians from military installations
44 189 273 351 470 572	60 A.L.R.3d 550	Fixed liquidated damage sums in sign or billboard contracts
45 190 274 352 471 573	43 A.L.R.3d 971	Mental condition of the depositor as a factor
46 191 275 353 472 574	96 A.L.R.3d 22	Defective toys
47 192 276 354 473 575	24 A.L.R.3d 1193	Unjust enrichment theory of recovery
48 193 277 355 474 576	11 A.L.R.3d 918	Prejudicial effect of a jury's unauthorized visit to the scene of the accident or premises in question
49 194 278 356 475 577	50 A.L.R.3d 1164	Mind-altering drugs
50 195 279 357 476 578	23 A.L.R.3d 683	Pick-up service as a branch bank
51 196 280 358 477 579	41 A.L.R.3d 904	Child injured by unreasonable punishment
52 197 281 359 478 580	10 A.L.R. Fed. 940	Actions for violation of the Trust Indenture Act of 1939
53 198 282 360 479 581	7 A.L.R.3d 908	Right to set off with regard to deposits made in the name of a legatee
54 199 283 361 480 582	44 A.L.R.3d 1283	Relation to a direct civil action
55 200 284 362 481 583	46 A.L.R.3d 369	Unwholesome influence of women employed in bars
56 101 285 363 482 584	50 A.L.R.3d 1089	Discriminatory bussing plans
57 102 286 364 483 585	37 A.L.R.3d 645	Necessity of a hearing
58 103 287 365 484 586	19 A.L.R.3d 1297	Indorsement on allonge
59 104 288 366 485 587	43 A.L.R.3d 824	Actions on rent notes
60 105 289 367 486 588	48 A.L.R.3d 240	Surviving spouse's right to custody of a dead body
61 106 290 368 487 589	25 A.L.R.3d 1367	Whether the right to cancel depends on the noninterference with the intervening rights of other parties
62 107 291 369 488 590	49 A.L.R. Fed. 511	Seizure of a tape recorder
63 108 292 370 489 591	62 A.L.R. Fed. 733	Conduct in excess of simple negligence
64 109 293 371 490 592	19 A.L.R.4th 861	"Sudden hate" in a prosecution for manslaughter
65 110 294 372 491 593	20 A.L.R.4th 637	Intoxication as a bar to unemployment compensation
66 111 295 373 492 594	22 A.L.R.4th 321	Termination of an employee's group insurance coverage as a result of the employer's mistake
67 112 296 374 493 595	63 A.L.R. Fed. 446	Projects affecting marshlands

Problem #	A.L.R. Citation	(c) Topic
68 113 297 375 494 596	64 A.L.R. Fed. 552	Sufficiency of the notice
69 114 298 376 495 597	24 A.L.R.4th 870	Waiver by a guardian
70 115 299 377 496 598	25 A.L.R.4th 787	Aiding and abetting suicide of victim
71 116 300 378 497 599	26 A.L.R.4th 396	Actions against landlords
72 117 201 379 498 600	27 A.L.R.4th 864	Effect of summer employment
73 118 202 380 499 501	28 A.L.R.4th 227	Bail in treason cases
74 119 203 381 500 502	29 A.L.R.4th 104	Identification by pickpocket victim
75 120 204 382 401 503	48 A.L.R. Fed. 131	Wife's consent to a warrantless search and seizure
76 121 205 383 402 504	18 A.L.R.4th 360	Use of tape-recorded conversations
77 122 206 384 403 505	30 A.L.R.4th 414	Memory losses
78 123 207 385 404 506	31 A.L.R.4th 851	Use of expert witnesses
79 124 208 386 405 507	47 A.L.R. Fed. 490	Claims for cargo losses
80 125 209 387 406 508	32 A.L.R.4th 504	Failure of the judge to hold court because of illness
81 126 210 388 407 509	33 A.L.R.4th 663	Detention in a foreign country
82 127 211 389 408 510	34 A.L.R.4th 609	Disciplinary actions against physicians for fee splitting
83 128 212 390 409 511	35 A.L.R.4th 538	Punitive damages in oil pollution cases
84 129 213 391 410 512	36 A.L.R.4th 544	Timeliness of substitution of conforming tender
85 130 214 392 411 513	37 A.L.R.4th 10	Use of a walking test
86 131 215 393 412 514	38 A.L.R.4th 648	Riots at sporting events
87 132 216 394 413 515	39 A.L.R.4th 633	Use of a writ of attachment
88 133 217 395 414 516	65 A.L.R. Fed. 835	Notes taken by juror as evidence
89 134 218 396 415 517	66 A.L.R. Fed. 119	Search of the anal cavity
90 135 219 397 416 518	6 A.L.R.3d 973	Absence of a warranty clause in the deed
91 136 220 398 417 519	67 A.L.R. Fed. 282	Tolling of the statute
92 137 221 399 418 520	68 A.L.R. Fed. 861	Seizure of articles in plain view
93 138 222 400 419 521	46 A.L.R. Fed. 657	Fees charged by utility companies
94 139 223 301 420 522	58 A.L.R.3d 188	Accrued payments
95 140 224 302 421 523	69 A.L.R. Fed. 130	Reliance on novel theories
96 141 225 303 422 524	70 A.L.R. Fed. 427	Accidents related to work
97 142 226 304 423 525	21 A.L.R.3d 1383	Disability of preachers
98 143 227 305 424 526	71 A.L.R. Fed. 875	Applicability of state law
99 144 228 306 425 527	72 A.L.R. Fed. 191	Termination of gas service
100 145 229 307 426 528	73 A.L.R. Fed. 112	Disclosure in a television report

LIBRARY EXERCISE 16. ANNOTATIONS IN U.S. SUPREME COURT REPORTS, LAWYERS' EDITION. This exercise is designed to familiarize you with the annotations that accompany U.S. Supreme Court opinions published in Lawyers Co-operative's U.S. Supreme Court Reports, Lawyers' Edition. (a) Using the designated annotation in U.S. Supreme Court Reports, Lawyers' Edition, answer the question given with your problem number. Be sure to use the correct series. (b) Cite the reported Supreme Court case that accompanies the annotation to United States Reports without parallel citations. In L. Ed. 2d, that case is in the main part of the volume.

1 109 290 319 408 581   74 L. Ed. 677 When an improvement has been abandoned, can the amount of a special tax assessment paid on it be recovered under an assumpsit claim?
2 110 291 320 409 582   42 L. Ed. 688 Can a carrier limit its tort liability by means of a general notice of such a limitation?
3 111 292 321 410 583   1 L. Ed. 2d 1876 Does the death of an accused person ordinarily abate a criminal action against that person, including review proceedings pending at that time?
4 112 293 322 411 584   53 L. Ed. 826 Are reasonable attorneys' fees recoverable under the Sherman Antitrust Act?
5 113 294 323 412 585   98 L. Ed. 600 What is the name given to the statute codified at 40 U.S.C. § 276a et seq.?
6 114 295 324 413 586   78 L. Ed. 2d 914 Does a reasonable "possibility" that a petition for a writ of certiorari will ultimately be granted by the Court favor granting a stay of execution of a death sentence pending the Court's disposition of that writ?
7 115 296 325 414 587   97 L. Ed. 782 Does a witness waive the objection that Congress lacks constitutional power to investigate a matter as a defense to a contempt of congress action when the witness failed to raise that defense before the congressional committee?
8 116 297 326 415 588   94 L. Ed. 464 What is the name of the rule of construction dealing with general words appearing in a writing following a particular enumeration of subjects or classes of a persons?
9 117 298 327 416 589   93 L. Ed. 981 Is the double jeopardy provision of the Fifth Amendment violated when a person is retried after his first trial is unavoidably interrupted before its completion?
10 118 299 328 417 590   50 L. Ed. 204 Does the weight of authority hold that a municipal ordinance conferring an exclusive privilege to remove garbage is a valid exercise of state police power?
11 119 300 329 418 591   39 L. Ed. 742 What is the term used to designate the contribution made by the owners of the ship, freight, and goods on board, in proportion to their respective interests, toward any particular loss or expense sustained for the general safety of the ship and cargo?
12 120 201 330 419 592   26 L. Ed. 481 Is proof of "reputation" of marriage sufficient to prove a marriage under a bigamy statute?
13 121 202 331 420 593   45 L. Ed. 281 Under the early rule in the U.S. Supreme Court, was the opinion of the court below part of the record on appeal?
14 122 203 332 421 594   92 L. Ed. 281 What name is given to state laws excluding aliens from acquiring agricultural land within the borders of a state?
15 123 204 333 422 595   8 L. Ed. 2d 894 Can a reasonable attorney's fee be awarded under the Perishable Agricultural Commodities Act?
16 124 205 334 423 596   17 L. Ed. 2d 1067 Under the general rule, is it an unfair labor practice under the National Labor Relations Act for an employer to make a general increase in his employees' wages without consulting his employees' bargaining agent?
17 125 206 335 424 597   27 L. Ed. 769 Do corporations have the power to issue preferred stock in absence of express statutory authority or consent of the common shareholders?
18 126 207 336 425 598   4 L. Ed. 2d 1777 In general, is a seaman on shore leave still acting "in the course of his employment" under the Jones Act?
19 127 208 337 426 599   62 L. Ed. 189 What subject was regulated by the contract labor laws?
20 128 209 338 427 600   68 L. Ed. 814 Does a statute prescribing a minimum weight for loaves of bread unconstitutionally deprive a baker of his freedom to contract?

21 129 210 339 428 501 28 L. Ed. 809 Must fraud be a constituent of the act of barratry?
22 130 211 340 429 502 90 L. Ed. 1267 What name is given to legislative acts that inflict punishment without trial?
23 131 212 341 430 503 5 L. Ed. 2d 1056 Does the filing of a bond to dissolve an attachment constitute a waiver of an objection to venue?
24 132 213 342 431 504 34 L. Ed. 355 May the element of noise be considered in calculating damages in an abutter's action against the owners of an elevated railway?
25 133 214 343 432 505 70 L. Ed. 822 Does a threat to break a contract in itself constitute duress?
26 134 215 344 433 506 61 L. Ed. 2d 910 What four factors did the Supreme Court recognize in a 1977 Supreme Court decision as relevant in determining whether a private remedy is implicit in a federal statute that does not expressly provide one?
27 135 216 345 434 507 60 L. Ed. 2d 1107 Has the Supreme Court recognized that a reasonable amount of interest may be properly included "just compensation" when the United States condemns real property or an interest therein?
28 136 217 346 435 508 59 L. Ed. 2d 959 Does the Fourth Amendment prohibit per se the covert entry of a place to plant an electronic bugging device where the surveillance is otherwise lawful under the Fourth Amendment?
29 137 218 347 436 509 58 L. Ed. 2d 904 If a federal statute made extended absence from the United States a ground for the forfeiture of Social Security benefits, would such a statute violate the federal constitutional right of international travel?
30 138 219 348 437 510 57 L. Ed. 2d 1279 According to the Supreme Court, what is the threshold inquiry in determining whether a particular exercise of a state's police power permissibly interferes with obligations arising under an existing private contract?
31 139 220 349 438 511 56 L. Ed. 2d 918 Has the Supreme Court regarded pronouncements of individual legislators respecting the intent of a previously enacted statute as extremely important in construing the statute?
32 140 221 350 439 512 55 L. Ed. 2d 892 Can lawful acts be prohibited as part of federal antitrust injunctive relief in order to make that relief effective?
33 141 222 351 440 513 54 L. Ed. 2d 873 Is it now necessary for a person in state custody seeking federal habeas corpus relief to have first sought review by certiorari in the U.S. Supreme Court to satisfy the requirement that state remedies must be exhausted?
34 142 223 352 441 514 53 L. Ed. 2d 1273 Is it necessary that a formal legislative announcement of punishment be made in order to have a constitutionally prohibited bill of attainder?
35 143 224 353 442 515 52 L. Ed. 2d 824 On what theory did early decisions uphold a state's right to discriminate between residents and nonresidents with respect to the right of access to fish and wildlife within its jurisdiction?
36 144 225 354 443 516 51 L. Ed. 2d 826 When a tying product is patented, will courts assume that sufficient economic power exists to make a tying sale of an unpatented product under section 1 of the Sherman Act?
37 145 226 355 444 517 50 L. Ed. 2d 902 Has an association ever been recognized by the Supreme Court as having standing to assert the rights of its own members in challenging the constitutionality of legislation?
38 146 227 356 445 518 40 L. Ed. 2d 846 Does the Seventh Amendment require that a jury always be composed of twelve jurors in a civil case?
39 147 228 357 446 519 41 L. Ed. 2d 1193 Can a defense that is required to be raised by Rule 12(b)(2) in a pretrial motion be also raised by a motion under 28 U.S.C. § 2255?
40 148 229 358 447 520 42 L. Ed. 2d 870 Can a certification of a federal question, standing alone, be sufficient to support the Supreme Court's appellate jurisdiction?
41 149 230 359 448 521 43 L. Ed. 2d 833 Are states entitled to absolute immunity from liability under 42 U.S.C. § 1983 governing civil rights actions?
42 150 231 360 449 522 44 L. Ed. 2d 818 Are minimum fee schedules for attorneys enforced by a state bar association "price fixing" under section 1 of the Sherman Act?

43 151 232 361 450 523   46 L. Ed. 2d 955   If an article has begun its physical entry into the stream of exportation, is it an "export" within the meaning of the import-export clause?
44 152 233 362 451 524   47 L. Ed. 2d 975   Is the right of privacy implicit in the concept of liberty guaranteed by Section 1 of the Fourteenth Amendment?
45 153 234 363 452 525   48 L. Ed. 2d 917   Under the "drummer" cases, can a state validly tax the mere solicitation of interstate business for future delivery?
46 154 235 364 453 526   49 L. Ed. 2d 1296   Are corporations created by a federal statute "persons" protected by the equal protection clause?
47 155 236 365 454 527   30 L. Ed. 2d 952   Does a Circuit Justice have the power to grant an application for bail when the applicant's appeal from a state trial court's conviction is still pending in a state appellate court?
48 156 237 366 455 528   31 L. Ed. 2d 1006   After the Erie decision, does federal common law or state law apply to interstate water pollution issues?
49 157 238 367 456 529   32 L. Ed. 2d 942   Can the police in a "frisk" permissibly look for items other than concealed weapons unrelated to the protection of the officer?
50 158 239 368 457 530   33 L. Ed. 2d 865   Does the constitutional right of association include the right to associate for the assertion of mutual economic interests?
51 159 240 369 458 531   34 L. Ed. 2d 839   On what basis is the due process issue to be decided when the manner of conducting a police lineup is alleged to be unnecessarily suggestive?
52 160 241 370 459 532   36 L. Ed. 2d 1077   Must prior notice be given to an alleged parole violator of when and where his final revocation hearing will be held and which conditions of his parole agreement he or she is alleged to have violated?
53 161 242 371 460 533   38 L. Ed. 2d 835   In a prosecution under what act was the "clear and present danger" rule first announced by Mr. Justice Holmes?
54 162 243 372 461 534   37 L. Ed. 2d 1147   Do the First Amendment's religion clauses allow parents to withhold medical treatment from their children based upon the parents' religious beliefs?
55 163 244 373 462 535   39 L. Ed. 2d 942   Has the "deference rule" ever been applied in the construction of the Passport Act by the Department of State?
56 164 245 374 463 536   25 L. Ed. 2d 1025   In order for a guilty plea to be valid, must the accused understand the consequences of that plea?
57 165 246 375 464 537   26 L. Ed. 2d 916   According to the Supreme Court, what is the "most relevant criterion" for determining the seriousness of a particular offense for purposes of jury trial rights?
58 166 247 376 465 538   27 L. Ed. 2d 935   Prior to the Civil Rights Act of 1957, on what basis were women included or excluded from service on federal juries?
59 167 248 377 466 539   28 L. Ed. 2d 978   Can the police permissibly arrest more than one person for a crime when it is known by the police that the crime was committed by only one person?
60 168 249 378 467 540   29 L. Ed. 2d 1067   In order for the "plain view" doctrine to apply, must the police officer have had the right to be in the position to have that view?
61 169 250 379 468 541   18 L. Ed. 2d 1602   Under the Erie decision, which requires a federal court to follow state law in diversity cases, must a federal court generally follow a lower state court decision that is inconsistent with an earlier decision of the state's highest court?
62 170 251 380 469 542   19 L. Ed. 2d 1530   Based upon authority given in the annotation, is it unlawful for a wire service to require a subscriber to take a complete "package" news wire service when the subscriber did not need or want the complete service?
63 171 252 381 470 543   20 L. Ed. 2d 1623   What name is given to the doctrine that requires a federal court to defer a decision of a federal question until potentially controlling state-law issues are authoritatively decided?
64 172 253 382 471 544   21 L. Ed. 2d 905   Does the Sixth Amendment's guaranty of a right to a speedy trial apply to state criminal proceedings by virtue of the Fourteenth Amendment?
65 173 254 383 472 545   22 L. Ed. 2d 821   What three criteria has the Supreme Court established for determining whether a new rule announced by the Court will be retroactively applied?

66 174 255 384 473 546   23 L. Ed. 2d 915   Does the "arrest" under Article I, Section 6, Clause 1 of the U.S. Constitution include attachment of a senator's property to satisfy a prior judgment so as to give that senator immunity from such an attachment?
67 175 256 385 474 547   24 L. Ed. 2d 889   Has the U.S. Supreme Court held that discrimination against Negroes in purely private transactions involving real estate violates 42 U.S.C. § 1982?
68 176 257 386 475 548   9 L. Ed. 2d 1138   Is the good faith meeting the competition defense, when applicable, an absolute defense to a violation of the Robinson-Patman Act?
69 177 258 387 476 549   10 L. Ed. 2d 1397   In absence of statutory provisions to the contrary, are aliens returning to the United States after a temporary absence subject to all then current exclusionary provisions of the immigration laws?
70 178 259 388 477 550   11 L. Ed. 2d 1116   Is a free speech question presented by an income tax regulation that denies taxpayers a deduction for expenditures made to promote or defeat legislation?
71 179 260 389 478 551   12 L. Ed. 1282   Have lower federal courts held that the equal protection clause is violated when substantial disparities in population exist among voting districts for the election of municipal bodies?
72 180 261 390 479 552   13 L. Ed. 2d 1036   Under the current rule prevailing in federal civil trials, is a party's actual payment of travel expenses a prerequisite to recovering such expenses as costs?
73 181 262 391 480 553   14 L. Ed. 2d 784   Is a determination of the relevant "line of commerce" and "section of the country" a necessary predicate for finding a Section 7 Clayton Act violation?
74 182 263 392 481 554   16 L. Ed. 2d 1332   Do "simple" examinations of a person suspected of a crime violate the constitutional protection against self-incrimination?
75 183 264 393 482 555   15 L. Ed. 2d 1016   Does delay in making a Section 1404(a) transfer motion absolutely foreclose the granting of the motion?
76 184 265 394 483 556   2 L. Ed. 2d 1737   Does a simple refusal to sell to others who do not maintain the seller's fixed resale price violate Section 2 of the Robinson-Patman Act?
77 185 266 395 484 557   3 L. Ed. 1912   Is a "distinct physical place of business" one indicia that a particular business facility is an "establishment" for purposes of the retail or service establishment exemption of the Fair Labor Standards Act?
78 186 267 396 485 558   6 L. Ed. 2d 1510   Would the double jeopardy provision of the Fifth Amendment be violated if a defendant in a federal criminal prosecution were retried after a jury was discharged at a prior trial because the government was not prepared to go on with the prosecution?
79 187 268 397 486 559   7 L. Ed. 2d 959   Is a tort action within the scope of Section 301(a) of the Taft-Hartley Act?
80 188 269 398 487 560   86 L. Ed. 597   Do competitors have standing to sue to enjoin a final order of the Interstate Commerce Commission granting a permit to a motor carrier?
81 189 270 399 488 561   83 L. Ed. 567   In view of Section 42 of the Judicial Code, in which districts may prosecutions for conspiracies in violation of the laws of the United States be maintained?
82 190 271 400 489 562   85 L. Ed. 732   Does the remedy of attachment exist only by virtue of statute?
83 191 272 301 490 563   84 L. Ed. 1191   Does the defendant have the right to examine a transcript containing the testimony of the witnesses before a grand jury when the prosecution uses it to refresh a witness' memory at trial?
84 192 273 302 491 564   87 L. Ed. 1201   Is there a conflict among the decisions as to whether payment of a fine under protest precludes a review of the judgment imposing the fine?
85 193 274 303 492 565   88 L. Ed. 177   Are lobby expenses generally considered to be "ordinary and necessary expenses" deductible under the Internal Revenue Code?
86 194 275 304 493 566   89 L. Ed. 130   Are lunch periods included within "working time" for purposes of the overtime provisions of the Fair Labor Standards Act?
87 195 276 305 494 567   91 L. Ed. 146   What term is used to describe a suspension of operations by an employer resulting from a dispute with his employees over wages, hours, or working conditions?

88 196 277 306 495 568   96 L. Ed. 211   Is a longshoreman a "seaman" within the meaning of the Jones Act if he is injured while engaged in maritime service aboard a ship lying in navigable waters?
89 197 278 307 496 569   99 L. Ed. 403   Are merchant ships owned, controlled, and possessed by a foreign sovereign immune from suit in federal court?
90 198 279 308 497 570   100 L. Ed. 420   Are the federal statutes dealing with pretrial determination of mental competency of persons accused of a federal crime unconstitutional because they fail to provide a jury trial on the question of competency?
91 199 280 309 498 571   80 L. Ed. 785   Is a suit to restrain the warden of the state penitentiary as an agent of the state from selling convict-made goods without labeling them as such considered to be a suit "against the state"?
92 200 281 310 499 572   75 L. Ed. 528   Does the weight of authority support the view that a clause in an insurance policy that states an agent of the insurer shall not have authority to waive any policy condition unless it is endorsed on the policy apply to waivers, after the loss occurs, with respect to furnishing proof of loss within a stated time period?
93 101 282 311 500 573   76 L. Ed. 967   In considering the validity of a statute, will courts inquire into whether the legislature complied with its own rules in enacting the statute, provided no constitutional provision is violated?
94 102 283 312 401 574   77 L. Ed. 1213   Is a landowner's oral consent to the construction of a proposed system of municipal sewers considered to be revocable at any time by him?
95 103 284 313 402 575   79 L. Ed. 1133   Does a court in reorganization proceedings have jurisdiction over property of a corporation that is subject to a trust deed?
96 104 285 314 403 576   64 L. Ed. 482   Can counts at common law be joined in a complaint with counts under the Federal Employers' Liability Act in an action to recover for an alleged negligent injury to a railway employee?
97 105 286 315 404 577   66 L. Ed. 635   Is there an unconstitutional discrimination against a nonresident widow when she is denied by statute, unlike a resident widow, a dower interest in lands of which the husband was seized during coverture, but were conveyed prior to his death?
98 106 287 316 405 578   65 L. Ed. 511   On an appeal by either party in an admiralty case, must the appellate court consider changes in fact that have supervened since the decree of the lower court was entered?
99 107 288 317 406 579   67 L. Ed. 883   In determining whether state legislation impairs the obligation of a contract, will the Supreme Court independently determine whether a contract exists and to what extent it has been impaired?
100 108 289 318 407 580   60 L. Ed. 368   Has it been held that a party must give a satisfactory reason in order to be entitled to inspect judicial records?

LIBRARY EXERCISE 17. ENGLISH REPORTS, FULL REPRINT. This exercise is designed to familiarize you with English Reports, Full Reprint and to give you practice in citing cases in that series. (a) Find and cite the case that is reprinted in the volume of English Reports, Full Reprint and begins on the page listed below. For purposes of this exercise, a parallel citation to the original report reprinted should not be included in the citation. (b) List the original volume number, the reporter, and the page of the original report on which the case began, e.g., 19 Beavan 262, 1 B. & Ald. 405, etc. No special form is required for your answer to part (b).

Problem #					Vol.	Page	Problem #					Vol.	Page
1	111	251	361	471	581	3	5	51	161	201	311	421	531	98	69
2	112	252	362	472	582	4	372	52	162	202	312	422	532	128	943
3	113	253	363	473	583	6	1376	53	163	203	313	423	533	53	108
4	114	254	364	474	584	8	1576	54	164	204	314	424	534	41	937
5	115	255	365	475	585	29	103	55	165	205	315	425	535	47	1345
6	116	256	366	476	586	9	702	56	166	206	316	426	536	158	3
7	117	257	367	477	587	10	844	57	167	207	317	427	537	45	1131
8	118	258	368	478	588	142	956	58	168	208	318	428	538	105	552
9	119	259	369	479	589	11	825	59	169	209	319	429	539	48	531
10	120	260	370	480	590	58	435	60	170	210	320	430	540	138	648
11	121	261	371	481	591	40	624	61	171	211	321	431	541	2	708
12	122	262	372	482	592	145	1415	62	172	212	322	432	542	32	316
13	123	263	373	483	593	146	16	63	173	213	323	433	543	51	795
14	124	264	374	484	594	67	269	64	174	214	324	434	544	111	183
15	125	265	375	485	595	15	541	65	175	215	325	435	545	61	734
16	126	266	376	486	596	143	979	66	176	216	326	436	546	57	495
17	127	267	377	487	597	141	6	67	177	217	327	437	547	126	357
18	128	268	378	488	598	43	50	68	178	218	328	438	548	68	170
19	129	269	379	489	599	109	1335	69	179	219	329	439	549	1	150
20	130	270	380	490	600	17	327	70	180	220	330	440	550	49	1019
21	131	271	381	491	501	22	709	71	181	221	331	441	551	88	509
22	132	272	382	492	502	46	703	72	182	222	332	442	552	131	516
23	133	273	383	493	503	112	89	73	183	223	333	443	553	36	611
24	134	274	384	494	504	130	990	74	184	224	334	444	554	134	1160
25	135	275	385	495	505	26	400	75	185	225	335	445	555	60	703
26	136	276	386	496	506	27	603	76	186	226	336	446	556	54	511
27	137	277	387	497	507	127	939	77	187	227	337	447	557	133	456
28	138	278	388	498	508	101	279	78	188	228	338	448	558	25	389
29	139	279	389	499	509	16	450	79	189	229	339	449	559	132	792
30	140	280	390	500	510	30	961	80	190	230	340	450	560	142	695
31	141	281	391	401	511	31	414	81	191	231	341	451	561	28	584
32	142	282	392	402	512	63	491	82	192	232	342	452	562	56	237
33	143	283	393	403	513	55	307	83	193	233	343	453	563	66	1052
34	144	284	394	404	514	100	645	84	194	234	344	454	564	38	981
35	145	285	395	405	515	23	454	85	195	235	345	455	565	153	304
36	146	286	396	406	516	99	1191	86	196	236	346	456	566	148	724
37	147	287	397	407	517	39	96	87	197	237	347	457	567	13	932
38	148	288	398	408	518	14	415	88	198	238	348	458	568	42	461
39	149	289	399	409	519	52	770	89	199	239	349	459	569	147	616
40	150	290	400	410	520	104	594	90	200	240	350	460	570	7	250
41	151	291	301	411	521	33	690	91	101	241	351	461	571	136	536
42	152	292	302	412	522	35	4	92	102	242	352	462	572	103	255
43	153	293	303	413	523	70	385	93	103	243	353	463	573	64	90
44	154	294	304	414	524	62	669	94	104	244	354	464	574	107	639
45	155	295	305	415	525	135	844	95	105	245	355	465	575	65	510
46	156	296	306	416	526	137	424	96	106	246	356	466	576	152	796
47	157	297	307	417	527	125	1135	97	107	247	357	467	577	71	891
48	158	298	308	418	528	110	1172	98	108	248	358	468	578	140	14
49	159	299	309	419	529	37	396	99	109	249	359	469	579	129	573
50	160	300	310	420	530	59	435	100	110	250	360	470	580	50	640

A) *Lang v. Purves*, 15, English Reports, 541 (1862).

B) 15, Book 4, Edmund F. Moore, Volume XV Moore 388
Volume XV., ~~Judicial Committee of the Lords of the Privy Council~~,

LIBRARY EXERCISE 18. LAW REPORTS. This exercise familiarizes you with the semi-official English Law Reports series and gives you practice in citing modern English cases. To complete this exercise, find the case that begins on the page listed below in the designated volume of Law Reports. For your answer, cite the case using the proper form. Use a pen to write in the brackets in the citation if you are giving typewritten answers and brackets are not included on the key board.

	Problem #					Division	Volume Year	Volume Number	Page
1	122	227	321	425	506	Ch.	1929	1	253
2	123	228	322	426	507	Ch.	1929	2	368
3	124	229	323	427	508	Ch.	1930	1	138
4	125	230	324	428	509	Ch.	1930	2	93
5	126	231	325	429	510	Ch.	1931	1	138
6	127	232	326	430	511	Ch.	1931	2	183
7	128	233	327	431	512	Q.B.	1958	2	110
8	129	234	328	432	513	Q.B.	1959	1	114
9	130	235	329	433	514	Q.B.	1959	2	84
10	131	236	330	434	515	Q.B.	1960	1	197
11	132	237	331	435	516	Q.B.	1960	2	384
12	133	238	332	436	517	Ch.	1924	1	45
13	134	239	333	437	518	Ch.	1924	2	53
14	135	240	334	438	519	Q.B.	1961	1	232
15	136	241	335	439	520	Ch.	1926	1	897
16	137	242	336	440	521	Ch.	1927	1	75
17	138	243	337	441	522	Ch.	1927	2	150
18	139	244	338	442	523	Q.B.	1961	2	57
19	140	245	339	443	524	Q.B.	1962	1	676
20	141	246	340	444	525	Q.B.	1962	2	350
21	142	247	341	445	526	Q.B.	1963	1	528
22	143	248	342	446	527	Ch.	1969	1	20
23	144	249	343	447	528	Q.B.	1963	2	383
24	145	250	344	448	529	Q.B.	1970	1	357
25	146	251	345	449	530	Q.B.	1970	2	541
26	147	252	346	450	531	Q.B.	1971	1	300
27	148	253	347	451	532	Q.B.	1971	2	691
28	149	254	348	452	533	Q.B.	1972	1	326
29	150	255	349	453	534	Ch.	1921	2	59
30	151	256	350	454	535	Ch.	1922	1	364
31	152	257	351	455	536	Ch.	1922	2	256
32	153	258	352	456	537	Ch.	1923	1	192
33	154	259	353	457	538	Ch.	1923	2	372
34	155	260	354	458	539	Q.B.	1969	2	599
35	156	261	355	459	540	Q.B.	1969	1	272
36	157	262	356	460	541	Q.B.	1968	2	390
37	158	263	357	461	542	Q.B.	1968	1	455
38	159	264	358	462	543	Q.B.	1967	2	584
39	160	265	359	463	544	Q.B.	1967	1	29
40	161	266	360	464	545	Q.B.	1966	2	602
41	162	267	361	465	546	Q.B.	1966	1	273
42	163	268	362	466	547	Q.B.	1965	2	367
43	164	269	363	467	548	Q.B.	1965	1	334
44	165	270	364	468	549	Q.B.	1964	2	23
45	166	271	365	469	550	Q.B.	1958	1	439
46	167	272	366	470	551	Q.B.	1957	2	352
47	168	273	367	471	552	Q.B.	1957	1	294
48	169	274	368	472	553	Q.B.	1956	2	99
49	170	275	369	473	554	Q.B.	1956	1	658
50	171	276	370	474	555	Q.B.	1955	2	429
51	172	277	371	475	556	Q.B.	1955	1	253
52	173	278	372	476	557	Q.B.	1954	2	267
53	174	279	373	477	558	Q.B.	1954	1	191
54	175	280	374	478	559	Q.B.	1953	2	464
55	176	281	375	479	560	Q.B.	1953	1	86
56	177	282	376	480	561	Q.B.	1972	2	250

	Problem #				Division	Volume Year	Volume Number	Page
56	177	282	376	480	561	Q.B.	1972	2	250
57	178	283	377	481	562	K.B.	1930	1	393
58	179	284	378	482	563	K.B.	1930	2	364
59	180	285	379	483	564	K.B.	1931	1	374
60	181	286	380	484	565	K.B.	1931	2	583
61	182	287	381	485	566	K.B.	1932	1	458
62	183	288	382	486	567	K.B.	1932	2	309
63	184	289	383	487	568	K.B.	1933	1	551
64	185	290	384	488	569	K.B.	1933	2	251
65	186	291	385	489	570	K.B.	1934	1	357
66	187	292	386	490	571	K.B.	1934	2	299
67	188	293	387	491	572	K.B.	1901	2	596
68	189	294	388	492	573	K.B.	1935	1	146
69	190	295	389	493	574	K.B.	1902	2	743
70	191	296	390	494	575	K.B.	1903	1	861
71	192	297	391	495	576	K.B.	1903	2	657
72	193	298	392	496	577	K.B.	1904	1	84
73	194	299	393	497	578	K.B.	1904	2	824
74	195	300	394	498	579	K.B.	1905	1	336
75	196	201	395	499	580	K.B.	1905	2	723
76	197	202	396	500	581	K.B.	1935	2	282
77	198	203	397	401	582	K.B.	1936	1	697
78	199	204	398	402	583	K.B.	1921	2	799
79	200	205	399	403	584	K.B.	1921	3	32
80	101	206	400	404	585	K.B.	1922	1	693
81	102	207	301	405	586	K.B.	1922	2	674
82	103	208	302	406	587	K.B.	1941	1	396
83	104	209	303	407	588	K.B.	1941	2	321
84	105	210	304	408	589	K.B.	1942	1	269
85	106	211	305	409	590	K.B.	1942	2	253
86	107	212	306	410	591	K.B.	1928	2	501
87	108	213	307	411	592	K.B.	1929	2	249
88	109	214	308	412	593	K.B.	1927	2	181
89	110	215	309	413	594	K.B.	1925	1	141
90	111	216	310	414	595	K.B.	1925	2	646
91	112	217	311	415	596	K.B.	1948	1	459
92	113	218	312	416	597	K.B.	1948	2	394
93	114	219	313	417	598	K.B.	1949	1	250
94	115	220	314	418	599	K.B.	1949	2	372
95	116	221	315	419	600	K.B.	1950	1	455
96	117	222	316	420	501	K.B.	1950	2	208
97	118	223	317	421	502	K.B.	1951	1	752
98	119	224	318	422	503	K.B.	1951	2	420
99	120	225	319	423	504	K.B.	1952	1	89
100	121	226	320	424	505	K.B.	1936	2	226

LIBRARY EXERCISE 19. WEST'S DIGESTS: KEY NUMBER DIGESTS IN WEST'S REPORTER VOLUMES. This exercise is designed to familiarize you with the "Key Number Digest" section in West's National Reporter Syestem and to give you further practice in citing cases. To complete this exercise, find the volume of the reporter listed below. Turn to the "Key Number Digest" section (usually) located at the end of the volume. This section is an index to the digest topics and key numbers contained in the volume you are examining. Find the digest topic "Appeal and Error" in the digest section. Locate the first key number given under this topic. Find the first case digested under this key number in the main part of the volume. Cite the case in proper form. Use Shepard's Citations to find parallel citations when necessary. Since some volumes occasionally are bound without including the "Key Digest" section, check for the section in a duplicate copy of the reporter or complete a different problem if you have difficulty locating the section.

Problem #	Citation	Problem #	Citation
1 121 241 331 421 521	11 S.E.2d	51 171 291 381 471 571	237 A.2d
2 122 242 332 422 522	10 S.E.2d	52 172 292 382 472 572	239 A.2d
3 123 342 333 423 523	7 S.E.2d	53 173 293 383 473 573	240 A.2d
4 124 244 334 424 524	99 A.2d	54 174 294 384 474 574	91 A.2d
5 125 245 335 425 525	146 S.E.2d	55 175 295 385 475 575	92 A.2d
6 126 246 336 426 526	148 S.E.2d	56 176 296 386 476 576	93 A.2d
7 127 247 337 427 527	188 S.W.2d	57 177 297 387 477 577	94 A.2d
8 128 248 338 428 528	100 A.2d	58 178 298 388 478 578	95 A.2d
9 129 249 339 429 529	190 S.W.2d	59 179 299 389 479 579	588 F.2d
10 130 250 340 430 530	697 S.W.2d	60 180 300 390 480 580	566 F.2d
11 131 251 341 431 531	255 S.W.2d	61 181 201 391 481 581	530 F.2d
12 132 252 342 432 532	254 S.W.2d	62 182 202 392 482 582	529 F.2d
13 133 253 343 433 533	376 N.W.2d	63 183 203 393 483 583	528 F.2d
14 134 254 344 434 534	167 N.W.2d	64 184 204 394 484 584	527 F.2d
15 135 255 345 435 535	188 N.W.2d	65 185 205 395 485 585	526 F.2d
16 136 256 346 436 536	602 P.2d	66 186 206 396 486 586	525 F.2d
17 137 257 347 437 537	387 P.2d	67 187 207 397 487 587	524 F.2d
18 138 258 348 438 538	603 P.2d	68 188 208 398 488 588	523 F.2d
19 139 259 349 439 539	98 A.2d	69 189 209 399 489 589	479 F.2d
20 140 260 350 440 540	384 P.2d	70 190 210 400 490 590	478 F.2d
21 141 261 351 441 541	91 N.E.2d	71 191 211 301 491 591	477 F.2d
22 142 262 352 442 542	93 N.E.2d	72 192 212 302 492 592	510 F.2d
23 143 263 353 443 543	90 N.E.2d	73 193 213 303 493 593	475 F.2d
24 144 264 354 444 544	109 N.E.2d	74 194 214 304 494 594	487 F.2d
25 145 265 355 445 545	95 N.E.2d	75 195 215 305 495 595	485 F.2d
26 146 266 356 446 546	190 So. 2d	76 196 216 306 496 596	775 F.2d
27 147 267 357 447 547	179 So. 2d	77 197 217 307 497 597	483 F.2d
28 148 268 358 448 548	44 So. 2d	78 198 218 308 498 598	482 F.2d
29 149 269 359 449 549	43 So. 2d	79 199 219 309 499 599	481 F.2d
30 150 270 360 450 550	30 N.W.2d	80 200 220 310 500 600	305 F.2d
31 151 271 361 451 551	29 N.W.2d	81 101 221 311 401 501	307 F.2d
32 152 272 362 452 552	28 N.W.2d	82 102 222 312 402 502	309 F.2d
33 153 273 363 453 553	31 N.W.2d	83 103 223 313 403 503	310 F.2d
34 154 274 364 454 554	63 P.2d	84 104 224 314 404 504	311 F.2d
35 155 275 365 455 555	62 P.2d	85 105 225 315 405 505	312 F.2d
36 156 276 366 456 556	61 P.2d	86 106 226 316 406 506	322 F.2d
37 157 277 367 457 557	59 P.2d	87 107 227 317 407 507	318 F.2d
38 158 278 368 458 558	131 P.	88 108 228 318 408 508	316 F.2d
39 159 279 369 459 559	590 P.2d	89 109 229 319 409 509	315 F.2d
40 160 280 370 460 560	133 P.	90 110 230 320 410 510	314 F.2d
41 161 281 371 461 561	134 P.	91 111 231 321 411 511	365 F.2d
42 162 282 372 462 562	45 N.E.2d	92 112 232 322 412 512	767 F.2d
43 163 283 373 463 563	42 N.E.2d	93 113 233 323 413 513	367 F.2d
44 164 284 374 464 564	39 N.E.2d	94 114 234 324 414 514	368 F.2d
45 165 285 375 465 565	33 N.E.2d	95 115 235 325 415 515	375 F.2d
46 166 286 376 466 566	36 N.E.2d	96 116 236 326 416 516	376 F.2d
47 167 287 377 467 567	236 A.2d	97 117 237 327 417 517	378 F.2d
48 168 288 378 468 568	234 A.2d	98 118 238 328 418 518	379 F.2d
49 169 289 379 469 569	233 A.2d	99 119 239 329 419 519	370 F.2d
50 170 290 380 470 570	231 A.2d	100 120 240 330 420 520	574 F.2d

34

LIBRARY EXERCISE 20. WEST'S DIGESTS: FINDING CASES USING KNOWN TOPICS AND KEY NUMBERS. The purpose of this exercise is to give you practice in using known topic and key numbers to find relevant cases in West's digests. Assume that you have located a reference to the topic and key number (listed below) which appears to bear directly on a point of law that you are researching. Using West's Southern Digest, find a case decided in the year listed and arising in the state listed that is abstracted under that topic and key number. Find that case in the relevant volume of West's Southern Reporter, and cite the case in proper form. Do not include the subsequent history of the case in your citation. Disregard the reference to the WESTLAW topic heading number listed below for purposes of this exercise. It is used in conjunction with a later exercise.

Problem #	WESTLAW Topic No.	Topic & Key No.	Year	State
1 143 231 380 477 526	30	Appeal & Error 1133	1912	Ala.
2 144 232 381 478 527	30	Appeal & Error 1006(3)	1937	Miss.
3 145 233 382 479 528	30	Appeal & Error 880(2)	1965	Ala.
4 146 234 383 480 529	30	Appeal & Error 655(1)	1893	Miss.
5 147 235 384 481 530	30	Appeal & Error 262(2)	1908	Fla.
6 148 236 385 482 531	30	Appeal & Error 197(5)	1909	Miss.
7 149 237 386 483 532	56	Bills & Notes 519	1930	Ala.
8 150 238 387 484 533	52	Banks & Banking 270(10)	1924	Ala.
9 151 239 388 485 534	48A	Automobiles 357	1931	La.
10 152 240 389 486 535	48A	Automobiles 79	1949	Ala.
11 153 241 390 487 536	45	Attorney & Client 39	1931	Miss.
12 154 242 391 488 537	20	Adverse Possession 112	1902	Miss.
13 155 243 392 489 538	11	Account Stated 5	1969	Fla.
14 156 244 393 490 539	70	Carriers 320(27)	1943	Fla.
15 157 245 394 491 540	92	Constitutional Law 296(1)	1950 1984	La.
16 158 246 395 492 541	73	Certiorari 47	1947	Fla.
17 159 247 396 493 542	95	Contracts 155	1956	Miss.
18 160 248 397 494 543	101	Corporations 523	1926	Miss.
19 161 249 398 495 544	106	Courts 204	1938	Ala.
20 162 250 399 496 545	110	Criminal Law 241	1910	Miss.
21 163 251 400 497 546	110	Criminal Law 351(7)	1904	Miss.
22 164 252 301 498 547	110	Criminal Law 518(2)	1924	Fla.
23 165 253 302 499 548	104	Counties 199	1930	Miss.
24 166 254 303 500 549	307	Powers 32	1922	Miss.
25 167 255 304 401 550	134	Divorce 206	1953	Fla.
26 168 256 305 402 551	122	Depositions 38	1945	Ala.
27 169 257 306 403 552	120	Deeds 114(1)	1890	Fla.
28 170 258 307 404 553	115	Damages 131(4)	1901	La.
29 171 259 308 405 554	116	Dead Bodies 9	1941	Fla.
30 172 260 309 406 555	115	Damages 198	1929	Fla.
31 173 261 310 407 556	110	Criminal Law 799	1934	Miss.
32 174 262 311 408 557	157	Evidence 147	1914	Ala.
33 175 263 312 409 558	150	Equity 245	1908	Ala.
34 176 264 313 410 559	146	Embezzlement 39	1904	Fla.
35 177 265 314 411 560	167	Factors 1	1933	Miss.
36 178 266 315 412 561	162	Executors & Admin. 206(2)	1904	Ala.
37 179 267 316 413 562	157	Evidence 543(4)	1921	Ala.
38 180 268 317 414 563	186	Fraudulent Conveyances 299(10)	1924	La.
39 181 269 318 415 564	200	Highways 153	1927	Fla.
40 182 270 319 416 565	203	Homicide 181	1910	Ala.
41 183 271 320 417 566	205	Husband & Wife 129(3)	1917	Miss.
42 184 272 321 418 567	211	Infants 10	1909	Ala.
43 185 273 322 419 568	217	Insurance 104(1)	1979	Ala.
44 186 274 323 420 569	217	Insurance 730.1	1926	Ala.
45 187 275 324 421 570	219	Interest 46(1)	1902	Fla.
46 188 276 325 422 571	228	Judgment 107	1932	Fla.
47 189 277 326 423 572	230	Jury 42	1914	Ala.
48 190 278 327 424 573	232A	Labor Relations 924	1954	La.
49 191 279 328 425 574	238	Licenses 8(1)	1943	Fla.
50 192 280 329 426 575	268	Municipal Corp. 725	1937	Fla.

35

	Problem #				WESTLAW Topic No.	Topics & Key No.	Year	State
51	193	281	330	427 576	268	Municipal Corp. 284(4)	1950	Ala.
52	194	282	331	428 577	266	Mortgages 307	1898	Ala.
53	195	283	332	429 578	257A	Mental Health 55	1961	Miss.
54	196	284	333	430 579	255	Master & Servant 240(2)	1916	La.
55	197	285	334	431 580	250	Mandamus 73(1)	1943	Fla.
56	198	286	335	432 581	321	Rape 59 (16)	1925	Miss.
57	199	287	336	433 582	302	Pleading 280	1925	Ala.
58	200	288	337	434 583	313	Process 79	1917	Miss.
59	101	289	338	435 584	302	Pleading 36(3)	1944	Fla.
60	102	290	339	436 585	289	Partnership 242(7)	1929	La.
61	103	291	340	437 586	283	Officers 83	1927	La.
62	104	292	341	438 587	269	Names 18	1910	Ala.
63	105	293	342	439 588	369	Sunday 4	1920	Miss.
64	106	294	343	440 589	361	Statutes 130	1927	Fla.
65	107	295	344	441 590	354	Shipping 29	1956	La.
66	108	296	345	442 591	344	Salvage 39	1921	Miss.
67	109	297	346	443 592	343	Sales 54	1919	Miss.
68	110	298	347	444 493	348	Seamen 29(1)	1937	Miss.
69	111	299	348	445 594	403	Warehousemen 15(2)	1938	Fla.
70	112	300	349	446 595	390	Trusts 203	1928	Fla.
71	113	201	350	447 596	388	Trial 133(5)	1953	Miss.
72	114	202	351	448 597	381	Towns 59	1947	Fla.
73	115	203	352	449 598	372	Telecommunications 89	1954	Fla.
74	116	203	353	450 599	414	Zoning 613	1959	Fla.
75	117	205	354	451 600	413	Workmen's Compensation 1545	1949	Fla.
76	118	206	355	452 501	413	Workmen's Comepnsation 712	1930	Ala.
77	119	207	356	453 502	410	Witnesses 302	1966	La.
78	120	208	357	454 503	409	Wills 618	1925	Fla.
79	121	209	358	455 504	409	Wills 67	1955	Fla.
80	122	210	359	456 505	404	Waste 9	1956	Ala.
81	123	211	360	457 506	409	Wills 754	1942	Fla.
82	124	212	361	458 507	412	Work & Labor 22	1930	Fla.
83	125	213	362	459 508	413	Workmen's Compensation 799	1956	Miss.
84	126	214	363	460 509	413	Workmen's Compensation 1552	1946	Ala.
85	127	215	364	461 510	413	Workmen's Compensation 1966	1940	Fla.
86	128	216	365	462 511	268	Municipal Corporations 5	1956	Fla.
87	129	217	366	463 512	266	Mortgages 2	1929	Miss.
88	130	218	367	464 513	263	Money Paid 4	1932	Fla.
89	131	219	368	465 514	255	Master & Servant 256 (3)	1905	Ala.
90	132	220	369	466 515	247	Lotteries 6	1938	Ala.
91	133	221	370	467 516	16	Admiralty 4	1938	Miss.
92	134	222	371	468 517	101	Corporations 507(5)	1931	Miss.
93	135	223	372	469 518	95	Contracts 345	1905	Ala.
94	136	224	373	470 519	28	Animals 50(1)	1894	Ala.
95	137	225	374	471 520	71	Cemeteries 21	1895	Ala.
96	138	226	375	472 521	53	Bastards 78	1939	Fla.
97	139	227	376	473 522	65	Brokers 74	1912	Ala.
98	140	228	377	474 523	48A	Automobiles 238(2)	1914	Ala.
99	141	229	378	475 524	94	Continuance 48	1964	Ala.
100	142	230	379	476 525	67	Burglary 46(4)	1890	Fla.

LIBRARY EXERCISE 21. WEST'S DIGESTS: DESCRIPTIVE WORD INDEXES. This exercise gives you practice in using a descriptive word approach to find relevant topic and key numbers. Using the word(s) underlined for your problem below as one of the word(s) to be checked for relevant entries in the designated digest's Descriptive Word Index, find the the most relevant digest paragraph which answers the problem posed. Be sure to use the digest designated with your problem number (e.g., Modern Federal Practice Digest, Federal Practice Digest 2d, etc.). (a) Answer the question based upon the most relevant digest paragraph found in that digest (if appropriate). (b) List the topic and key number under which the digest paragraph was found. (c) Cite the case from which the digest paragraph was abstracted. Use Shepard's Citations to find missing parallel citations; for Supreme Court cases, however, cite only United States Reports. Consult the case to find missing information. Do not include the subsequent history of the case in your citation. (d) List the entry in the Descriptive Word Index from which you were directed to your answer (e.g., Pool Tables/Licensing and Regulation).

1 118 227 318 415 523   A purchaser of a plantation binds himself in an agreement to transfer one-half of the plantation to his son-in-law as soon as his son-in-law pays for one-half the cost, either with his own funds or with one-half of the profits of the plantation. Is there case authority denying specific performance of this type of agreement on the ground of want of mutuality of obligation? [West's U.S. Supreme Court Digest]
2 119 228 319 416 524   Under Illinois law, does the issuance of an unauthorized oil and gas lease in a cemetery [cemeteries] give rise to a damage action for mental suffering based upon the resulting disturbance of the cemetery land and its sacred and sentimental character? [Seventh Decennial]
3 120 229 320 417 525   Are state workmen's compensation laws included within the "common law remedies" referred to in statutes [28 U.S.C. § 1251, 1333 et seq.] giving to United States District Courts jurisdiction of all civil causes of admiralty and maritime jurisdiction but saving to suitors the right of common law remedies? [Modern Federal Practice Digest]
4 121 230 321 418 526   Cite a case which states that artistic jewelry constitutes a copyrightable subject matter. [Modern Federal Practice Digest]
5 122 231 322 419 527   In California, are statutes presumed to alter or repeal the common law even though the statute does not expressly so provide? In other words, is there such a presumption? [Seventh Decennial]
6 123 232 323 420 528   Under the Louisiana law of fixtures, when can immobilization by destination only occur? [Federal Practice Digest Second]
7 124 233 324 421 529   Cite a case holding that shipping commissioners do not have the power to resolve seamen's unliquidated demands for cure, for maintenance, or for damage growing out of unseaworthiness or negligence. [Federal Practice Digest Second]
8 125 234 325 422 530   Does the fact that a lessor acquired a quitclaim deed from a competing lessor of the same property estop [estoppel] the grantee from asserting superiority of his title? [Federal Practice Digest Second]
9 126 235 326 423 531   Find a Rhode Island precedent for the proposition that a representation by a workmen's compensation insurer's adjuster that an employee cannot receive both compensation and his regular wages for the same period of disability, though false, will not waive or estop an employer's right to assert that the employee's claim is barred by the statute of limitations. [Seventh Decennial]
10 127 236 327 424 532   Assume that you are trying to determine what factors are considered in determining disability benefits. Specifically, you want to know whether an otherwise vigorous and able-bodied forty year old man is "disabled" within the Social Security Act's definition of "disability" if he is subject to fairly regular epileptic seizures (grand mal)? Assume that he is usually able to work, but has had difficulty obtaining continuous employment because of his affliction and because of insurance companies' opposition. [Seventh Decennial]
11 128 237 328 425 533   In Indiana, what is the measure of damages for breach of the covenant [covenants] of the right to convey as a general rule? [First Decennial]
12 129 238 329 426 534   Under Indiana law, can a right to the use of a party wall be acquired by prescription by placing beams of a building in a wall located on adjoining land? [Modern Federal Practice Digest]

13 130 239 330 427 535   Cite a 1971 case holding that an action in the nature of mandamus is an improper remedy to obtain retraction of a post office department employee's dismissal or removal. [Federal Practice Digest Second]
14 131 240 331 428 536   Is it a proper ground for quashing an indictment under a California statute prohibiting the presence of unauthorized persons in the grand jury room if the inspector of the city police department is present during the time that his child testified with respect to a violation of the criminal code? [Seventh Decennial]
(15) 132 241 332 429 537   In a criminal prosecution for seduction in Kentucky, is evidence of the character of the female which tends to affect a woman's chastity within a reasonable time previous to the alleged seduction admissible? [Fifth Decennial]
16 133 242 333 430 538   In Florida, is the marriage of a person whose mental condition or capacity is that of an idiot or lunatic void ab initio? [Fourth Decennial]
17 134 243 334 431 539   If a note given in connection with a release is not paid, does that failure of consideration make the release void? [Federal Practice Digest Second]
18 135 244 335 432 540   Concerning the elements of the offense, does the commission of indecent acts by a mature man with a female child in private, where no physical injury resulted, come with the provisions of an Oklahoma lewdness statute, commonly known as the statute against outraging public decency? [Third Decennial]
19 136 245 336 433 541   Is a cause of action based upon deceit and misrepresentation (fraud) assignable in Nebraska? [Third Decennial]
20 137 246 337 434 542   In Nebraska, is a will valid if it was correctly written in the testator's presence according to his dictation and then executed by him in a manner required by statute even though the testator did not actually read it? In other words, did the testator have sufficient notice or knowledge of the contents of the will in this situation? [Fifth Decennial]
21 138 247 338 435 543   Is it part of a licensed pilot's [pilots] authority or function to determine the course and speed of a ship he or she is piloting? [Federal Practice Digest Second]
22 139 248 339 436 544   Under Arizona Law, can a person abandoning [abandonment] a mining claim reacquire his interest by resuming work? [Fourth Decennial]
23 140 249 340 437 545   Is a permanent obstruction of a public highway or road that interferes with travel a "nuisance per se" [nuisances] in Georgia? Cite two Georgia supreme court cases supporting your answer. [Sixth Decennial]
24 141 250 341 438 546   Is an injured skier barred from recovery by the doctrine of assumption of risks when the skier's injuries resulted from a collision with a chair lift tower while the skier was skiing down the slope? [Federal Practice Digest Second]
25 142 251 342 439 547   Cite a Florida supreme court case holding that an order denying a motion to dismiss for improper venue may be reviewed by a writ of certiorari. [Seventh Decennial]
26 143 252 343 440 548   Under a New York federal district court precedent, does the failure of the owners of a copyright to object to television showings or to make any attempt to restrict the exhibition of the film during a long period of time alone result in the abandonment [abandonments] of rights in the copyrighted work? [Federal Practice Digest Second]
27 144 253 344 441 549   Is consent a complete defense to a charge of kidnapping under the federal statute? [Modern Federal Practice Digest]
28 145 254 345 442 550   In the construction of a will [wills] in New Mexico, must all words within the "four corners of the will" be considered? [Eighth Decennial]
29 146 255 346 443 551   Under Nebraska law, where a principal entrusts property to his agent for a particular purpose and the agent embezzles it, will a subsequent offer or agreement to make restitution be recognized as a defense and defeat a prosecution for embezzlement? [Fifth Decennial]
30 147 256 347 444 552   Cite a 1968 Montana federal district court case that holds that Montana law does not grant to Indians special rights-of-way across private lands. [Federal Practice Digest Second]
31 148 257 348 445 553   Under Missouri law, is a child adopted either by deed of adoption method or by court decree an "heir" of adopting parents for purposes of inheritance? [Fifth Decennial]

32 149 258 349 446 554   Under Michigan law, is a sheriff who, in good faith and obedience to a mandatory writ of supersedeas, valid on its face, released a prisoner civilly liable to the person who had caused the sheriff to take the prisoner into custody? [Fifth Decennial]

33 150 259 350 447 555   Are recklessly made statements which are intended to be acted upon, without regard to their truth or falsity, sufficient to constitute fraud? Cite a Kentucky federal district court decision in support of your answer. [Fifth Decennial]

34 151 260 351 448 556   Under Arkansas law, is a devise for the maintenance of a church a charitable [charities] devise promoting religion? [First Decennial]

35 152 261 352 449 557   Under Florida law, may an action be maintained for money had and received when the money was wrongfully obtained by undue advantage? [Federal Practice Digest Second]

36 153 262 353 450 558   In a tenancy in common, does execution and sale of a tenant's interest by a third-party judgment creditor affect the title of the other tenants in common? [Federal Practice Digest Second]

37 154 263 354 451 559   Under a United States-France treaty of 1778, alien citizens of France [aliens] were given the right to hold real property in the United States. Did the abrogation of that treaty divest title to land that had vested under the treaty? [West's U.S. Supreme Court Digest]

38 155 264 355 452 560   Cite a Texas case holding that a conviction for "carrying on or about a person" a pistol is warranted from proof showing that the accused carried the weapon [weapons] in the glove compartment of his automobile. [Eighth Decennial]

39 156 265 356 453 561   Must a charitable trust [charities] benefit an indefinite number of beneficiaries in order to be valid? [West's U.S. Supreme Court Digest]

40 157 266 357 454 562   Cite a United States Supreme Court decision which holds that the overt acts of aid and comfort to the enemy, to constitute treason, must be intentional as distinguished from merely negligent or misdesigned ones. [Modern Federal Practice Digest]

41 158 267 358 455 563   In Connecticut, is an innkeeper liable for loss of goods occasioned by guests' contributory negligence? [Fourth Decennial]

42 159 268 359 456 564   Is an employee a person who is entitled to seek an injunction for violation of the Fair Labor Standards Act of 1938 regulating wages and hours [wages and hours regulations]? Cite a Second Circuit case arising out of New York as authority for your answer. [Modern Federal Practice Digest]

43 160 269 360 457 565   Are both delivery by bailor and acceptance by bailee required to constitute "bailment" under the law of North Carolina? [Fifth Decennial]

44 161 270 361 458 566   Under Michigan law, are reciprocal negative easements retroactive? [Sixth Decennial]

45 162 271 362 459 567   Where money is entrusted to an attorney to be paid to a borrower on satisfactory security being given, the relation of attorney and client being established, will the attorney be subject to punishment in Pennsylvania for embezzlement if he fraudulently converts the money to his own use? [First Decennial]

46 163 272 363 460 568   Under Alabama law, are damages recoverable for a principal's breach of contract in refusing to pay for services where an owner revokes a broker's contract after the broker [brokers] had found a purchaser as agreed? [Third Decennial]

47 164 273 364 461 569   Under the law of Arkansas, is a person who is a surety for a contractor for the construction of a building entitled to claim a mechanic's lien for material furnished by him at the request of the contractor? [Second Decennial]

48 165 274 365 462 570   In Maine, is estoppel a question for the jury or a question of law? [Second Decennial]

49 166 275 366 463 571   Cite a Circuit Court of Appeal case arising out of Colorado supporting the proposition that a colored photograph of natural scenery may be copyrighted [copyrights]. [First Decennial]

50 167 276 367 464 572   Cite an 1856 Supreme Court decision that states that parol evidence may be used to extablish a resulting trust? [West's U.S. Supreme Court Digest]

51 168 277 368 465 573   Cite a California case in which an application for a writ of habeas corpus to procure a release from custody under commitment for violating a Railroad Commission's order was denied. [Fifth Decennial]
52 169 278 369 466 574   Under Florida law, what are the two essentials to a valid common-law marriage? [Modern Federal Practice Digest]
53 170 279 370 467 575   Is contributory negligence chargeable, under the law of negligence in Louisiana, to one who suffers injury by reason of risking danger to his life to save others' lives and failing to exercise his best judgment in the emergency [emergencies]? [Second Decennial]
54 171 280 371 468 576   In a prosecution for obtaining money by false pretenses, must the prosecution show that the defrauded owner relied solely on the pretended fact as the basis for parting with his money? [Federal Practice Digest Second]
55 172 281 372 469 577   Under Idaho law, how much force may a person use in resisting an illegal arrest without becoming criminally liable for an assault and battery? [Second Decennial]
56 173 282 373 470 578   Under California law, how many acts of vagrancy are required in evidence to support a conviction of vagrancy? [Fourth Decennial]
57 174 283 374 471 579   In North Carolina, to what extent are insane persons liable for their torts? [Fifth Decennial]
58 175 284 375 472 580   Should an attorney be allowed to act as surety for clients [attorney and client] in legal proceedings? [Fifth Decennial]
59 176 285 376 473 581   Give a definition of a vagrant as set forth by the Supreme Court of Missouri that delineates the elements of the offense of vagrancy. [Second Decennial]
60 177 286 377 474 582   Where a deed is delivered in escrow, and the grantee fails in performance of the agreement on which delivery depends, can there be vesting of title in the grantee by the unauthorized transfer by the depository of possession of the conveyance to the grantee under the law of Alabama? [Third Decennial]
61 178 287 378 475 583   Under Iowa law, is one who has contributed to a tort [torts] personally or jointly and severally liable to the person injured for the entire damage if he was not present at the doing of the act? [First Decennial]
62 179 288 379 476 584   In Washington, whose property are fish caught in traps operated illegally during season? [Fourth Decennial]
63 180 289 380 477 585   Are judicial sales of real property (such as a sheriff's sale) within the Maryland Statute of Frauds and thus require a written memorandum to be valid? [West's U.S. Supreme Court Digest]
64 181 290 381 478 586   If a real estate developer arranged for removal of the remains of persons buried over 125 years ago in a cemetery [cemeteries] without permission, should the developer be found guilty of violating Ohio's grave-robbing statute (§ 2923.07)? [Eighth Decennial]
65 182 291 382 479 581   Cite a case holding that sensitivity to thermofax paper is an occupational disease for workmen's compensation purposes. [Eighth Decennial]
66 183 292 383 480 588   Is "burning" an essential element of the crime of arson? [Federal Practice Digest Second]
67 184 293 384 481 589   May parol or extrinsic evidence be used to establish the date of a written instrument or contract if noe appears on its face? [West's U.S. Supreme Court Digest]
68 185 294 385 482 590   When a turnpike is constructed, will it be presumed that the minimum width was laid out when only maximum and minimum widths of a turnpike [turnpikes] were specified in the charter? [Fifth Decennial]
69 186 295 386 483 591   Is fraudulent removal or disposition of property a ground for arrest in Vermont? [Fifth Decennial]
70 187 296 387 484 592   Under Virginia law, does the failure of a person renting an automobile to return it as agreed constitute embezzlement? [Eighth Decennial]
71 188 297 388 485 593   Under the Mississippi Code, were aliens given the capacity to take title to real property given to them under a will (devise)? [Federal Practice Digest Second]
72 189 298 389 486 594   Does a state have the power to regulate and protect its fish and game by prohibiting the taking or catching of oysters with a scoop or drag? [West's U.S. Supreme Court Digest]

73 190 299 390 487 595   Under Washington law, are courts bound by parties' stipulations of law? [Eighth Decennial]

74 191 300 391 488 596   Is the offense of robbery committed by a person who is not a citizen of the United States on the high seas on board a ship belonging exclusively to subjects of a foreign state "piracy" under the Act of April 30, 1790 and punishable in the courts of the United States? [West's U.S. Supreme Court Digest]

75 192 201 392 489 597   Under the law of Kansas, are "common barratry" and "champerty" synonymous? [Seventh Decennial]

76 193 202 393 490 598   Under Minnesota law, is evidence of the good reputation of the defendant in a civil action for damages for assault [assault and battery] admissible? [Third Decennial]

77 194 203 394 491 599   Under Arkansas law, does a lender who contracts for usuarious rates forfeit [forfeitures] only the interest or the principal as well? [Federal Practice Digest Second]

78 195 204 395 492 600   Is a religious corporation a person entitled to claim title to land by adverse possession or prescription? [West's U.S. Supreme Court Digest]

79 196 205 396 493 501   Where a limited partnership agreement provided for a partnership for one year and at the expiration of the year the parties continued to do business but did not record a renewal of their agreement as required by the statutory provisions of Uniform Limited Partnership Act, are the parties liable to creditors as general partners after termination of the contract? [Fourth Decennial]

80 197 206 397 494 502   May an invention be patentable [patents] as possessing utility in the sense of the law, though an improvement may be necessary to its commercial success? [Third Decennial]

81 198 207 398 495 503   Pennsylvania law makes a person criminally liable for being a "common gambler." What is a "common gambler"? [Federal Practice Digest Second]

82 199 208 399 496 504   Under Iowa law, is a savings account as represented by a bank book property subject to replevin? [Fourth Decennial]

83 200 209 400 497 505   Cite a federal Court of Appeals case holding that it is necessary to fence [fences] or enclose grazing land in order to establish adverse possession in Mississippi. [Sixth Decennial]

84 101 210 301 498 506   Under a 1942 Kentucky decision discussing the nature of constructive trusts, what is a "constructive trust"? [Fifth Decennial]

85 102 211 302 499 507   Is recantation an absolute defense to a charge of perjury or merely relevant to show circumstantially the absence of intent? Cite a New York federal district court decision in support of your answer. [Seventh Decennial]

86 103 212 303 500 508   Will a writ of prohibition issue in Montana when there is another plain, speedy, and adequate remedy of law available? [Sixth Decennial]

87 104 213 304 401 509   Can seamen be subjected to a penalty for the offense of desertion if they have signed a merchant vessel's shipping articles and then fail to appear? [West's U.S. Supreme Court Digest]

88 105 214 305 402 510   Cite a Missouri case supporting the rule that specific performance rests in the discretion of the court and if there be any want of good faith on the part of the plaintiff, that relief will not be granted to him. [First Decennial]

89 106 215 306 403 511   If a salesman at an automobile dealership were to refuse to return the keys to a potential customer's automobile after the customer decided not to trade, would the salesman be guilty of trover and conversion of the automobile, not just the keys? [Eighth Decennial]

90 107 216 307 404 512   If a trial court enters a finding of fact stating that none of the allegations in certain paragraphs were true, does such a finding contain a "negative pregnant" so as to imply the affirmative? [Sixth Decennial]

91 108 217 308 405 513   Under New York law, liverymen may have a lien upon each animal kept. Is the stablemen's lien specific, attaching to a specific animal as distinguished from maintenance of any other animals [livery stable keepers]? [Federal Practice Digest Second]

92 109 218 309 406 514   Is there a public policy requirement in New York that members of a partnership must act in good faith or show good cause in order to expel a partner when the partnership agreement expressly provides for

involuntary expulsion? In other words, is good or bad faith of the other members of the group relevant? [Eighth Decennial]

93 110 219 310 407 515   Does a reservation in a conveyance that the grantors shall have the right and privilege to remove any and all timber [logs] from the land reserve title in timber to the grantors or only a profit a pendre? [Eighth Decennial]

94 111 220 311 408 516   At common law, according to the Supreme Court of Idaho, of what elements did kidnapping consist? [Sixth Decennial]

95 112 221 312 409 517   Cite a 1962 federal Court of Appeals decision arising out of Nebraska holding that a person's domicile, once acquired, is presumed to continue until it is shown to have been changed. [Federal Practice Digest Second]

96 113 222 313 410 518   During war, are neutral merchant steamers carrying mails privileged from visit and search by blockading vessels? [West's U.S. Supreme Court Digest]

97 114 223 314 411 519   Cite a 1967 federal Court of Appeals decision arising out of Illinois holding that a person seeking indemnity to recover damages paid may use as a form of remedy an action ex delicto. [Federal Practice Digest Second]

98 115 224 315 412 520   Under Nebraska law, is intent to kill (purpose) an essential element of second-degree murder homicide prosecution? [Seventh Decennial]

99 116 225 316 413 521   Can a person be properly indicted for the offense of "counterfeiting" if the subject he has forged is a Spanish head pistareen? [West's U.S. Supreme Court Digest]

100 117 226 317 414 522   May a contingent remainder [remainders] be conveyed or disposed of by deed in Virginia under the controlling Virginia statute? [Federal Practice Digest Second]

LIBRARY EXERCISE 22. LAWYERS CO-OPERATIVE'S DIGESTS. This exercise familiarizes you with Lawyers Co-operative's <u>U.S. Supreme Court Digest</u> and gives you practice in citing cases in proper form. To complete this exercise, find the digest entry listed below in the <u>U.S. Supreme Court Digest, Lawyers' Edition</u>. Cite the Supreme Court case that <u>distinguished</u> the digested case noted below. Find the distinguishing case in <u>United States Reports</u> to determine additional information (e.g., case name, date, volume number, page number) needed for your citation. Note that the Digest often cites the page of treatment, <u>not</u> the beginning page of the case you will be citing. For this exercise, do <u>not</u> give parallel citations to the <u>Supreme Court Reporter</u> or <u>Lawyers' Edition</u>.

	Problem #				Digest Topic	Digested Case	Distinguishing Case
1	103	217	320	423	555	Abatement & Revival § 16	Watson	205 U.S.
2	104	218	321	424	556	Administrative Law § 238	Silberschien	311 U.S.
3	105	219	322	425	557	Admiralty § 65	Post	172 U.S.
4	106	220	323	426	558	Alteration of Instruments § 7	Wood	112 U.S.
5	107	221	324	427	559	Appeal & Error § 80.5	Osborne	166 U.S.
6	108	222	325	428	560	Appeal & Error § 383	Rogers	214 U.S.
7	109	223	326	429	561	Appeal & Error § 544	Mitchell	188 U.S.
8	110	224	327	430	562	Appeal & Error § 707	Field	203 U.S.
9	111	225	328	431	563	Appeal & Error § 822	Marshall	21 Wall.
10	112	226	329	432	564	Appeal & Error § 917	Knox County	219 U.S.
11	113	227	330	433	565	Appeal & Error § 1071	Davis	143 U.S.
12	114	228	331	434	566	Appeal & Error § 1170	Johnson	322 U.S.
13	115	229	332	435	567	Appeal & Error § 1296	Roy	180 U.S.
14	116	230	333	436	568	Appeal & Error § 1553	Baldwin	124 U.S.
15	117	231	334	437	569	Appeal & Error § 1656	St. Pierre	329 U.S.
16	118	232	335	438	570	Bailment § 2	Prescott	15 Wall.
17	119	233	336	439	571	Banks § 94	Armstrong	176 U.S.
18	120	234	337	440	572	Bonds § 14	Pauly	183 U.S.
19	121	235	338	441	573	Carriers § 122	Piper	360 U.S.
20	122	236	339	442	574	Citizenship § 11	Campbell	204 U.S.
21	123	237	340	443	575	Claims § 2	Smith	273 U.S.
22	124	238	341	444	576	Commerce § 45	Erie R.R.	298 U.S.
23	125	239	342	445	577	Commerce § 97	Fry	426 U.S.
24	126	240	343	446	578	Commerce § 299	Morf	300 U.S.
25	127	241	344	447	579	Constitutional Law § 78	Duncan	170 U.S.
26	128	242	345	448	580	Constitutional Law § 174	Yard	173 U.S.
27	129	243	346	449	581	Constitutional Law § 299	Gantly	290 U.S.
28	130	244	347	450	582	Constitutional Law § 805	Turner	263 U.S.
29	131	245	348	451	583	Constitutional Law § 484	Louisville	184 U.S.
30	132	246	349	452	584	Constitutional Law § 731	Sands	147 U.S.
31	133	247	350	453	585	Contracts § 107	McMullen	174 U.S.
32	134	248	351	454	586	Contracts § 153	Gavinzel	105 U.S.
33	135	249	352	455	587	Corporations § 16	James	268 U.S.
34	136	250	353	456	588	Corporations § 164	Webster	165 U.S.
35	137	251	354	457	589	Courts § 115	Erie R.R.	236 U.S.
36	138	252	355	458	590	Courts § 381	Ambler	235 U.S.
37	139	253	356	459	591	Courts § 848	Moore-Mansfield	281 U.S.
38	140	254	357	460	592	Criminal Law § 29	Ball	199 U.S.
39	141	255	358	461	593	Criminal Law § 49	Diaz	291 U.S.
40	142	256	359	462	594	Damages § 117	Benson Min.	237 U.S.
41	143	257	360	463	595	Descent & Distribution § 8	Blythe	239 U.S.
42	144	258	361	464	596	Discovery & Inspection § 16	Botsford	177 U.S.
43	145	259	362	465	597	Domicil § 2	Penfield	147 U.S.
44	146	260	363	466	598	Ejectment § 16	Christy	124 U.S.
45	147	261	364	467	599	Eminent Domain § 7	Shoemaker	261 U.S.
46	148	262	365	468	600	Eminent Domain § 106	Sweet	200 U.S.
47	149	263	366	469	501	Estoppel & Waiver § 11	Swann	111 U.S.
48	150	264	367	470	502	Evidence § 272	Jennings	107 U.S.
49	151	265	368	471	503	Evidence § 683	Pierce	168 U.S.
50	152	266	369	472	504	Extradition § 4	Ker	148 U.S.
51	153	267	370	473	505	Food & Drugs § 5	Blockburger	357 U.S.

		Problem #			Digest Topic	Digested Case	Distinguishing Case
52	154	268	371	474	506	Gift & Taxes § 4	Smith	318 U.S.
53	155	269	372	475	507	Habeas Corpus § 62	Lange	218 U.S.
54	156	270	373	476	508	Highways & Streets § 17	St. Louis	172 U.S.
55	157	271	374	477	509	Insolvency § 19	Union Bank	133 U.S.
56	158	272	375	478	510	Insurance § 78	Warnock	222 U.S.
57	159	273	376	479	511	Interest § 35	No. Carolina	229 U.S.
58	160	274	377	480	512	International Law § 14	The Exchange	183 U.S.
59	161	275	378	481	513	Interstate Commerce Commission § 82	Merchants' & Mfgrs.' Traffic Ass'n	295 U.S.
60	162	276	379	482	514	Limitation of Actions § 61	Prevost	2 Wall.
61	163	277	380	483	515	Labor § 129	Virginian R.	312 U.S.
62	164	278	381	484	516	Levy & Seizure § 3	Stevens	105 U.S.
63	165	279	382	485	517	Limitation of Actions § 17	Southern P. Co.	270 U.S.
64	166	280	383	486	518	Limitation of Actions § 201	Greene	145 U.S.
65	167	281	384	487	519	Master & Servant § 5	Standard Oil	284 U.S.
66	168	282	385	488	520	Master & Servant § 61	Raymond	349 U.S.
67	169	283	386	489	521	Mines § 29	Deffeback	221 U.S.
68	170	284	387	490	522	Mortgage § 148	Miltenberger	197 U.S.
69	171	285	388	491	523	Parties § 3	Perkins	330 U.S.
70	172	286	389	492	524	Patents § 27	Hoyt	155 U.S.
71	173	287	390	493	525	Patents § 240	Bauer	247 U.S.
72	174	288	391	494	526	Pleading § 274	Southern P. Co.	151 U.S.
73	175	289	392	495	527	Principal & Surety § 9	Smith	112 U.S.
74	176	290	393	496	528	Private Land Claims § 87	Hornsby	97 U.S.
75	177	291	394	497	529	Public Lands § 56	Leavenworth	127 U.S.
76	178	292	395	498	530	Public Lands § 83	Kissell	9 Wall.
77	179	293	396	499	531	Public Lands § 239	Davis	154 U.S.
78	180	294	397	500	532	Public Utilities § 16	So. Iowa Elec.	268 U.S.
79	181	295	398	401	533	Receivers § 59	St. Louis R.R.	136 U.S.
80	182	296	399	402	534	Salvage § 11	Cope	191 U.S.
81	183	297	400	403	535	Seamen § 15	O'Donnell	328 U.S.
82	184	298	301	404	536	Shipping § 74	The Freeman	24 How.
83	185	299	302	405	537	Specific Performance § 10	Marshall	138 U.S.
84	186	300	303	406	538	States § 45	Clark	366 U.S.
85	187	201	304	407	539	Statutes § 39	Pollock	220 U.S.
86	188	202	305	408	540	Statutes § 132	Brewster	141 U.S.
87	189	203	306	409	541	Statutes § 246	King	113 U.S.
88	190	204	307	410	542	Succession & Estate Taxes § 6	Keeney	253 U.S.
89	191	205	308	411	543	Taxes § 45	Baltic Mininig	245 U.S.
90	192	206	309	412	544	Taxes § 177	State Assessors	206 U.S.
91	193	207	310	413	545	Territories, Dependencies, Possessions § 17	Miners' Bank	186 U.S.
92	194	208	311	414	546	Trial § 324	Winston	225 U.S.
93	195	209	312	415	547	Trusts § 41	Magruder	318 U.S.
94	196	210	313	416	548	War § 10	Hiatt	271 U.S.
95	197	211	314	417	549	War § 17	Hamilton	197 U.S.
96	198	212	315	418	550	Waters § 16	Wisconsin	180 U.S.
97	199	213	316	419	551	Witnesses § 84	Counselman	161 U.S.
98	200	214	317	420	552	Writ & Process § 27	Davis	218 U.S.
99	101	215	318	421	553	Banks § 16	Bramwell	288 U.S.
100	102	216	319	422	554	Bills & Notes § 76	Hortsman	252 U.S.

LIBRARY EXERCISE 23. SHEPARD'S CASE CITATIONS: SUBSEQUENT HISTORY. This exercise teaches you how to find the subsequent judicial history (certiorari denied, reversed, vacated, modified, certiorari dismissed, affirmed, affirmed per curiam, reversed per curiam, etc.) of a case. listed below in the appropriate volume of Shepard's Citations. Cite the case showing its subsequent history; however, do not show the history on remand or a denial of a rehearing in the citation. If there is no subsequent history, answer "none." Use Shepard's Citations to find any missing parallel citations. For Supreme Court actions, cite only United States Reports.

Problem #					Citation
1	190	270	350	430	520	269 A.2d 737
2	191	271	351	431	521	276 A.2d 18
3	192	272	352	432	522	329 A.2d 376
4	193	273	353	433	523	239 A.2d 409
5	194	274	354	434	524	315 A.2d 501
6	195	275	355	435	525	284 A.2d 700
7	196	276	356	436	526	352 A.2d 4
8	197	277	357	437	527	356 A.2d 897
9	198	278	358	438	528	288 A.2d 863
10	199	279	359	439	529	273 A.2d 361
11	200	280	360	440	530	420 P.2d 693
12	101	281	361	441	531	450 P.2d 364
13	102	282	362	442	532	455 P.2d 34
14	103	283	263	443	533	455 P.2d 395
15	104	284	364	444	534	524 P.2d 97
16	105	285	365	445	535	503 P.2d 1322
17	106	286	366	446	536	408 P.2d 116
18	107	287	367	447	537	466 P.2d 961
19	108	288	368	448	538	435 P.2d 692
20	109	289	369	449	539	213 N.E.2d 438
21	110	290	370	450	540	218 N.E.2d 428
22	111	291	371	451	541	219 N.E.2d 194
23	112	292	372	452	542	241 N.E.2d 419
24	113	293	373	453	543	244 N.E.2d 89
25	114	294	374	454	544	245 N.E.2d 771
26	115	295	375	455	545	193 N.E.2d 449
27	116	296	376	456	546	190 N.E.2d 719
28	117	297	377	457	547	134 N.E.2d 914
29	118	298	378	458	548	256 So. 2d 98
30	119	299	379	459	549	241 So. 2d 390
31	120	300	380	460	550	197 So. 2d 241
32	121	201	381	461	551	123 F. 817
33	122	202	382	462	552	128 F. 527
34	123	203	383	463	553	374 F. Supp. 301
35	124	204	384	464	554	239 F.2d 97
36	125	205	385	465	555	262 F.2d 501
37	126	206	386	466	556	281 F.2d 59
38	127	207	387	467	557	240 N.W.2d 729
39	128	208	388	468	558	221 N.W.2d 357
40	129	209	389	469	559	219 N.W.2d 920
41	130	210	390	470	560	377 F. Supp. 1065
42	131	211	391	471	561	211 N.W.2d 642
43	132	212	392	472	562	199 N.W.2d 480
44	133	213	393	473	563	182 N.W.2d 887
45	134	214	394	474	564	174 N.W.2d 504
46	135	215	395	475	565	149 N.W.2d 557
47	136	216	396	476	566	163 S.E.2d 589
48	137	217	397	477	567	197 S.E.2d 502
49	138	218	398	478	568	176 S.E.2d 818
50	139	219	399	479	569	199 S.E.2d 183
51	140	220	400	480	570	188 S.E.2d 296
52	141	221	301	481	571	236 S.E.2d 353
53	142	222	302	482	572	216 S.E.2d 608
54	143	223	303	483	573	215 S.E.2d 540

Problem #						Citation
55	144	224	304	484	574	214 S.E.2d 742
56	145	225	305	485	575	307 S.W.2d 385
57	146	226	306	486	576	389 S.W.2d 774
58	147	227	307	487	577	481 S.W.2d 473
59	148	228	308	488	578	277 S.W.2d 125
60	149	229	309	489	579	278 S.W.2d 398
61	150	230	310	490	580	418 S.W.2d 708
62	151	231	311	491	581	362 S.W.2d 695
63	152	232	312	492	582	518 S.W.2d 207
64	153	233	313	493	583	520 S.W.2d 424
65	154	234	314	494	584	337 F.2d 891
66	155	235	315	495	585	335 F.2d 1021
67	156	236	316	496	586	431 F.2d 1282
68	157	237	317	497	587	500 F.2d 144
69	158	238	318	498	588	505 F.2d 426
70	159	239	319	499	589	320 F.2d 285
71	160	240	320	500	590	317 F.2d 838
72	161	241	321	401	591	251 F.2d 69
73	162	242	323	403	593	236 F.2d 708
74	163	243	323	403	593	65 F. Supp. 130
75	164	244	324	404	594	76 F. Supp. 604
76	165	245	325	405	595	99 F. Supp. 81
77	166	246	326	406	596	100 F. Supp. 198
78	167	247	327	407	597	88 F. Supp. 64
79	168	248	328	408	598	98 F. Supp. 455
80	169	249	329	409	599	111 F. Supp. 912
81	170	250	330	410	600	116 F. Supp. 15
82	171	251	331	411	501	119 F. Supp. 295
83	172	252	332	412	502	100 Cal. Rptr. 618
84	173	253	333	413	503	549 F.2d 89
85	174	254	334	414	504	125 Cal. Rptr. 265
86	175	255	335	415	505	384 F. Supp. 1231
87	176	256	336	416	506	442 F. Supp. 1000
88	177	257	337	417	507	82 Cal. Rptr. 473
89	178	258	338	418	508	67 Cal. Rptr. 409
90	179	259	339	419	509	90 Cal. Rptr. 15
91	180	260	340	420	510	42 Cal. Rptr. 169
92	181	261	341	421	511	258 N.Y.S.2d 109
93	182	262	342	422	512	175 N.Y.S.2d 794
94	183	263	343	423	513	264 N.Y.S.2d 557
95	184	264	344	424	514	265 N.Y.S.2d 899
96	185	265	345	425	515	386 N.Y.S.2d 691
97	186	266	346	426	516	383 N.Y.S.2d 573
98	187	267	347	427	517	255 N.Y.S.2d 833
99	188	268	348	428	518	228 N.Y.S.2d 641
100	189	269	349	429	519	282 N.Y.S.2d 491

LIBRARY EXERCISE 24. SHEPARD'S CASE CITATIONS: SUBSEQUENT TREATMENT. This exercise teaches you how to use Shepard's Citations to find the subsequent treatment of a case. Note that there are two answers required for this exercise.

(a) Using the appropriate volume(s) of Shepard's Citations, find and cite in proper form the first case listed in Shepard's Citations that has treated the case identified below in the manner noted. Be sure to note the citation listed below carefully (e.g., whether it is to the first or second series of the reporter) and to begin your search with the volume of Shepard's Citations in which the case first appeared. Note that you may have to check later Shepard's volumes or paper-bound supplements in order to find the required entry. Note also that Shepard's cites the page of treatment, not the beginning page of the case that you will be citing. If there is no entry in Shepard's treating the case in the manner noted, answer "none."

(b) To which headnote number does the cited treatment in part (a) refer? If no headnote is specifically treated, answer "none."

Problem #					Citation	Treatment
1	190	270	350	430	520	91 A.2d 428	Followed
2	191	271	351	431	521	588 F.2d 319	Distinguished
3	192	272	352	432	522	47 A. 579	Distinguished
4	193	273	353	433	523	74 A. 1051	Distinguished
5	194	274	354	434	524	51 A.2d 19	Distinguished
6	195	275	355	435	525	90 A. 677	Distinguished
7	196	276	356	436	526	103 A. 511	Explained
8	197	277	357	437	527	126 A. 224	Explained
9	198	278	358	438	528	162 A. 441	Questioned
10	199	279	359	439	529	267 A.2d 481	Distinguished
11	200	280	360	440	530	454 P.2d 993	Distinguished
12	101	281	361	441	531	460 P.2d 578	Followed
13	102	282	362	442	532	454 P.2d 987	Distinguished
14	103	283	363	443	533	244 P. 343	Distinguished
15	104	284	364	444	534	206 P. 178	Questioned
16	105	285	365	445	535	199 P. 396	Distinguished
17	106	286	366	446	536	117 P.2d 707 *195 FS*	Distinguished
18	107	287	367	447	537	52 P. 944	Distinguished
19	108	288	368	448	538	47 P. 521 *172*	Distinguished
20	109	289	369	449	539	29 N.E. 517	Criticized
21	110	290	370	450	540	64 N.E. 442	Criticized
22	111	291	371	451	541	33 N.E. 746	Distinguished
23	112	292	372	452	542	33 N.E. 1054	Explained
24	113	293	373	453	543	63 N.E. 110	Criticized
25	114	294	374	454	544	153 N.E.2d 563	Explained
26	115	295	375	455	545	204 N.E.2d 842	Questioned
27	116	296	376	456	546	212 N.E.2d 279	Questioned
28	117	297	377	457	547	273 N.E.2d 592	Explained
29	118	298	378	458	548	99 So. 716	Explained
30	119	299	379	459	549	99 So. 27	Followed
31	120	300	380	460	550	11 So. 2d 225	Limited
32	121	201	381	461	551	104 F.2d 837	Harmonized
33	122	202	382	462	552	161 F.2d 636	Questioned
34	123	203	383	463	553	516 F.2d 411	Explained
35	124	204	384	464	554	512 F.2d 527	Questioned
36	125	205	385	465	555	495 F.2d 1026	Criticized
37	126	206	386	466	556	281 F. 744	Followed
38	127	207	387	467	557	112 N.W. 748	Distinguished
39	128	208	388	468	558	99 N.W. 395	Distinguished
40	129	209	389	469	559	103 N.W. 137	Questioned
41	130	210	390	470	560	165 N.W. 297	Questioned
42	131	211	391	471	561	109 N.W. 744	Explained
43	132	212	392	472	562	181 N.W. 135	Explained
44	133	213	393	473	563	113 N.W. 858	Questioned
45	134	214	394	474	564	235 N.W. 185	Overruled
46	135	215	395	475	565	252 N.W. 650	Distinguished

47

		Problem #			Citation	Treatment
47	136	216	396	476	566	86 S.E. 552	Distinguished
48	137	217	397	477	567	86 S.E. 340	Questioned
49	138	218	398	478	568	79 S.E. 806	Distinguished
50	139	219	399	479	569	23 S.E. 784	Questioned
51	140	220	400	480	570	17 S.E. 812	Criticized
52	141	221	301	481	571	81 S.E. 418	Distinguished
53	142	222	302	482	572	399 F. Supp. 208	Followed
54	143	223	303	483	573	122 S.E. 327	Harmonized
55	144	224	304	484	574	84 S.E. 69	Explained
56	145	225	305	485	575	180 S.W. 663	Questioned
57	146	226	306	486	576	180 S.W. 839	Explained
58	147	227	307	487	577	63 S.W. 624	Questioned
59	148	228	308	488	578	80 S.W. 516	Overruled
60	149	229	309	489	579	83 S.W. 680	Harmonized
61	150	230	310	490	580	107 S.W. 496	Questioned
62	151	231	311	491	581	262 S.W. 387	Distinguished
63	152	232	312	492	582	145 S.W. 582	Distinguished
64	153	233	313	493	583	91 S.W. 834	Distinguished
65	154	234	314	494	584	190 U.S. 197	Limited
66	155	235	315	495	585	191 U.S. 78	Harmonized
67	156	236	316	496	586	196 U.S. 217	Distinguished
68	157	237	317	497	587	205 U.S. 322	Questioned
69	158	238	318	498	588	234 U.S. 52	Explained
70	159	239	319	499	589	328 U.S. 781	Harmonized
71	160	240	320	500	590	335 U.S. 464	Criticized
72	161	241	321	401	591	348 U.S. 176	Questioned
73	162	242	322	402	592	389 U.S. 429	Distinguished
74	163	243	323	403	593	102 F. Supp. 399	Followed
75	164	244	324	404	594	36 F.R.D. 37	Distinguished
76	165	245	325	405	595	226 F. Supp. 56	Distinguished
77	166	246	326	406	596	235 F. Supp. 984	Explained
78	167	247	327	407	597	249 F. Supp. 681	Distinguished
79	168	248	328	408	598	264 F. Supp. 146	Distinguished
80	169	249	329	409	599	195 F. Supp. 795	Criticized
81	170	250	330	410	600	192 F. Supp. 373	Distinguished
82	171	251	331	411	501	149 F. Supp. 272	Distinguished
83	172	252	332	412	502	43 Cal. Rptr. 14	Overruled
84	173	253	333	413	503	55 Cal. Rptr. 1	Criticized
85	174	254	334	414	504	63 Cal. Rptr. 13	Followed
86	175	255	335	415	505	101 Cal. Rptr. 4	Explained
87	176	256	336	416	506	82 Cal. Rptr. 489	Explained
88	177	257	337	417	507	102 Cal. Rptr. 36	Distinguished
89	178	258	338	418	508	105 Cal. Rptr. 318	Distinguished
90	179	259	339	419	509	102 Cal. Rptr. 547	Followed
91	180	260	340	420	510	105 Cal. Rptr. 568	Explained
92	181	261	341	421	511	82 N.Y.S. 773	Questioned
93	182	262	342	422	512	172 N.Y.S. 673	Followed
94	183	263	343	423	513	247 N.Y.S.2d 21	Distinguished
95	184	264	344	424	514	247 N.Y.S.2d 269	Questioned
96	185	265	345	425	515	117 N.Y.S. 45	Distinguished
97	186	266	346	426	516	101 N.Y.S. 1031	Distinguished
98	187	267	347	427	517	99 N.Y.S. 721	Explained
99	188	268	348	428	518	396 N.Y.S.2d 883	Questioned
100	189	269	349	429	519	225 N.Y.S.2d 193	Questioned

LIBRARY EXERCISE 25. WEST'S WORDS AND PHRASES. The purpose of this exercise is to give you practice in using the West's <u>Words and Phrases</u> set. To complete this exercise, locate the following word or phrase in West's <u>Words and Phrases</u>. Find the case squib indicated for your problem that defines that word or phrase. If you cannot locate the squib in the bound part of the volume, be sure to check the pocket supplement. Give the citation to the case including the page on which that definition can be found, e.g., Variable Expenses [Waukeska] <u>Ans</u>. M/B: <u>Waukeska Motor Co. v. United States</u>, 322 F. Supp. 752, 756 (E.D. <u>Wis</u>. 1971). Note that the case begins on page 752 and the definition is on page 756. Consult the case to find any missing information. Do not rely on the form used in the squib for your citation. Use <u>Shepard's Citations</u> to find any missing parallel citations. Do not indicate the subsequent history of the case. Cite U.S. Supreme Court actions to <u>United States Reports</u>.

Note also that the page on which the definition appears in each parallel source should be indicated, e.g., M/B: <u>Kearney Electric Co. v. Laughlin</u>, 45 Neb. 390, 404, 63 N.W. 941, 946 (1895). If the exact page on which the definition is given in a parallel source is not noted in West's <u>Words and Phrases</u>, the missing page should be indicated in the following manner for the purposes of this exercise: e.g., M/B: <u>Kearney Electric Co. v. Laughlin</u>, 45 Neb. 390, ___, 63 N.W. 941, 946 (1895).

```
    Problem #                Word or Phrase/Case Name (Party)

 1  130 252 356 435 508     A-B-C Test [Wilson]
 2  131 253 357 436 509     Accident Policy [Noel's Estate]
 3  132 254 358 437 510     Account Current Basis [Holbrook]
 4  133 255 359 438 511     Act of War [Thomas]
 5  134 256 360 439 512     After-Acquired Title [Texas Sand]
 6  135 257 361 440 513     Aleatory Promise [Tyree]
 7  136 258 362 441 514     Alibi [Massen]
 8  137 259 363 442 515     Apparent Use [Stuart]
 9  138 260 364 443 516     Closing of the Class [Liddle's Estate]
10  139 261 365 444 517     Cleared Land [Marvel]
11  140 262 366 445 518     Conditional Vendee [King]
12  141 263 367 446 519     Contingent Estate [Houston]
13  142 264 368 447 520     Confession and Avoidance [Sievers]
14  143 265 369 448 521     Attestation Clause [Succession of Peterson]
15  144 266 370 449 522     Articulo Mortis [Beard]
16  145 267 371 450 523     Assault with Whip or Cowhide [Brenneman]
17  146 268 372 451 524     Counter Wills [Wright]
18  147 269 373 452 525     Conversion Rule [Am. Fidelity]
19  148 270 374 453 526     C. & F. [Maideirense]
20  149 271 375 454 527     Burford Doctrine [Clutchette]
21  150 272 376 455 528     Bill Payable [Guaranty Bond State Bank]
22  151 273 377 456 529     Detachable Warrant [Miller]
23  152 274 378 457 530     Deception Doctrine [Chapman]
24  153 275 379 458 531     Empty Chair Doctrine [Carraturo]
25  154 276 380 459 532     Embezzlement by Agent [Groves]
26  155 277 381 460 533     Dying with Issue [Turner's Will]
27  156 278 382 461 534     Dragnet Clause [Kenneally]
28  157 279 383 462 535     Disability Insurance Benefits [Banks]
29  158 280 384 463 536     Fuse Plug Levees [Sponenbarger]
30  159 281 385 464 537     F.O.B. Trucks [Garrett]
31  160 282 386 465 538     Filled Milk [Milnot Co.]
32  161 283 387 466 539     Fathometer [Soriano]
33  162 284 388 467 540     Excess Outage [Hunter-Wilson Distilling Co.]
34  163 285 389 468 541     Estate by Inheritance [Larrabee]
35  164 286 390 469 542     Intent to Maim [Richardson]
36  165 287 391 470 543     Irresistible Force [Palacio]
37  166 288 392 471 544     High-Water Mark [Bonelli Cattle Co.]
38  167 289 393 472 545     Heaving Line [Marincovich]
39  168 290 394 473 546     Great Writ [Harvey]
40  169 291 395 474 547     General Revenue Cases [Fla. Citrus Comm'n]
41  170 292 396 475 548     Kinetic Energy [Friedman]
42  171 293 397 476 549     Joint Will [Ellexson]
```

Problem #					Word or Phrase/Case Name (Party)
43	172	294	398	477 550	Illuminating Articles [New York Merchandise Co.]
44	173	295	399	478 551	Inclination and Opportunity Rule [Levitz]
45	174	296	400	479 552	Integrated Gas Company [Arkansas Louisana Gas]
46	175	297	301	480 553	Land Warehousing [Connor]
47	176	298	302	481 554	Lapping [Randecker]
48	177	299	303	482 555	Mach Speed Indicator [Bell]
49	178	300	304	483 556	McNaghten Rule [White]
50	179	201	305	484 557	Locus Penitentiae [Morris]
51	180	202	306	485 558	Limited Capacity Wells [Zimmerman]
52	181	203	307	486 559	Letter Stock [Kaufman]
53	182	204	308	487 560	Organoleptic Test [Commercial Creamery]
54	183	205	309	488 561	Oil Payment [Alamo]
55	184	206	310	489 562	Oath of Affirmation [Sullivan]
56	185	207	311	490 563	Net Worth Theory [O'Connor]
57	186	208	312	491 564	Neuroma [Skidmore]
58	187	209	313	492 565	Natural Gas Royalty [Huber]
59	188	210	314	493 566	Monition [Hunt]
60	189	211	315	494 567	Pettifoggery [Kraft]
61	190	212	316	495 568	Per My Et Per Tout [Gerling's Estate]
62	191	213	317	496 569	Pedis Possessio Doctrine [Ranchers Exploration]
63	192	214	318	497 470	Parens Patriae [Wilson]
64	193	215	319	498 571	Ready-to-Serve Charges [Finnigan]
65	194	216	320	499 572	Pug Mill [Schultz & Lindsay Construction Co.]
66	195	217	321	500 573	Pulmonary Fibrosis [Koshorek]
67	196	218	322	401 574	Pruno [Herr]
68	197	219	323	402 575	Property Ratione Soli [Alford]
69	198	220	324	403 576	Prejudicial Surprise [Hoffman]
70	199	221	325	404 577	Stowers Doctrine [Lacy]
71	200	222	326	405 578	Straight Line Method of Depreciation [Chadwick]
72	101	223	327	406 579	Spite Fence [Welsh]
73	102	224	328	407 580	Sic Utere Tuo Ut Alienum Non Laedas [Chapman]
74	103	225	329	408 581	Service Mark [National Trailways]
75	104	226	330	409 582	Sculling [Young]
76	105	227	331	410 583	Rest, Residue, and Remainder [Sinnott]
77	106	228	332	411 584	Res Integra [Reynolds]
78	107	229	333	412 585	Res Inter Alios Acta [Roosth]
79	108	230	334	413 586	Red-Blue-Yellow Technique [SCM Corp.]
80	109	231	335	414 587	Ullage [Blum]
81	110	232	336	415 588	Treasury Bill [Manufacturers Hanover Trust]
82	111	233	337	416 589	Treasury Stock [Fuller]
83	112	234	338	417 590	Touting [Owens]
84	113	235	339	418 591	Trade Acceptance [Gilliland]
85	114	236	340	419 592	Testamentary Class Gift [Lux]
86	115	237	341	420 593	Tachycardia [Bertrand]
87	116	238	342	421 594	Tacking [Cheatham]
88	117	239	343	422 595	Windstorm [Napanoch]
89	118	240	344	423 596	Wood Butcher [Rapisardi]
90	119	241	345	424 597	Wharfage [Howmet]
91	120	242	346	425 598	With Her Consent [Torres]
92	121	243	347	426 599	Valued Policy [Houston]
93	122	244	348	427 600	Unlimited Arbitration Clause [Ross]
94	123	245	349	428 501	Uttering of Forged Instrument [Reyes]
95	124	246	350	429 502	Vapor Lock [ACF Industries]
96	125	247	351	430 503	Warranty of Seaworthiness [Young]
97	126	248	352	431 504	Washout [Reagan]
98	127	249	353	432 505	Willfully Negligent [Hannon]
99	128	250	354	433 506	Work Stoppage [Moore]
100	129	251	355	434 507	Xylem [Rico Import]

Nelse Mortensen & Co. v. Treadwell, 217 F.2d 325 (1955).

LIBRARY EXERCISE 26. TABLE OF CASES AND POPULAR NAME TABLES. Using the information provided below, find the relevant entry in the designated Table of Cases, Defendant/Plaintiff Table, or Popular Name Table. Be especially careful to use the correct table. For your answer, cite the case in proper form. Do not show the subsequent history of the case in your citation. Cite Supreme Court cases only to <u>United States Reports</u>. The following abbreviations are used below: P = <u>Plaintiff</u>; D = <u>Defendant</u>; T/C = Table of Cases: D/P = Defendant/Plaintiff Table; PNT = Popular Name Table; Dec. = Decennial; Dig. = Digest; Shep PNT = <u>Shepard's Acts and Cases By Popular Names--Federal and State</u>; and S. Ct. = U.S. Supreme Court. Note that the listing of popular names of cases is located at the end of the <u>Shepard's</u> volume. Do not rely on the form used in the table for your citation. Consult the case to find missing information.

Problem #	Name or Party	Table
1 104 233 344 452 579	Schumaat (P)	3d Dec. Dig. T/C
2 105 234 345 453 580	Spreading Fire Case	Shep. PNT
3 106 235 346 454 581	Electric Theater Co. (P)	4th Dec. Dig. T/C
4 107 236 347 455 582	Densen's Estate	5th Dec. Dig. T/C
5 108 237 348 456 583	Hodson (D)	Mod. Fed. Prac. Dig. D/P
6 109 238 349 457 584	World's Fair Min. Co.(P)	West's S. Ct. Dig. T/C
7 110 239 350 458 585	Hlavaty (P)	Mod. Fed. Prac. Dig. T/C
8 111 240 351 459 586	Landa Cotton Oil Co. (D)	West's S. Ct. Dig. D/P
9 112 241 352 460 587	Rouselle (D)	Fed. Prac. Dig. 2d D/P
10 113 242 353 461 588	Vandike (P)	7th Dec. Dig. T/C
11 114 243 354 462 589	Heckman (P)	Sup. Ct. Dig. L. Ed. T/C
12 115 244 355 463 590	Am. Quasar Petroleum Co. of N.M. (D)	Fed. Prac. Dig. 2d D/P
13 116 245 356 464 591	Hindle (P)	6th Dec. Dig. T/C
14 117 246 357 465 592	In re West's Will	5th Dec. Dig. T/C
15 118 247 358 466 593	Nelse Mortensen & Co.(P)	6th Dec. Dig. T/C
16 119 248 359 467 594	Hartline (P)	7th Dec. Dig. T/C
17 120 249 360 468 595	Cow Palace, Ltd. (P)	8th Dec. Dig. T/C
18 121 250 361 469 596	Lebosky (P)	8th Dec. Dig. T/C
19 122 251 362 470 597	Yellowwolf (P)	8th Dec. Dig. T/C
20 123 252 363 471 598	Taylor v. Leesnitzer	S. Ct. Dig. L. Ed. T/C
21 124 253 364 472 599	Cappis (P)	1st Dec. & Cent. Dig. T/C
22 125 254 365 473 600	Leonidas, The	1st Dec. & Cent. Dig. T/C
23 126 255 366 474 501	Sehy (P)	2d Dec. Dig. T/C
24 127 256 367 475 502	Rutland Provision Co.(P)	1st Dec. & Cent. Dig T/C
25 128 257 368 476 503	Yamataya v. Fisher	S. Ct. Dig. L. Ed. T/C
26 129 258 369 477 504	Roschen v. Ward	S. Ct. Dig. L. Ed. T/C
27 130 259 370 478 505	First National Bank of Bellevue (P)	Fed. Prac. Dig. 2d T/C
28 131 260 371 479 506	Wiskie (P)	1st Dec. & Cent. Dig. T/C
29 132 261 372 480 507	Hamberger (P)	3d Dec. Dig. T/C
30 133 262 373 481 508	Sabbatino Case	Shep. PNT
31 134 263 374 482 509	Tenore (P)	4th Dec. Dig. T/C
32 135 264 375 483 510	Burkley (P)	5th Dec. Dig. T/C
33 136 265 376 484 511	Dri Mark Products, Inc.(D)	Mod. Fed. Prac. Dig. D/P
34 137 266 377 485 512	Federal Reserve Bank of Richmond (P)	West's S. Ct. Dig. T/C
35 138 267 378 486 513	Cech (P)	Mod Fed. Prac. Dig. T/C
36 139 268 379 487 514	Van Dolsen (D)	West's S. Ct. Dig. D/P
37 140 269 380 488 515	Redus (D)	Fed. Prac. Dig. 2d D/P
38 141 270 381 489 516	Riggs Optical Co. (P)	7th Dec. Dig. T/C
39 142 271 382 490 517	Burdell (P)	Sup. Ct. Dig. L. Ed. T/C
40 143 272 383 491 518	Carrell (D)	Fed. Prac. Dig. 2d D/P
41 144 273 384 492 519	Farin (P)	6th Dec. Dig. T/C
42 145 274 385 493 520	Smith v. Finkel	5th Dec. Dig. T/C
43 146 275 386 494 521	Bottle-Stopper Case	6th Dec. Dig. PNT
44 147 276 387 495 522	Cradic (P)	7th Dec. Dig. T/C
45 148 277 388 496 523	C-Line, Inc. (P)	8th Dec. Dig. T/C
46 149 278 389 497 524	Kenler (P)	8th Dec. Dig. T/C
47 150 279 390 498 525	Troglione (P)	8th Dec. Dig. T/C
48 151 280 391 499 526	Blair v. Bemis	1st Dec. & Cent. Dig. T/C

147 FS 708

Problem #		Name or Party	Table
49 152 281 392 500 527		Danielly v. Cheeves	1st Dec. & Cent. Dig. T/C
50 153 282 393 401 528		Indianapolis Brewing Co. (P)	1st Dec. & Cent. Dig. T/C
51 154 283 394 402 529		Clay Lumber Co. (P)	2d Dec. Dig. T/C
52 155 284 395 403 530		Morico v. U.S.	S. Ct. Dig. L. Ed. T/C
53 156 285 396 404 531		U.S. v. Rembrandt Electronics	Fed. Prac. Dig. 2d T/C
54 157 286 397 405 532		Loughrey (P)	Fed. Prac. Dig. 2d T/C
55 158 287 398 406 533		Laue (P)	Fed. Prac. Dig. 2d T/C
56 159 288 399 407 534		Sage v. Halversen	1st Dec. & Cent. Dig. T/C
57 160 289 400 408 535		Board of Trade Livery Co. (P)	3d Dec. Dig. T/C
58 161 290 301 409 536		Parked Auto Injury Case	Shep. PNT
59 162 291 302 410 537		National Radiator Case	Shep. PNT
60 163 292 303 411 538		Ginder (P)	4th Dec. Dig. T/C
61 164 293 304 412 539		Yosemite Valley Case	5th Dec. Dig. PNT
62 165 294 305 413 540		General Shaver Corp.(D)	Mod. Fed. Prac. Dig. D/P
63 166 295 306 414 541		Terhune (D)	Mod. Fed. Prac. Dig. D/P
64 167 296 307 415 542		Frank F. Fasi Supply Co. (P)	Mod. Fed. Prac. Dig. T/C
65 168 297 308 416 543		Gormley v. Bunyan	S. Ct. Dig. L. Ed. T/C
66 169 298 309 417 544		Metzger v. Knox	7th Dec. Dig. T/C
67 170 299 310 418 545		Sewall v. Haymaker	S. Ct. Dig. L. Ed. T/C
68 171 300 311 419 546		Gallinghouse (D)	Fed. Prac. Dig. 2d D/P
69 172 201 311 420 547		Brockelsby (P)	6th Dec. Dig. T/C
70 173 202 313 421 548		Rimnik Corp. (P)	5th Dec. Dig. T/C
71 174 203 314 422 549		Kuehner v. Irving Trust	S. Ct. Dig. L. Ed. T/C
72 175 204 315 423 550		Phillips v. Lust	6th Dec. Dig. T/C
73 176 205 316 424 551		Allen v. McCarthy	7th Dec. Dig. T/C
74 177 206 317 425 552		In re Beasley-Gilbert's, Inc.	8th Dec. Dig. T/C
75 178 207 318 426 553		Highway Products, Inc. (P)	8th Dec. Dig. T/C
76 179 208 319 427 554		Lay v. Lay	S. Ct. Dig. L. Ed. T/C
77 180 209 320 428 555		In re Bryden's Estate	1st Dec. & Cent. Dig. T/C
78 181 210 321 429 556		Stefanich (P)	8th Dec. Dig. T/C
79 182 211 322 430 557		Farnsworth v. Farnsworth	1st Dec. & Cent. Dig. T/C
80 183 212 323 431 558		Hoon v. Hoon	1st Dec. & Cent. Dig. T/C
81 184 213 324 432 559		Huls (P)	2d Dec. Dig. T/C
82 185 214 325 433 560		Chamoy (P)	Fed. Prac. Dig. 2d T/C
83 186 215 326 434 561		Massi (P)	1st Dec. & Cent. Dig. T/C
84 187 216 327 435 562		Holstine (P)	Fed. Prac. Dig. 2d T/C
85 188 217 328 436 563		U.S. v. Carbo	Fed. Prac. Dig. 2d T/C
86 189 218 329 437 564		Taylor v. McFadden	1st Dec. & Cent. Dig. T/C
87 190 219 330 438 565		Sage v. Halversen	1st Dec. & Cent. Dig. T/C
88 191 220 331 439 566		Del Pilar (P)	Mod. Fed. Prac. Dig. T/C
89 192 221 332 440 567		King v. McGinnis	Mod. Fed. Prac. Dig. T/C
90 193 222 333 441 568		United States v. Beuttas	S. Ct. Dig. L. Ed. T/C
91 194 223 334 442 569		Hale v. Bimco Trading	S. Ct. Dig. L. Ed. T/C
92 195 224 335 443 570		Hurford Case	Shep. PNT
93 196 225 336 444 571		Corker v. Jones	S. Ct. Dig. L. Ed. T/C
94 197 226 337 445 572		Dotson v. Milliken	S. Ct. Dig. L. Ed. T/C
95 198 227 338 446 573		Faas (D)	Mod. Fed. Prac. Dig. D/P
96 199 228 339 447 574		Sheff (D)	Mod. Fed. Prac. Dig. D/P
97 200 229 340 448 575		Brucker (D)	West's S. Ct. Dig. D/P
98 101 230 341 449 576		Royal Spy Case	Shep. PNT
99 102 231 342 450 577		Southern Ice Co. (D)	Fed. Prac. Dig. 2d D/P
100 103 232 343 451 578		Hader (D)	Fed. Prac. Dig. 2d D/P

LIBRARY EXERCISE 27. AMERICAN JURISPRUDENCE SECOND. Locate the following title and section in _American Jurisprudence Second_. Cite the section using the proper form. Abbreviate "and" to "&" when it appears in an _Am. Jur. 2d_ title.

```
   Problem #                    Title/Section
 1 155 206 322 421 533   Abandoned, Lost, & Unclaimed Property § 27
 2 156 207 323 422 534   Homestead § 179
 3 157 208 324 423 535   Laundries, Dyers, & Dry Cleaners § 12
 4 158 209 325 424 536   Public Lands § 89
 5 159 210 326 425 537   Restitution & Implied Contracts § 79
 6 160 211 327 426 538   Landlord & Tenant § 619
 7 161 212 328 427 539   Death § 304
 8 162 213 329 428 540   Abstracts of Title § 12
 9 163 214 330 429 541   Abuse of Process § 16
10 164 215 331 430 542   Mortgages § 371
11 165 216 332 431 543   Highways, Streets, & Bridges § 178
12 166 217 333 432 544   Evidence § 217
13 167 218 334 433 545   Carriers § 871
14 168 219 335 434 546   Landlord & Tenant § 878
15 169 220 336 435 547   Fraud & Deceit § 403
16 170 221 337 436 548   Acknowledgments § 117
17 171 222 338 437 549   Boundaries § 85
18 172 223 339 438 550   Carriers § 521
19 173 224 340 439 551   International Law § 83
20 174 225 341 440 552   Adverse Possession § 9
21 175 226 342 441 553   Labor & Labor Relations § 1757
22 176 227 343 442 554   Incompetent Persons § 137
23 177 228 344 443 555   Insolvency § 19
24 178 229 345 444 556   Federal Tort Claims Act § 54
25 179 230 346 445 557   Admiralty § 130
26 180 231 347 446 558   Parent & Child § 101
27 181 232 348 447 559   Adultery & Fornication § 13
28 182 233 349 448 560   Deeds § 294
29 183 234 350 449 561   Negligence § 223
30 184 235 351 450 562   Husband & Wife § 487
31 185 236 352 451 563   Banks § 772
32 186 237 353 452 564   Costs § 52
33 187 238 354 453 565   Municipal Corporations, Counties, & Other Political
                           Subdivisions § 55
34 188 239 355 454 566   Life Tenants & Remaindermen § 56
35 189 240 356 455 567   Sales § 519
36 190 241 357 456 568   Appeal & Error § 345
37 191 242 358 457 569   Pardon & Parole § 43
38 192 243 359 458 570   Fixtures § 91
39 193 244 360 459 571   Railroads § 201
40 194 245 361 460 572   Mobs & Riots § 5
41 195 246 362 461 573   Patents § 330
42 196 247 363 462 574   Electricity, Gas, & Steam § 136
43 197 248 364 463 575   Champerty & Maintenance § 4
44 198 249 365 464 576   Judgments § 724
45 199 250 366 465 577   Damages § 30
46 200 251 367 466 578   Infants § 84
47 101 252 368 467 579   Ne Exeat § 18
48 102 253 369 468 580   Bankruptcy § 772
49 103 254 370 469 581   Monopolies, Restraints of Trade, & Unfair Trade
                           Practices § 206
50 104 255 371 470 582   Banks § 428
51 105 256 372 471 583   Bigamy § 16
52 106 257 373 472 584   Labor & Labor Relations § 37
53 107 258 374 473 585   Federal Employers' Liability & Compensation Acts § 38
54 108 259 375 474 586   Extradition § 30
55 109 260 376 475 587   Drugs, Narcotics, & Poisons § 28
56 110 261 377 476 588   Domicil § 87
57 111 262 378 477 589   Gifts § 92
```

53

Problem #					Title/Section

```
 58 112 263 379 478 590   Malicious Prosecution § 128
 59 113 264 380 479 591   Death § 219
 60 114 265 381 480 592   Insurance § 1386
 61 115 266 382 481 593   Mobs & Riots § 14
 62 116 267 383 482 594   Irrigation § 97
 63 117 268 384 483 595   Jury § 213
 64 118 269 385 484 596   Cemeteries § 39
 65 119 270 386 485 597   Certiorari § 39
 66 120 271 387 486 598   Libel & Slander § 60
 67 121 272 388 487 599   Rape § 82
 68 122 273 389 488 600   Public Works & Contracts § 70
 69 123 274 390 489 501   Civil Service § 20
 70 124 275 391 490 502   Public Officers & Employees § 15
 71 125 276 392 491 503   Money § 14
 72 126 277 393 492 504   Interest & Usury § 194
 73 127 278 394 493 505   Customs Duties & Import Regulations § 101
 74 128 279 395 494 506   Collection & Credit Agencies § 22
 75 129 280 396 495 507   Improvements § 12
 76 130 281 397 496 508   Extradition § 13
 77 131 282 398 497 509   Copyright & Literary Property § 6
 78 132 283 399 498 510   Community Property § 92
 79 133 284 400 499 511   Gambling § 172
 80 132 285 301 500 512   Public Utilities § 189
 81 135 286 302 401 513   Conspiracy § 7
 82 136 287 303 402 514   Records & Recording Laws § 102
 83 137 288 304 403 515   Inheritance, Estate, & Gift Taxes § 82
 84 138 289 305 404 516   Contempt § 115
 85 139 290 306 405 517   Gas & Oil § 259
 86 140 291 307 406 518   Contracts § 324
 87 141 292 308 407 519   Lobbying § 7
 88 142 293 309 408 520   Markets & Marketing § 42
 89 143 294 310 409 521   Mines & Minerals § 165
 90 144 295 311 410 522   Fires § 30
 91 145 296 312 411 523   Cotenancy & Joint Ownership § 9
 92 146 297 313 412 524   Lost & Destroyed Instruments § 40
 93 147 298 314 413 525   Libel & Slander § 454
 94 148 299 315 414 526   New Trial § 148
 95 149 300 316 415 527   Prenatal Injuries § 22
 96 150 201 317 416 528   Logs & Timber § 125
 97 151 202 318 417 529   Names § 24
 98 152 203 319 418 530   Dead Bodies § 42
 99 153 204 320 419 531   Occupations, Trades, & Professions § 61
100 154 205 321 420 532   Private Franchise Contracts § 15
```

LIBRARY EXERCISE 28. CORPUS JURIS SECUNDUM. Locate the following title and section in <u>Corpus Juris Secundum</u> (<u>C.J.S.</u>). (a) Cite the section (in the main part of the volume). Note that many of the <u>C.J.S.</u> volumes used in this exercise also are used to complete Library Exercise 29.

<u>Problem #</u>					<u>Title/Section</u>
1	170	236	344	485 592	Territories § 1
2	171	237	345	486 593	Property § 15
3	172	238	346	487 594	States § 195
4	173	239	347	488 595	Witnesses § 527
5	174	240	348	489 596	Wills § 1308
6	175	241	349	490 597	Wills § 1066
7	176	242	350	491 598	Wills § 514
8	177	243	351	492 599	Waters § 308
9	178	244	352	493 600	Waste § 19
10	179	245	353	494 501	Venue § 86
11	180	246	354	495 502	Usury § 79
12	181	247	355	496 503	Trusts § 288
13	182	248	356	497 504	Trial § 631
14	183	249	357	498 505	Trial § 242
15	184	250	358	499 506	Trespass § 44
16	185	251	359	500 507	Territories § 38
17	186	252	360	401 508	Taxation § 1093
18	187	253	361	402 509	Taxation § 349
19	188	254	362	403 510	Subrogation § 57
20	189	255	363	404 511	Statutes § 357
21	190	256	364	405 512	States § 82
22	191	257	365	406 513	Sodomy § 15
23	192	258	366	407 514	Shipping § 11
24	193	259	367	408 515	Sequestration § 9
25	194	260	368	409 516	Salvage § 1
26	195	261	369	410 517	Replevin § 171
27	196	262	370	411 518	Religious Societies § 29
28	197	263	371	412 519	Rape § 58
29	198	264	372	413 520	Quo Warranto § 28
30	199	265	373	414 521	Public Lands § 282
31	200	266	374	415 522	Post Office § 47
32	101	267	375	416 523	Pleading § 269
33	102	268	376	417 524	Perjury § 77
34	103	269	377	418 525	Patents § 269
35	104	270	378	419 526	Partnership § 427
36	105	271	379	420 527	Officers § 143
37	106	272	380	421 528	New Trial § 77
38	107	273	381	422 529	Negligence § 220.7
39	108	274	382	423 530	Negligence § 63(9)
40	109	275	383	424 531	Municipal Corporations § 2058
41	110	276	384	425 532	Municipal Corporations § 931
42	111	277	385	426 533	Municipal Corporations § 93
43	112	278	386	427 534	Motor Vehicles § 632(1)
44	113	279	387	428 535	Motor Vehicles § 518(14)
45	114	280	388	429 536	Motor Vehicles § 270
46	115	281	389	430 537	Motor Vehicles § 5
47	116	282	390	431 538	Mortgages § 313
48	117	283	391	432 539	Monopolies § 81
49	118	284	392	433 540	Mechanics' Liens § 171
50	119	285	393	434 541	Marriage § 16
51	120	286	394	435 542	Mandamus § 228
52	121	287	395	436 543	Lis Pendens § 43
53	122	288	396	437 544	Licenses § 30
54	123	289	397	438 545	Homesteads § 187
55	124	290	398	439 546	Fraud § 13
56	125	291	399	440 547	Garnishment § 251
57	126	292	400	441 548	Larceny § 143
58	127	293	301	442 549	Associations § 13
59	128	294	302	443 550	Justices of the Peace § 22(1)
60	129	295	303	444 551	Juries § 111

55

Problem #						Title/Section
61	130	296	304	445	552	Bail § 44
62	131	297	305	446	553	Attachment § 49
63	132	298	306	447	554	Assignments § 39
64	133	299	307	448	555	Embezzlement § 35
65	134	300	308	449	556	Arrest § 15
66	135	201	309	450	557	Appearances § 51
67	136	202	310	451	558	Contracts § 548
68	137	203	311	452	559	Continuances § 94(1)
69	138	204	312	453	560	Contracts § 397
70	139	205	313	454	561	Railroads § 439
71	140	206	314	455	562	Certiorari § 144
72	141	207	315	456	563	Carriers § 334
73	142	208	316	457	564	Brokers § 95
74	143	209	317	458	565	Boundaries § 34
75	144	210	318	459	566	Brokers § 22
76	145	211	319	460	567	Animals § 51
77	146	212	320	461	568	Criminal Law § 1959
78	147	213	321	462	569	Damages § 41
79	148	214	322	463	570	Dead Bodies § 8(4)
80	149	215	323	464	571	Deeds § 32
81	150	216	324	465	572	Agency § 548
82	151	217	325	466	573	Death § 107
83	152	218	326	467	574	Admiralty § 127
84	153	219	327	468	575	Embezzlement § 27
85	154	220	328	469	576	Eminent Domain § 419
86	155	221	329	470	577	Equity § 454
87	156	222	330	471	578	Estoppel § 43
88	157	223	331	472	579	Executions § 383
89	158	224	332	473	580	Evidence § 1022
90	159	225	333	474	581	Evidence § 638
91	160	226	334	475	582	Evidence § 58
92	161	227	335	476	583	Depositaries § 2
93	162	228	336	477	584	Disorderly Houses § 11
94	163	229	337	478	585	Divorce § 137
95	164	230	338	479	586	Electricity § 41
96	165	231	339	480	587	Drains § 12
97	166	232	340	481	588	Divorce § 312
98	167	233	341	482	589	Homesteads § 78
99	168	234	342	483	590	Fraud § 95
100	169	235	343	484	591	False Imprisonment § 9

LIBRARY EXERCISE 29. TOPIC METHOD OF SEARCH IN LEGAL ENCYCLOPEDIAS. Using the "Analysis" and "Sub-Analysis" at the beginning of the topic in Corpus Juris Secundum listed below, find the section of Corpus Juris Secundum that most directly treats the question given with your problem number. (a) Answer the question based upon the material discussed in the section. (b) List the "Analysis" and "Sub-Analysis" entries (including the section entry) that directed you to the relevant section.

1 170 236 344 485 592   Theaters and Shows   May a theater owner make an admission ticket nontransferable by printing that condition on it?
2 171 237 345 486 593   Public Utilities   Is inability to comply with an order a defense to proceedings for contempt of a public utility commission?
3 172 238 346 487 594   States   Are state warrants generally considered to be negotiable instruments?
4 173 239 347 488 595   Work and Labor   When services are rendered in contemplation of marriage, without expectation of pecuniary compensation, may the person performing the services recover compensation when the recipient dies before the marriage?
5 174 240 348 489 596   Witnesses   Under the common law, are witnesses entitled to compensation for testifying?
6 175 241 349 490 597   Wills   Does an advancement bear interest during the lifetime of the testator?
7 176 242 350 491 598   Wills   May a testator properly delegate to a third party the power to execute a revocation of a will at his option after the death of the testator?
8 177 243 351 492 599   Wills   According to the weight of authority, may a person dispose of his own dead body by will?
9 178 244 352 493 600   Warehousemen and Safe Depositaries   In general, does a public warehouseman have a duty to receive goods delivered to him, provided the goods are within the class he is authorized to receive and store?
10 179 245 353 494 501   Venue   In most jurisdictions, where does an action to foreclose a lien on personal property have to be brought?
11 180 246 354 495 502   United States   Are Senators privileged from arrest in civil cases when they are returning from a session of Congress?
12 181 247 355 496 503   Trusts   Can a person be a "de facto" trustee when there is no de jure trusteeship?
13 182 248 356 497 504   Trusts   May an express trust be declared by means of several instruments rather than one trust document?
14 183 249 357 498 505   Trial   May a demurrer to the evidence be made before all the plaintiff's proof is heard?
15 184 250 358 499 506   Towns   Are anticipation warrants considered to be demand warrants?
16 185 251 359 500 507   Tenancy in Common   Are statutes that authorize treble damages for waste committed by tenants in common strictly construed?
17 186 252 360 401 508   Taxation   If a specific form of a tax deed is not prescribed by statute, will a common-law conveyance be sufficient if it is in such a form as to transfer the title of the former owner and vest the estate in the purchaser?
18 187 253 361 402 509   Taxation   Does taxation of trust property to both the trustee and the cestui que trust constitute improper double taxation?
19 188 254 362 403 510   Subrogation   Will an indemnitor of a surety be subrogated to the surety's rights when the indemnitor is compelled to satisfy the surety's liability?
20 189 255 363 404 511   Statutes   When the proper construction of a statute is in doubt, must the court refer to the statute's preamble in order to ascertain the legislature's intent?
21 190 256 364 405 512   States   Must a state use its property only for public purposes?
22 191 257 365 406 513   Social Security and Public Welfare   Has the federal Social Security Act been extended to cover self-employed persons (who otherwise meet the statutory requirements)?
23 192 258 366 407 514   Shipping   After a wrecked vessel has been abandoned by its owners, may a person be prosecuted for destroying the wrecked vessel?
24 193 259 367 408 515   Seamen   In cases of an aggravated character, may a seaman be punished by forfeiture of his clothing and effects on board ship?

25 194 260 368 409 516   Salvage   Is the pendency of a suit for salvage a bar to a subsequent action by other salvors against the same property to recover salvage for other services performed during the same voyage?
26 195 261 369 410 517   Replevin   Will replevin lie for the recovery of a corpse?
27 196 262 370 411 518   Religious Societies   As a general rule, is the property of a religious society divided among its members upon dissolution of the society?
28 197 263 371 412 519   Rape   Can a railroad company be held civilly liable for a rape when the rape was committed by one of its employees on one of its passengers?
29 198 264 372 413 520   Quieting Title   Is there a split of authority under quieting title statutes whether a holder of an easement has the right to bring an action to quiet title?
30 199 265 373 414 521   Public Utilities   Is good will normally considered in setting the value of a public utility for the purposes of rate making?
31 200 266 374 415 522   Process   Is a person confined in jail ordinarily exempt from service of civil process?
32 101 267 375 416 523   Pleading   Do some jurisdictions permit the use of a demurrer to attack the failure to attach necessary exhibits to a pleading when such attaching is required by statute?
33 102 268 376 417 524   Physicians and Surgeons   May practice of a profession under a trade name be prohibited by statute?
34 103 269 377 418 525   Patents   What rights are transferred when an expired patent is assigned?
35 104 270 378 419 526   Partnership   May a partner engage in business of the same nature as that of the partnership without the consent of his copartners (unless otherwise provided by the partnership agreement)?
36 105 271 379 420 527   Officers   In general, are de facto officers entitled to the emoluments of an office where there is a de jure officer also claiming the office?
37 106 272 380 421 528   Nuisances   May a structure which heats the property of another so as to make it untenantable be a nuisance?
38 107 273 381 422 529   Negligence   In determining whether a child is capable of exercising any care for his own safety for purposes of the law of contributory negligence, must consideration be given to all factors bearing on his capacity, not just his age?
39 108 274 382 423 530   Navigable Waters   May an individual obtain an absolute exclusive right to possession of an island in the sea by virtue of discovering it?
40 109 275 383 424 531   Municipal Corporations   In absence of a statute or ordinance controlling the matter, may claims against a municipal corporation be assigned?
41 110 276 384 425 532   Municipal Corporations   In general, is a municipal corporation liable in tort for injuries resulting from defects in a street not yet opened for public use?
42 111 277 385 426 533   Municipal Corporations   In general, may proceedings for annexation of territory to a municipal corporation be attacked collaterally on the ground that they are absolutely void for want of jurisdiction?
43 112 278 386 427 534   Motor Vehicles   Is a spectator's right to recover for injuries because of a speed contest along a public way affected by the fact the spectator was a trespasser on land adjacent to the highway?
44 113 279 387 428 535   Securities Regulation   Does a plaintiff have the privilege of nationwide service of process in a civil action based upon a violation of the federal securities laws (the Securities Act of 1933 and the Securities Exchange Act of 1934)?
45 114 280 388 429 536   Products Liability   May a manufacturer limit by contract his strict liability for injuries resulting from product defects? 46 115 281 389 430 537   Motor Vehicles   What is an auto stage?
47 116 282 390 431 538   Mortgages   May a creditor (not a judgment creditor), who is not a party to a mortgage, question or impeach the consideration supporting a mortgage?
48 117 283 391 432 539   Monopolies   Under the federal antitrust laws, are reasonable attorney's fees expressly granted to a successful plaintiff in an action for damages?

49 118 284 392 433 540   Mechanics' Liens   Is scire facias used as a proceeding to enforce a mechanic's lien in some jurisdictions?
50 119 285 393 434 541   Marriage   At common law, what was the age of legal consent to marriage for a female?
51 120 286 394 435 542   Marriage   What is jactitation of marriage?
52 121 287 395 436 543   Master and Servant   Does the insanity of an employee which prevents the performance of his contract terminate his employment contract unless the parties have agreed otherwise?
53 122 288 396 437 544   Licenses   Is a license in respect of real property ordinarily assignable by the licensee without the consent of the licensor?
54 123 289 397 438 545   Homesteads   Are there ordinarily moral qualification requirements that must be met in order to obtain a homestead exemption?
55 124 290 398 439 546   Fraud   Where an injury sufficient to sustain an action for fraud has been established, is the plaintiff entitled to at least nominal damages?
56 125 291 399 440 547   Garnishment   Does securing a garnishment on the basis of false allegations of fact ordinarily render the garnishment "wrongful"?
57 126 292 400 441 548   Larceny   May lost property be the subject of larceny?
58 127 293 301 442 549   Attachment   May vested interests under contracts be attached?
59 128 294 302 443 550   Justices of the Peace   In a civil case, as a general rule does a judgment of a justice of the peace prior to execution create a lien on property in absence of a statute regulating the matter?
60 129 295 303 444 551   Juries   In absence of a statute regulating the matter, is it necessary for the court to issue a formal written summons for talesmen?
61 130 296 304 445 552   Bail   Has it been held that a recital of the defendant's arrest in a bail bond in a civil action is not essential to the validity of the bail bond?
62 131 297 305 446 553   Attachment   Is a voidable writ of attachment amendable?
63 132 298 306 447 554   Assignments   Is an action for injury to reputation assignable in absence of a statute regulating the matter?
64 133 299 307 448 555   Eminent Domain   Is the establishment of a public ferry considered to be a public use for which private property may be condemned?
65 134 300 308 449 556   Assignments   Is an action for tortious injury to a person's property generally assignable in absence of a statute regulating the matter?
66 135 201 309 450 557   Arbitration   Is a party competent to act as an arbitrator in his own dispute?
67 136 202 310 451 558   Contracts   Must a contract generally be rescinded in toto or can any contract be rescinded in part and affirmed in part?
68 137 203 311 452 559   Continuances   Is the loss of papers in the case a good ground for a continuance when the applicant for the continuance is not at fault and the papers cannot readily be replaced?
69 138 204 312 453 560   Civil Rights   Is racial discrimination in the use of public facilities unlawful?
70 139 205 313 454 561   Railroads   After two railroads have been consolidated, are actions on a cause arising prior to consolidation generally maintainable against the consolidated company?
71 140 206 314 455 562   Charities   Is a gift for the care of a public burial ground a gift for a charitable use?
72 141 207 315 456 563   Carriers   According to the usually accepted view, does a carrier have a right to a common law lien for demurrage charges in absence of usage, statute, or contract providing such a right?
73 142 208 316 457 564   Brokers   Under what power does a state have the authority to regulate the business or occupation of a broker?
74 143 209 317 458 565   Boundaries   Does a conveyance of land bounded by a wall carry title to the center of the wall unless a contrary intention appears?
75 144 210 318 459 566   Burglary   Under the common law, is the breaking and entering of a railroad car with the intent to steal burglary?

76 145 211 319 460 567   Animals   In general, what is the difference between a rescue and a pound breach?
77 146 212 320 461 568   Criminal Law   May the age of the accused be considered in fixing the accused's punishment?
78 147 213 321 462 569   Customs Duties   In order to recover excessive duties paid, is it necessary that they were paid under some form of protest?
79 148 214 322 463 570   Death   Where it is shown that a person was alive at a certain time, will it be presumed that this person was alive at a subsequent time, unless the contrary is shown by proof or a different presumption arises?
80 149 215 323 464 571   Deeds   Is the affixing of a revenue stamp to a deed, in absence of an intent to evade the revenue law, essential to the validity of the deed?
81 150 216 324 465 572   Agency   Does an agent have a specific lien upon the principal's property in his possession for his expenses during the course of the agency with respect to that property?
82 151 217 325 466 573   Death   Is justifiable homicide recognized as a defense to a wrongful death action?
83 152 218 326 467 574   Admiralty   Is a charter party a contract within admiralty jurisdiction so as to be enforceable in admiralty?
84 153 219 327 468 575   Eminent Domain   May the powers of eminent domain be conferred on a territory by implication?
85 154 220 328 469 576   Eminent Domain   Is a market, public in character, a public use for which private property may be condemned?
86 155 221 329 470 577   Equity   Does a court have the power to render and enter a decree nunc pro tunc, assuming it has exercised proper discretion?
87 156 222 330 471 578   Estoppel   Must estoppel ordinarily be specially pleaded?
88 157 223 331 472 579   Executions   Is a franchise subject to execution under the common law?
89 158 224 332 473 580   Evidence   Under the best evidence rule, is parol evidence ordinarily admissible to prove the contents of a newspaper?
90 159 225 333 474 581   Evidence   Will a nonexpert witness be permitted to state his opinion as to the cause of a sound?
91 160 226 334 475 582   Evidence   May an application for a continuance that contains admissions be introduced in evidence as a judicial admission?
92 161 227 335 476 583   Descent and Distribution   May community property be the subject of an advancement?
93 162 228 336 477 584   Dismissal and Nonsuit   What is a retraxit?
94 163 229 337 478 585   Divorce   Is adultery a generally recognized ground for divorce in most jurisdictions?
95 164 230 338 479 586   Electricity   Is there a duty, independent of statute, imposed on an electric company to serve without discrimination all similarity situated members of the public it professes to serve, provided they have complied with all proper conditions precedent for service?
96 165 231 339 480 587   Drains   Does a drainage assessment constitute a lien on lands within the district in absence of a statute so providing?
97 166 232 340 481 588   Divorce   Does the full faith and credit provision of the federal Constitution apply to a decree rendered in a foreign country?
98 167 233 341 482 589   Drugs and Narcotics   May the ownership of a pharmacy be restricted to persons who are licensed or registered pharmacists?
99 168 234 342 483 590   Attorney and Client   Is an attorney's possessory lien assignable?
100 169 235 343 484 591   False Imprisonment   Is there a right to at least nominal damages as a result of an illegal restraint amounting to false imprisonment?

LIBRARY EXERCISE 30. LEGAL PERIODICALS. Find and cite the article, comment, note, case comment, or case note that begins on the page of the volume of the designated law review listed below in proper form.

Problem #					Citation
1	119	209	375	470	584	61 Mich. L. Rev. 425
2	120	210	376	471	585	57 Mich. L. Rev. 945
3	121	211	377	472	586	39 Mich. L. Rev. 561
4	122	212	378	473	587	37 Mich. L. Rev. 841
5	123	213	379	474	588	44 Mich. L. Rev. 955
6	124	214	380	475	589	63 Calif. L. Rev. 926
7	125	215	381	476	590	64 Calif. L. Rev. 678
8	126	216	382	477	591	42 Mich. L. Rev. 383
9	127	217	383	478	592	36 Mich. L. Rev. 56
10	128	218	384	479	593	50 Mich. L. Rev. 1291
11	129	219	385	480	594	49 Mich. L. Rev. 1103
12	130	220	386	481	595	77 Mich. L. Rev. 63
13	131	221	387	482	596	48 Mich. L. Rev. 745
14	132	222	388	483	597	47 Mich. L. Rev. 775
15	133	223	389	484	598	65 Calif. L. Rev. 546
16	134	224	390	485	599	66 Calif. L. Rev. 935
17	135	225	391	486	600	54 Mich. L. Rev. 71
18	136	226	392	487	501	59 Mich. L. Rev. 1017
19	137	227	393	488	502	56 Mich. L. Rev. 33
20	138	228	394	489	503	41 Mich. L. Rev. 815
21	139	229	395	490	504	60 Mich. L. Rev. 169
22	140	230	396	491	505	23 Stanford L. Rev. 1
23	141	231	397	492	506	52 Mich. L. Rev. 479
24	142	232	398	493	507	24 Stanford L. Rev. 439
25	143	233	399	494	508	58 Mich. L. Rev. 55
26	144	234	400	495	509	74 Mich. L. Rev. 1258
27	145	235	301	496	510	25 Minn. L. Rev. 730
28	146	236	302	497	511	20 Minn. L. Rev. 1
29	147	237	303	498	512	30 Minn. L. Rev. 435
30	148	238	304	499	513	125 U. Pa. L. Rev. 947
31	149	239	305	500	514	23 Minn. L. Rev. 879
32	150	240	306	401	515	36 Minn. L. Rev. 1
33	151	241	307	402	516	5 Minn. L. Rev. 493
34	152	242	308	403	517	127 U. Pa. L. Rev. 581
35	153	243	309	404	518	33 Minn. L. Rev. 331
36	154	244	310	405	519	24 Minn. L. Rev. 607
37	155	245	311	406	520	12 Minn. L. Rev. 129
38	156	246	312	407	521	14 Minn. L. Rev. 124
39	157	247	313	408	522	9 Minn. L. Rev. 101
40	158	248	314	409	523	11 Minn. L. Rev. 313
41	159	249	315	410	524	10 Minn. L. Rev. 1
42	160	250	316	411	525	128 U. Pa. L. Rev. 361
43	161	251	317	412	526	17 Minn. L. Rev. 689
44	162	252	318	413	527	18 Minn. L. Rev. 269
45	163	253	319	414	528	22 Minn. L. Rev. 1008
46	164	254	320	415	529	13 Minn. L. Rev. 439
47	165	255	321	416	530	59 Calif. L. Rev. 1091
48	166	256	322	417	531	15 Minn. L. Rev. 261
49	167	257	323	418	532	31 Minn. L. Rev. 301
50	168	258	324	419	533	35 Minn. L. Rev. 262
51	169	259	325	420	534	44 Yale L.J. 782
52	170	260	326	421	535	45 Yale L.J. 1201
53	171	261	327	422	536	46 Yale L.J. 52
54	172	262	328	423	537	47 Yale L.J. 724
55	173	263	329	424	538	48 Yale L.J. 195
56	174	264	330	425	539	49 Yale L.J. 18
57	175	265	331	426	540	50 Yale L.J. 1376
58	176	266	332	427	541	51 Yale L.J. 213
59	177	267	333	428	542	86 Yale L.J. 809
60	178	268	334	429	543	88 Yale L.J. 1623
61	179	269	335	430	544	54 Yale L.J. 809

	Problem #					Citation
62	180	270	336	431	545	55 Yale L.J. 76
63	181	271	337	432	546	56 Yale L.J. 605
64	182	272	338	433	547	57 Yale L.J. 1207
65	183	273	339	434	548	58 Yale L.J. 213
66	184	274	340	435	549	29 U. Fla. L. Rev. 789
67	185	275	341	436	550	28 U. Fla. L. Rev. 1
68	186	276	342	437	551	26 U. Fla. L. Rev. 191
69	187	277	343	438	552	44 U. Chi. L. Rev. 271
70	188	278	344	439	553	43 U. Chi. L. Rev. 667
71	189	279	345	440	554	46 U. Chi. L. Rev. 3
72	190	280	346	441	555	47 U. Chi. L. Rev. 1
73	191	281	347	442	556	79 Colum. L. Rev. 1227
74	192	282	348	443	557	76 Colum. L. Rev. 48
75	193	283	349	444	558	77 Colum. L. Rev. 511
76	194	284	350	445	559	75 Colum. L. Rev. 771
77	195	285	351	446	560	74 Colum. L. Rev. 40
78	196	286	352	447	561	62 Harv. L. Rev. 987
79	197	287	353	448	562	63 Harv. L. Rev. 27
80	198	288	354	449	563	64 Harv. L. Rev. 417
81	199	289	355	450	564	89 Harv. L. Rev. 1685
82	200	290	356	451	565	86 Harv. L. Rev. 1380
83	101	291	357	452	566	85 Harv. L. Rev. 537
84	102	292	358	453	567	68 Harv. L. Rev. 257
85	103	293	359	454	568	69 Harv. L. Rev. 1
86	104	294	360	455	569	70 Harv. L. Rev. 1183
87	105	295	361	456	570	71 Harv. L. Rev. 1401
88	106	296	362	457	571	72 Harv. L. Rev. 609
89	107	297	363	458	572	73 Harv. L. Rev. 625
90	108	298	364	459	573	74 Harv. L. Rev. 473
91	109	299	365	460	574	75 Harv. L. Rev. 1532
92	110	300	366	461	575	76 Harv. L. Rev. 303
93	111	201	367	462	576	77 Harv. L. Rev. 1037
94	112	202	368	463	577	78 Harv. L. Rev. 1578
95	113	203	369	464	578	79 Harv. L. Rev. 733
96	114	204	370	465	579	80 Harv. L. Rev. 1432
97	115	205	371	466	580	81 Harv. L. Rev. 1439
98	116	206	372	467	581	82 Harv. L. Rev. 42
99	117	207	373	468	582	83 Harv. L. Rev. 1362
100	118	208	374	469	583	84 Harv. L. Rev. 281

LIBRARY EXERCISE 31. INDEX TO LEGAL PERIODICALS: ARTICLES. Find the article listed below in the Index to Legal Periodicals and cite the article in proper form based upon the information given in the Index. Note that the volume of the Index to Legal Periodicals used to complete this Exercise is also used in many instances to complete Library Exercise 32.

#					Citation
1	172	289	355	428 534	E.H. Levi, "The sovereignty of the courts" (1983).
2	173	290	356	429 535	R.E. Epstein, "Blackmail, Inc." (1983).
3	174	291	357	430 536	M. Gibson, "The case of the Burnside Foundry" (1984).
4	175	292	358	431 537	E. Warren, "Formal and operative rules under common law and code" (1983).
5	176	293	359	432 538	J Reno, Dealing with child abuse and neglect: a prosecutor's viewpoint" (1984).
6	177	294	360	433 539	R.H. Coase, "Lighthouse in economics" (1974).
7	178	295	361	434 540	E.D. Eshelman, "Proposed joint tenancy statute" (1971).
8	179	296	362	435 541	R.H. Neuman, "Oil on troubled waters: the international control of marine pollution" (1971).
9	180	297	363	436 542	M.H. Redish, "Campaign spending laws and the first amendment" (1971).
10	181	298	364	437 543	R. Nimmer, "Public drunk: formalizing the police role as a social help agency" (1970).
11	182	299	365	438 544	C.P. Paquin, "Valuation of wrongful death actions in Georgia" (1973).
12	183	300	366	439 545	W.G. Rothenberg, "Stockholder loans to insolvent corporations" (1971).
13	184	201	367	440 546	D.R. Packard, "Fair procedure in welfare hearings" (1969).
14	185	202	368	441 547	H.H. Hackley, "Our discriminatory banking structure" (1969).
15	186	203	369	442 548	E.G. West, "Agency shops and the public sector: an economic analysis" (1979).
16	187	204	370	443 549	E.Y. Semerjian, "Right of confrontation" (1969).
17	188	205	371	444 550	L.V. Kaplan, "Civil commitment 'as you like it'" (1969).
18	189	206	372	445 551	J.K. Weeks, "Broker-dealer disclosure of corporate inside information" (1969).
19	190	207	373	446 552	D.F. Clifford, "Colorado's 'short arm' jurisdiction" (1965).
20	191	208	374	447 553	L.D. Lowenfels, "Rule 10b-5 and the stockholder's derivative action" (1965).
21	192	209	375	448 554	M.W. Macey, "Bring your fixtures up to date" (1965).
22	193	210	376	449 555	W.E. Knepper, "Alimony for accident victims?" (1966).
23	194	211	377	450 556	M. Domke, "American arbitral awards: enforcement in foreign countries" (1965).
24	195	212	378	451 557	R.F. Shryock, "Survey evidence in contested trademark cases" (1967).
25	196	213	379	452 558	D.S. Coham, "Pennsylvania tentative trusts: problems and problem areas" (1962).
26	197	214	380	453 559	A. Lenhoff, "New procedural code in New York" (1963).
27	198	215	381	454 560	L.B. Orfield, "Consolidation in federal criminal procedure" (1961).
28	199	216	382	455 561	G.J. Weiser, "Antitrust aspects of the joint venture in the European economic community" (1963).
29	200	217	383	456 562	H.B. Stover, Jr., "Longshoremen-shipowner-stevedore: the circle of liability" (1963).
30	101	218	384	457 563	J.K. Weeks, "Comparative law of privacy" (1963).
31	102	219	385	458 564	H. Griese, "Marine insurance contracts in the conflict of laws: a comparative study of the case law" (1959).
32	103	220	386	459 565	H.W. Felton, "Federal tax liens, their priority and enforcement" (1960).
33	104	221	387	460 566	G.M. Fenner and J.L. Koley, "Rights of the press and the closed court criminal proceeding" (1978).

Economics (E)

34	105	222	388	461	567	R.E. Keeton, "Conditional fault in the law of torts" (1959).
35	106	223	389	462	568	R.C. Bernhard, "English law and American law on monopolies and restraints of trade" (1960).
36	107	224	390	463	569	F.M. Covey, Jr., "French law of eminent domain" (1959).
37	108	225	391	464	570	I.R. Kaufman, "Masters in the federal courts: rule 53" (1958).
38	109	226	392	465	571	C.W. Ehrhardt, "Using convictions to impeach under the Florida Evidence Code" (1982).
39	110	227	393	466	572	T. Scribner, "Professional goodwill in dissolution proceedings: the personification of property" (1982).
40	111	228	394	467	573	C. Hancock, "State court activism and searches incident to arrest" (1982).
41	112	229	395	468	574	B. Tarlow, "RICO revisited" (1983).
42	113	230	396	469	575	R.W. Peterson "Few things you should know about paternity test (but were afraid to ask)" (1982).
43	114	231	397	470	576	G.W. Goble, "Alternative to the strike" (1955).
44	115	232	398	471	577	J.W. Castles, III, "Personal contract doctrine: an anomaly in American maritime law" (1953).
45	116	233	399	472	578	C.L. Newman, "Should trial by jury be modernized?" (1953).
46	117	234	400	473	579	R.M. Perkins, "Self-defense re-examined" (1954).
47	118	235	301	474	580	R. Pound, "Chinese Civil Code in action" (1955).
48	119	236	302	475	581	G. Gilmore, "Commercial doctrine of good faith purchase" (1954).
49	120	237	303	476	582	T.W. Samuels, "Drafting a partnership agreement" (1950).
50	121	238	304	477	583	R.P. Hoff, Implications for farm ownership of the tax preferred status of pension trust investment in real estate" (1981).
51	122	239	305	478	584	K.S. Abraham, "Judge-made law and judge-made insurance: honoring the reasonable expectations of the insured" (1981).
52	123	240	306	479	585	R.F. Pannier, "Nature of the judicial process and judicial discretion" (1981).
53	124	241	307	480	586	D.H. Haynes, "Language and logic of law: a case study" (1981).
54	125	242	308	481	587	J.N. Hazard, "Soviet socialism and embezzlement" (1951).
55	126	243	309	482	588	H.A. Kooman, "Judicial supervision of trusts" (1948).
56	127	244	310	483	589	A.T. Spence, "Parental liability" (1948).
57	128	245	311	484	590	M.H. Merrill, "Basic doctrine of Oklahoma public law" (1948).
58	129	246	312	485	591	B. Reich, "Entertainment industry and the Federal Antitrust Laws" (1946).
59	130	247	313	486	592	J.T. Ganoe, "The Yamashita case and the Constitution" (1946).
60	131	248	314	487	593	L. Garment, "Real evidence: use and abuse" (1948).
61	132	249	315	488	594	C.B. Nutting, "Policy making by the Supreme Court" (1947).
62	133	250	316	489	595	F.F. Stone, "Modern problems in ancient dress" (1980).
63	134	251	317	490	596	W.B. Stoebuck, "Police power, takings, and due process" (1980).
64	135	252	318	491	597	J. Dolan, "Good faith purchase study: true owners and the warehouse lien" (1981).
65	136	253	319	492	598	R.M. Twiss, "Impact of RICO upon labor unions" (1980).
66	137	254	320	493	599	R.N. Jackson, "Right to bail and suspensive appeal in the Louisiana juvenile courts" (1946).
67	138	255	321	494	600	D. Williams, "Care and custody of children in Mississippi" (1944).

68	139	256	322	495	501	D. Dowling, "Parents' usufruct of child's estate during marriage" (1945).
69	140	257	323	496	502	D.J. Snyder, Jr., "Computing municipal indebtedness under Pennsylvania constitutional limitations" (1941).
70	141	258	324	497	503	E.B. Cass, "The blackout and its relation to civil liabilities" (1942).
71	142	259	325	498	504	J.H. Ottman, "Partition in Missouri" (1941).
72	143	260	326	499	505	S.O. Bates, "Holographic Wills" (1942).
73	144	261	327	500	506	P. Shirley, "Special issue submission in workmen's compensation cases" (1940).
74	145	262	328	401	507	R. Magill, "Relief from excess profits tax" (1941).
75	146	263	329	402	508	P. Schiff, "Married women's suretyship contracts in the United States" (1939).
76	147	264	330	403	509	M.S. Isseks, "The executive and his use of the militia" (1937).
77	148	265	331	404	510	F.B. McCall, "Destructibility of contingent remainders in North Carolina" (1938).
78	149	266	332	405	511	M.M. Harrison, "Remission in the Civil Law" (1940).
79	150	267	333	406	512	W.C. Johnstone, "New commercial treaty with Siam" (1938).
80	151	268	334	407	513	S.P. Sandrock, "Tort liability of a non-manufacturing franchisor for acts of its franchisee" (1979).
81	152	269	335	408	514	M. Siegel, "Implication doctrine and the foreign corrupt practices act" (1979).
82	153	270	336	409	515	R.H. Coase, "Payola in radio and television broadcasting" (1979).
83	154	271	337	410	516	H.W. Brill, "Protection for the hard of hearing: state and federal regulation of hearing aid dealers" (1977).
84	155	272	338	411	517	J.M. Hughes, "'Notice of claim' as a condition precedent to suit: is the proprietary-governmental distinction important?" (1979).
85	156	273	339	412	518	L.S. May, "Scientific methods of criminal investigation" (1935).
86	157	274	340	413	519	R.H. Schnell, "Co-tenancy of personal property in New York" (1936).
87	158	275	341	414	520	B. Eskin, "Legality of 'peaceful coercion' in labor disputes" (1937).
88	159	276	342	415	521	P. Bordwell, "Alienability and perpetuities" (1937).
89	160	277	343	416	522	R.F. Fuchs, "The French law of collective labor agreements" (1932).
90	161	278	344	417	523	M. Radin, "Fraudulent conveyances at Roman law" (1931).
91	162	279	345	418	524	M.S. Culp, "Process in actions against non-resident motorists" (1934).
92	163	280	346	419	525	G.R. Farnum, "Admiralty jurisdiction and amphibious torts" (1933).
93	164	281	347	420	526	B.R. Desenberg, "Torrens system of title registration" (1932).
94	165	282	348	421	527	G. May, "Experiments in legal control of sex expression" (1929).
95	166	283	349	422	528	J.C. Biggs, "Religious belief as qualification of a witness" (1929).
96	167	284	350	423	529	J.J. Kenney, "Illegitimacy under the Children's Code" (1929).
97	168	285	351	424	530	R.C. Clark, "Duties of the corporate debtor to its creditors" (1977).
98	169	286	352	425	531	M.E. Price, "First amendment and television broadcasting by satellite" (1976).
99	170	287	353	426	532	A.V. Lowe, "Right of entry into maritime ports in international law" (1977).
100	171	288	354	427	533	R.N. Clinton, "Right to present a defense: an emergent constitutional guarantee in criminal trials" (1976).

LIBRARY EXERCISE 32.   INDEX TO LEGAL PERIODICALS: CASE NOTES AND COMMENTS.
Find the case comment[s] or note[s] on the following case using the Index to
Legal Periodicals. Cite the legal periodicals in which they can be found. No
special form is required.

	Problem #					Year of Comment	Case
1	172	289	355	428	534	1983	Grant v. Arizona Pub. Serv. Co. [652 P.2d 507]
2	173	290	356	429	535	1984	Riley v. Northern Commercial Co. [648 P.2d 961]
3	174	291	357	430	536	1984	Sax v. Votteler [648 S.W.2d 661]
4	175	292	358	431	537	1983	State v. Berge [634 P.2d 947]
5	176	293	359	432	538	1983	Sutter v. Groen [687 F.2d 197]
6	177	294	360	433	539	1973	Baker v. Hamilton [345 F. Supp. 345]
7	178	295	361	434	540	1973	In re Lynch [503 P.2d 921]
8	179	296	362	435	541	1973	McKinney v. State [260 So. 2d 444]
9	180	297	363	436	542	1972	McMillen v. Klingensmith [467 S.W.2d 193]
10	181	298	364	437	543	1970	Appeal of McNeil [257 A.2d 835]
11	182	299	365	438	544	1971	Maddox v. Fortson [172 S.E.2d 595]
12	183	300	366	439	545	1973	Manson v. Edwards [345 F. Supp. 719]
13	184	201	367	440	546	67-68	Pierson v. Ray [87 S. Ct. 1213]
14	185	202	368	441	547	1968	Pinto v. Pierce [88 S. Ct. 192]
15	186	203	369	442	548	1969	Pittman v. State [434 S.W.2d 352]
16	187	204	370	443	549	1969	Succession of Plunkett [213 So. 2d 793]
17	188	205	371	444	550	1967	Powers v. Temple [156 S.E.2d 759]
18	189	206	372	445	551	1967	Prentzler v. Schneider [411 S.W.2d 135]
19	190	207	373	446	552	1965	Fish v. State [159 So. 2d 866]
20	191	208	374	447	553	1965	Flesher v. United States [238 F. Supp. 119]
21	192	209	375	448	554	1964	Fonte v. State [373 S.W.2d 445]
22	193	210	376	449	555	1964	Foy v. Dayko [196 A.2d 535]
23	194	211	377	450	556	1965	Franklin v. Parker [223 F. Supp. 724]
24	195	212	378	451	557	1966	Frasier v. Pierce [398 S.W.2d 955]
25	196	213	379	452	558	1964	Swift v. Wimberly [370 S.W.2d 500]
26	197	214	380	453	559	1964	System Meat Co. v. Stewart [122 N.W.2d 1]
27	198	215	381	454	560	1962	Texaco v. Goldstein [229 N.Y.S.2d 51]
28	199	216	382	455	561	1962	In re Thacher [10 N.Y.2d 439]
29	200	217	383	456	562	1963	Thome v. Thome [127 S.E.2d 916]
30	101	218	384	457	563	1962	Thompson v. Reedman [199 F. Supp. 120]
31	102	219	385	458	564	1955	People v. Thompson [271 P.2d 507]
32	103	220	386	459	565	1957	People v. Horowitz [131 N.E.2d 715]
33	104	221	387	460	566	1955	People v. Wilson [135 N.Y.S.2d 893]
34	105	222	388	461	567	1956	Stone v. Dunn Bros. [80 So. 2d 802]
35	106	223	389	462	568	1956	Stuart v. Pilgrim [74 N.W.2d 212]
36	107	224	390	463	569	1957	Swigert v. Welk [133 A.2d 428]
37	108	225	391	464	570	1956	Swift v. Beaty [282 S.W.2d 655]
38	109	226	392	465	571	1982	Griffin v. Ocean Contractors, Inc. [102 S. Ct. 3245]
39	110	227	393	466	572	1982	Hartman v. Shambaugh [630 P.2d 758]
40	111	228	394	467	573	1981	Hlodan v. Ohio Barge Line [611 F.2d 71]
41	112	229	395	468	574	1982	McMinn v. Oyster Bay [445 N.Y.S.2d 859]
42	113	230	396	469	575	1982	Logan v. Zimmerman Brush Co. [102 S. Ct. 1148]
43	114	231	397	470	576	1952	Jawish v. Morlet [86 A.2d 96]
44	115	232	398	471	577	1952	Jersey Ins. Co. v. Roddam [56 So. 2d 631]
45	116	233	399	472	578	1954	Johnson v. Baltimore & O.R.R. [208 F.2d 633]
46	117	234	400	473	579	54-55	Johnson v. Chicago, B. & Q.R.R. [66 N.W.2d 763]
47	118	235	401	474	580	1955	Johnson v. Safreed [273 S.W.2d 545]
48	119	236	302	475	581	1952	Joliet Contractors Ass'n v. NLRB [193 F.2d 833]
49	120	237	303	476	582	1950	Standfur v. Standfur [223 S.W.2d 111]
50	121	238	304	477	583	1982	Kaiser Steel Corp. v. Mullins [102 S. Ct. 851]

Problem #		Year of Comment	Case
51 122 239 305 478 584		1981	Jain v. INS [612 F.2d 683]
52 123 240 306 479 585		1981	McClain v. Meier [637 F.2d 1159]
53 124 241 307 480 586		1951	State v. Crittenden [49 So. 2d 418]
54 125 242 308 481 587		1952	State v. Fowler [83 A.2d 67]
55 126 243 309 482 588		1946	NLRB v. Inter-City Advertising Co. [154 F.2d 244]
56 127 244 310 483 589		1947	NLRB v. Packard Motor Car [157 F.2d 80]
57 128 245 311 484 590		1946	National Surety Corp. v. City Bank and Trust Co. [20 N.W.2d 559]
58 129 246 312 485 591		1946	Navarro v. Fiorita [62 N.Y.S.2d 730]
59 130 247 313 486 592		1948	Neal v. State [192 P.2d 294]
60 131 248 314 487 593		1947	Neff v. Firth [47 A.2d 193]
61 132 249 315 488 594		1947	Neitsch v. Tyrrell [171 P.2d 241]
62 133 250 316 489 595		1980	MacDonald v. MacDonald [412 A.2d71]
63 134 251 317 490 596		1980	Livingston v. Ewing [601 F.2d 1110]
64 135 252 318 491 597		1980-81	Lepis v. Lepis [416 A.2d 45]
65 136 253 319 492 598		1980	Lau v. Nelson [601 P.2d 527]
66 137 254 320 493 599		1945	In re Cope's Estate [41 A.2d 617]
67 138 255 321 494 600		1946	Corder v. Corder [189 S.W.2d 100]
68 139 256 322 495 501		1945	Corlew v. State [180 S.W.2d 900]
69 140 257 323 496 502		1942	Hacker v. Nitschke [39 N.E.2d 644]
70 141 258 324 497 503		1941	Hagerty v. Clement [196 So. 330]
71 142 259 325 498 504		1942	Hale v. Campbell [40 F. Supp. 584]
72 143 260 326 499 505		1941	Hancock v. Moore [146 S.W.2d 369]
73 144 261 327 500 506		1942	Haney v. Cheatham [111 P.2d 1003]
74 145 262 328 401 507		1940	Hanley v. Central Sav. Bank [21 N.E.2d 213
75 146 263 329 402 508		1937	Harper v. City of Wichita Falls [105 S.W.2d 743]
76 147 264 330 403 509		1938	Appeal of Harr [194 A. 395]
77 148 265 331 404 510		1937	Harris v. Harris [186 S.E. 29]
78 149 266 332 405 511		1938	Estate of Harrison [70 P.2d 522]
79 150 267 333 406 512		1939	Hart v. McClusky [118 S.W.2d 1077]
80 151 268 334 407 513		78-79	Sherlock v. Stillwater Clinic [260 N.W.2d 169]
81 152 269 335 408 514		1979	State v. Sobel [363 So. 2d 324]
82 153 270 336 409 515		1978	Sunday v. Statton Corp. [390 A.2d 398]
83 154 271 337 410 516		1979	Suntide Inn Operating Corp. v. State ex rel. Oklahoma State Highway Commission [571 P.2d 1207]
84 155 272 338 411 517		79-80	Zweig v. Hearst Corp. [594 F.2d 1261]
85 156 273 339 412 518		1936	Kuhn v. Carlin Const. Co. [278 N.Y.S. 635]
86 157 274 340 413 519		1937	In re Kuntz' Will [290 N.Y.S. 867]
87 158 275 341 414 520		1935	Laird v. Gulf Production Co. [64 S.W.2d 1080]
88 159 276 342 415 521		1936	In re Lalla's Estate [1 N.E.2d 50]
89 160 277 343 416 522		1931	Christian v. Canfield [155 A. 788]
90 161 278 344 417 523		1931	Cisler v. Ray [2 P.2d 987]
91 162 279 345 418 524		1933	City Ice & Fuel Co. v. McKee [57 S.W.2d 443]
92 163 280 346 419 525		1932	City of Houston v. Scanlan [37 S.W.2d 718]
93 164 281 347 420 526		1931	City of El Paso v. Jackson [40 S.W.2d 845]
94 165 282 348 421 527		1930	McHugh v. Mason [283 P. 184]
95 166 283 349 422 528		29-30	McKee v. Suez [167 N.E. 720]
96 167 284 350 423 529		1930	Estate of McLaughlin [275 P. 874]
97 168 285 351 424 530		1976	Long v. City of Weirton [214 S.E.2d 832]
98 169 286 352 425 531		1978	Shevin v. Sunbeam Television Corp. [351 So. 2d 723]
99 170 287 353 426 532		1976	Muncie Aviation Corp. v. Party Doll Fleet [519 F.2d 1178]
100 171 288 354 427 533		76-77	Muzquiz v. San Antonio [528 F.2d 499]

LIBRARY EXERCISE 33. TEXTS AND TREATISES. (a) Briefly answer the question based upon the treatise or text given for your problem number, and (b) cite the treatise or text on which your answer is based. Note that when a text or treatise is organized by sections running consecutively throughout the entire work, the relevant section should be cited; when a section is cited, the relevant page numbers should be added (e.g., § 52, at 102-03) to identify the specific portion of the section on which your answer is based (when necessary). Rule 15, 3.4. Follow the rules for multiple page numbers containing repetitious digits noted in the instructions to Library Exercise 5.

For problem numbers 1-25, 128-152, 250-274, 301-325, 426-450, 551-575, use the third edition (1982) of Perkins and Boyce's Criminal Law treatise.

1 128 250 301 426 551   How was the crime of mayhem defined under English common law? Was it a felony or misdemeanor?
2 129 251 302 427 552   Was dueling a crime at common law?
3 130 252 303 428 553   What elements make up the crime of common-law burglary?
4 131 253 304 429 554   Can one be lawfully convicted for common-law arson if one intentionally burns down his own dwelling?
5 132 254 305 430 555   What is the common-law crime of "houseburning"?
6 133 255 306 431 556   What are the common-law elements of the crime of larceny?
7 134 256 307 432 557   What is an unlawful assembly?
8 135 257 308 433 558   What does "reading the riot act" mean?
9 136 258 309 434 559   Under the treason provision in the United States Constitution, can a person be convicted of that crime if there is one witness to an overt act of treason even though there is no confession of guilt in open court?
10 137 259 310 435 560   What is the difference between the common-law crimes of perjury and false swearing?
11 138 260 311 436 561   What is the difference between the common-law crimes of escape and breach of prison?
12 139 261 312 437 562   What is misprision of felony?
13 140 262 313 438 563   Under English common law, was compounding a misdemeanor punishable as a crime?
14 141 263 314 439 564   What did the common misdemeanor of maintenance involve?
15 142 264 315 440 565   What are the requisites for a person's conviction as an accessory after the fact?
16 143 265 316 441 566   Was seduction a crime under the common law of England?
17 144 266 317 442 567   To what crime does the phrase "infamous crime against nature" usually refer?
18 145 267 318 443 568   At common law was it unlawful to throw a dead body into a river?
19 146 268 319 444 569   Was an "affray" indictable at common law?
20 147 269 320 445 570   Can a "riot" consist of two persons acting together in the commission of a crime by open force?
21 148 270 321 446 571   What acts constitute the common law crime of extortion?
22 149 271 322 447 572   What elements are usually required for conviction of the offense of receiving stolen property under most statutes in the United States?
23 150 272 323 448 573   Was bigamy a crime under the common law of England?
24 151 273 324 449 574   Under many modern statutes can a man be prosecuted for the crime of "seduction" even though the parties subsequently marry?
25 152 274 325 450 575   What does the term "corpus delicti" mean?

For Problems 26-50, 153-177, 275-299, 326-350, 451-475, 576-600, use the third edition (1985) of James and Hazard's Civil Procedure.

26 153 275 326 451 576   Did trial by jury largely begin as a trial by witnesses who judged facts within their knowledge?
27 154 276 327 452 577   What was the "local-action rule" of jurisdiction?
28 155 277 328 453 578   How is the "law of the case" different from res judicata?

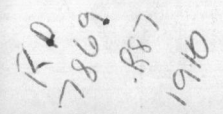

29 156 278 329 454 579   Is the use of remittitur to control verdicts likely to be overturned on constitutional grounds at this late date?
30 157 279 330 455 580   Does the weight of modern judicial authority hold that an amendment relates back to the time of the original pleading whenever the claim or defense asserted in the amendment arose out of the transaction or occurrence set forth or attempted to be set forth in the original pleading?
31 158 280 331 456 581   With what general problem does the case of <u>Erie v. Tompkins</u> deal?
32 159 281 332 457 582   May a void judgment be attacked by a Rule 60(b) motion even if the motion is made more than one year after entry of the judgment?
33 160 282 333 458 583   Under the common law and the codes, was a "variance" ground for objection to the admissibility of evidence outside the limits set by the pleadings?
34 161 283 334 459 584   What is the doctrine of forum non conveniens?
35 162 284 335 460 585   What was the size of a jury at common law?
36 163 285 336 461 586   Which Federal Rule of Civil Procedure governs intervention?
37 164 286 337 462 587   At common law, the special verdict device emerged as a means by which the jury might protect itself from what danger?
38 165 287 338 463 588   Do the Federal Rules of Civil Procedure provide a definition of "privileged" matter for discovery purposes?
39 166 288 339 464 589   Is discovery permitted of insurance coverage under the Federal Rules of Civil Procedure?
40 167 289 340 465 590   Which Federal Rule of Civil Procedure governs interpleader?
41 168 290 341 466 591   When is a reply required under the Federal Rules of Civil Procedure?
42 169 291 342 467 592   For what was the common-law "demurrer to the evidence" used?
43 170 292 343 468 593   Under a 1934 Supreme Court decision, is the conditioning a new trial on the defendant's consent to an additur in federal court constitutional?
44 171 293 344 469 594   May the driver of a vehicle in which the plaintiff was riding when the collision occurred that caused the plaintiff's injury be compelled to submit to a physical examination under Rule 35?
45 172 294 345 470 595   Is impleader a proper device for a defendant to bring in someone he contends is really the one liable to the plaintiff?
46 173 295 346 471 596   Is an order allowing intervention immediately appealable?
47 174 296 347 472 597   Under the common law, did married women have the capacity to sue alone as a party?
48 175 297 348 473 598   Are federal venue rules cast in terms of the citizenship of the parties?
49 176 298 349 474 599   If venue in a federal court is improper and there is a district of proper venue, must the court in which the action was brought dismiss the action?
50 177 299 350 475 600   Can parties to a lawsuit be compelled through discovery to identify each expert witness they expect to call at trial?

For problem numbers 51-75, 101-102, 178-200, 201-224, 300, 351-375, 476-500, 501-525, use the <u>fifth</u> edition (1984) of <u>Prosser and Keeton on the Law of Torts</u>.
For purposes of this exercise, cite this to (1) W. Keeton, D. Dobbs, R. Keeton & D. Owen as the authors, (2) use "Prosser and Keeton on the Law of Torts" as the title, and (3) indicate the edition in the parenthetical containing the date.

51 178 300 351 476 501   Under the Federal Tort Claims Act, is the local law of the place where the tort occurred applied?
52 179 201 352 477 502   Can the federal government be held liable for a claim arising out of abuse of process under the Federal Tort Act?
53 180 202 353 478 503   In negligence cases, have most cases held insane persons liable for failure to conform to the standard of conduct required of a sane man?

54 181 203 354 479 504   Under the common law of England, if the victim of a tort died before he recovered in tort, did the victim's right of action "survive" or did it "die"?
55 182 204 355 480 505   Are torts committed by the federal government immune under the Federal Tort Claims Act when they occur as a result of combatant activities of its military forces in time of war?
56 183 205 356 481 506   Have American courts consistently held (in absence of legislation) that there is no liability for "escape" of fire where the defendant was not negligent?
57 184 206 357 482 507   If a tiger, which X keeps as a house pet, escapes and bites Y, will X be strictly liable for the damage done?
58 185 207 358 483 508   What interest is protected by permitting recovery for batteries?
59 186 208 359 484 509   When did the action of trespass first emerge?
60 187 209 360 485 510   What is the basic difference or distinction between trespass and trespass on the case?
61 188 210 361 486 511   From what action did the tort of false imprisonment descend?
62 189 211 362 487 512   Could the common-law action of trespass be maintained without proof of any actual damage?
63 190 212 363 488 513   When may a private citizen arrest without a warrant?
64 191 213 364 489 514   When was negligence recognized as a separate tort?
65 192 214 365 490 515   Must there be actual loss or damage before a cause of action based upon negligence is stated?
66 193 215 366 491 516   Does a jury determine the existence of the "duty" element of a negligence cause of action?
67 194 216 367 492 517   What does the phrase "res ipsa loquitur" mean and when did it first appear in judicial arguments?
68 195 217 368 493 518   What is the "sine qua non" rule?
69 196 218 369 494 519   Who has the burden, according to the great majority of courts, to plead and prove contributory negligence?
70 197 219 370 495 520   Can unmarried consorts, such as live-in lovers, who are financially dependent on the deceased for support recover for wrongful death under modern wrongful death statutes?
71 198 220 371 496 521   What is the essence of a private nuisance claim? In other words, with what does a private nuisance interfere?
72 199 221 372 497 522   Are loud noises sufficient to constitute an actionable private nuisance if they adversely affect a hypersensitive individual?
73 200 222 373 498 523   What is the traditional definitional difference between "libel" and "slander"?
74 101 223 374 499 524   Who first recognized a separate tort based upon the right to privacy?
75 102 224 375 500 525   As originally developed, what are the elements of a cause of action for malicious prosecution?

For problem numbers 76-87, 103-114, 225-236, 376-387, 401-412, and 526-537, use the third edition (1984) of McCormick on Evidence. For purposes of this exercise, cite this work to (1) Charles McCormick as the author, (2) use "McCormick on Evidence" at the title, and (3) indicate parenthetically that the third edition was edited by Edward Cleary. See USOC Rule 15.1 and 15.2.

76 103 225 376 401 526   Do most courts reject proof of an actor's character for care given through expert testimony?
77 104 226 377 402 527   When the existence and scope of a partnership have been proved, is a statement of a partner made in the conduct of the business of the firm allowed as evidence of an admission of the partnership?
78 105 227 378 403 528   Traditionally, were contemporary entries in a family Bible admissible (as an exception to the hearsay rule) to prove family history or pedigree even though the author may not be identifiable?
79 106 228 379 404 529   Will courts take judicial notice of historical facts, such as when a war ended?
80 107 229 380 405 530   Under the common-law exception to the hearsay rule, what four elements had to be shown to use regularly kept business records to prove the facts recited in them?
81 108 230 381 406 531   Is lack of religious belief generally available as a ground to impeach the credibility of a witness?

82 109 231 382 407 532   Will a party's refusal to furnish handing examplars serve as a basis for drawing an adverse inference based on an admission by conduct?
83 110 232 383 408 533   When did the term res gestae come into common usage in discussing the admissibility of spontaneous statements accompanying material acts or situations?
84 111 233 384 409 534   Is it an accurate statement concerning the burden of proof to say that even though a party is required to plead a fact, that party is not required to prove that fact if his averment is negative rather than affirmative in form?
85 112 234 385 410 535   Will courts take judicial notice of the scientific principles on which radar is based even though those principles are not commonly known among the public?
86 113 235 386 411 536   Was a clergyman-penitent privilege recognized at common law?
87 114 236 387 412 537   Is evidence of payment or offers to pay medical expense of an injured person ordinarily admissible to prove liability for the injury?

For problem numbers 88-100, 115-127, 237-249, 388-400, 413-425, and 538-550, use Cunningham, Stoebuck, and Whitman's The Law of Property (1984).

88 115 237 388 413 538   Does the English rule give a possessor of land the absolute right to withdraw underground percolating water as he wishes for whatever purposes he wishes as long as he does not maliciously injure others?
89 116 238 389 414 539   With regard to surface water, what is the essential idea of the "common enemy doctrine?
90 117 239 390 415 540   For purposes of the law of trespass, does an ownership of land carry rights extending downward indefinitely?
91 118 240 391 416 541   Is title insurance a contract of indemnity?
92 119 241 392 417 542   Is the following statute a "race" type, a "notice" type, or a "notice-race" type of recording act: "Every conveyance not recorded is void as against any subsequent purchaser or mortgagee in good faith and for valuable consideration . . . whose conveyance is first duly recorded"?
93 120 242 393 418 543   What is the general distinction between a nuisance and a trespass?
94 121 243 394 419 544   Dictum in what American judicial decision is the source of the "correlative rights" doctrine for the use of percolating underground water?
95 122 244 395 420 545   Where does a proper "metes and bounds" description of land end up?
96 123 245 396 421 546   How long does title insurance last?
97 124 246 397 422 547   In order to run to the covenantee's grantee, must the burden of a real covenant "touch and concerns" some estate in land?
98 125 247 398 423 548   Do title insurance policies ordinarily exclude laws and governmental ordinances unless they appear on the public records?
99 126 248 399 424 549   What is the "American" doctrine of rights to percolating underground water sometimes called?
100 127 249 400 425 550   Have recent cases recognized a duty of a title insurer to make a title search and report the defects found to the insured?

LIBRARY EXERCISE 34. RESTATEMENTS OF THE LAW. Follow the directions given with your problem number below.

For problems 1-17, 101-117, 201-217, 301-317, 401-417, 501-517, use the Restatement (Second) of Trusts (1959). Using the index in Volume 2, find the section[s] (in Vol. 1 or 2) that answer[s] or govern[s] the question or subject listed with your problem number. (a) Cite the section[s] and (b) using the Appendix (Vol. 3), list the "Cross References" to "Digest System Key Numbers" (West) for the section[s].

    1 101 201 301 401 501   Is an equitable charge a trust?
    2 102 202 302 402 502   Can an interest that has ceased to exist be held in trust?
    3 103 203 303 403 503   Does an infant have the legal capacity to administer a trust?
    4 104 204 304 404 504   Duty of trustee to keep the trust property separate.
    5 105 205 305 405 505   Can a trust be created without notice to or acceptance by the beneficiary?
    6 106 206 306 406 506   Is a receiver appointed by a court a trustee?
    7 107 207 307 407 507   Duty of a trustee to keep and render clear and accurate accounts.
    8 108 208 308 408 508   Liability of a successor trustee for a breach of trust committed by a predecessor trustee.
    9 109 209 309 409 509   Amount which a trustee can properly lend on a mortgage upon real property.
    10 110 210 310 410 510   Can a trust be a "charitable trust" when the trust property is devoted to a private use?
    11 111 211 311 411 511   Are the duties of a trustee of a charitable trust similar to the duties of a trustee of a private trust?
    12 112 212 312 412 512   Does a resulting trust terminate if the legal title to the trust property and the entire beneficial interest become united in one person?
    13 113 213 313 413 513   Is consideration necessary for the creation of a charitable trust?
    14 114 214 314 414 514   If a trustee of a resulting trust repudiates the trust to the knowledge of the beneficiary, can the beneficiary then be barred by laches from enforcing the trust?
    15 115 215 315 415 515   Does the Attorney General have the power to enforce a charitable trust?
    16 116 216 316 416 516   Is a charitable trust invalid if it is created for an "illegal purpose," such as inducing a crime?
    17 117 217 317 417 517   Doctrine of cy pres applies to charitable trusts when there has been a failure of the purpose of the trust.

For problems 18-26, 118-126, 218-226, 318-326, 418-426, 518-526, use the Restatement (Second) of Torts (1965). Locate Volume 1, (covering §§ 1 to 280). Using the index in the back of Volume 1, find the section[s] that answer[s] or govern[s] the question or subject listed with your problem number. (a) Cite the section[s], and (b) using the Appendix volume covering that section, list the "Cross References" to "Digest System Key Numbers" (West) for the section[s].

    18 118 218 318 418 518   Special liability of a common carrier or other public utility for gross insults made by its servants.
    19 119 219 319 419 519   Ways of committing a trespass to chattel.
    20 120 220 320 420 520   Privilege to enter land in possession of another person based upon private necessity.
    21 121 221 321 421 521   Self-defense by use of reasonable force to defend oneself against negligent conduct.
    22 122 222 322 422 522   Privilege to enter land in another person's possession to abate a private nuisance.
    23 123 223 323 423 523   What constitutes confinement for purposes of determining whether the tort of false imprisonment has occurred.
    24 124 224 324 424 524   Ways of committing conversion.
    25 124 225 325 425 535   Trespass to land may occur by the failure to remove things tortiously placed on the land.

26 126 226 326 426 526   Privilege of distraint of chattels for rent.

For problems 27-37, 127-137, 227-237, 327-337, 427-437, 527-537, use the Restatement (Second) of Torts (1965). Locate Volume 2 (covering §§ 281 to 503). Using the index in the back of Volume 2, find the section[s] that answer[s] or govern[s] the question or subject listed with your problem number. (a) Cite the section[s], and (b) using the Appendix volume covering that section, list the "Cross References" to "Digest System Key Numbers" (West) for the section[s].

27 127 227 327 427 527   Definition of a trespasser.
28 128 228 328 428 528   Obstruction of a highway which thereby prevents a third person from rendering aid to prevent physical harm.
29 129 229 329 429 529   Definition of a licensee.
30 130 230 330 430 530   Master's duty to protect an endangered or hurt employee.
31 131 231 331 431 531   Definition of an invitee.
32 132 232 332 432 532   Liability for intentionally preventing aid necessary to prevent physical harm to third persons.
33 133 233 333 433 533   Custodian's duty of control of dangerous persons from harming others.
34 134 234 334 434 534   Intentional infliction of emotional distress causing bodily harm.
35 135 235 335 435 535   Possessor of land defined.
36 136 236 336 436 536   Liability of possessor of land for dangerous natural conditions in private rights of way.
37 137 237 337 437 537   Unintentional infliction of emotional distress causing bodily harm.

For problems 38-50, 138-150, 238-250, 338-350, 438-450, 538-550, use the Restatement (Second) of Agency (1958). Using the index in Volume 2, find the section[s] (in Vol. 1 or 2) that answer[s] or govern[s] the question or subject listed with your problem number. (a) Cite the section[s], and (b) list the "Cross References" to "Digest System Key Numbers" (West) for the section[s].

38 138 238 338 438 538   Statement of the fellow servant rule.
39 139 239 339 439 539   Admissibility in evidence of statements of agents as to their authority.
40 140 240 340 440 540   Definition of a "servant."
41 141 241 341 441 541   Definition of "ratification."
42 142 242 342 442 542   Termination of agency powers by disloyal conduct of the agent.
43 143 243 343 443 543   Definition of a "fellow servant."
44 144 244 344 444 544   Definition of "authority."
45 145 245 345 445 545   Liability of principal (master) for a servant's leaving the principal's instrumentality in a dangerous situation while pursuing a private purpose.
46 146 246 346 446 546   Definition of "affirmance."
47 147 247 347 447 547   Release as a defense of an agent against a principal.
48 148 248 348 448 548   Definition of "apparent authority."
49 149 249 349 449 549   Laches as a defense available to the agent against his principle.
50 150 250 350 450 550   Assault on a servant by other servants as affected by the fellow servant rule.

For problems 51-68, 151-168, 251-268, 351-368, 451-468, 551-568, use the Restatement (Second) of Conflict of Laws (1971). Using the index in Volume 2, find the section[s] (in Vol. 1 or 2) that answer[s] or govern[s] the question or subject listed with your problem number. (a) Cite the section[s], and (b) using the Appendix (Volume 3), list the "Cross References" to "Digest System Key Numbers" (West for the section[s] of the Restatement (Second).

51 151 251 351 451 551   Contribution and indemnity among tortfeasors.
52 152 252 352 452 552   Foreign nation decrees enjoining an act; recognition in the United States.

53 153 253 353 453 553	Contractual liability of partners.
54 154 254 354 454 554	Requisites of a valid judgment.
55 155 255 355 455 555	Statute of Frauds.
56 156 256 356 456 556	Joint torts.
57 157 257 357 457 557	Termination of corporate existence.
58 158 258 358 348 558	Law controlling escheat of land.
59 159 259 359 459 559	Construction of a will devising land.
60 160 260 360 460 560	Trespass to foreign land.
61 161 261 361 461 561	Equitable interests in land.
62 162 262 362 462 562	Recognition and enforcement of erroneous judgments in other states.
63 163 263 363 463 563	Subject matter of conflict of laws.
64 164 264 364 464 546	Domicil of a minor.
65 165 265 365 465 565	Transfer of chattel by an executor or administrator.
66 166 266 366 466 566	Nationality and citizenship.
67 167 267 367 467 567	Meaning of the term "shareholder."
68 168 268 368 468 568	Liability of majority shareholder.

For problems 69-80, 169-180, 269-280, 369-380, 469-480, 569-580, use the Restatement (Second) of Property (1977). Using the index in Volume 2, find the section[s] (in Vol. 1 or 2) that answer[s] or govern[s] the question or subject listed with your problem number. (a) Cite the section[s], and (b) using the "Table of Cross References" to "Digest System Key Numbers" (West) in the back of Volume 2, list the references. Cite only the section. Do not cite comments to a section.

69 169 269 369 469 569	Tenant's obligation to pay rent.
70 170 270 370 470 570	Assumption of a lease by a trustee in bankruptcy.
71 171 271 371 471 571	Bankruptcy proceedings as a default under a lease.
72 172 272 372 472 572	Definition of retaliatory action by landlord.
73 173 273 373 473 573	Validity of an agreement to make a lease.
74 174 274 374 474 574	Rejection of lease by landlord's trustee in bankruptcy.
75 175 275 375 475 575	Restraints on alienation generally.
76 176 276 376 476 576	Time factor for the restoration of property.
77 177 277 377 477 577	Rejection of a lease by the tenant's trustee in bankruptcy.
78 178 278 378 478 578	What constitutes a paramount title.
79 179 279 379 479 579	Tenant's share of a condemnation award.
80 180 280 380 480 580	Capacity and authority to enter into a landlord-tenant tenant relationship.

For problems 81-90, 181-190, 281-290, 381-390, 481-490, 581-590, use the Restatement (Second) of Contracts (1979). Using the index in Volume 3, find the section[s] (in Vols. 1-3) that answer[s] or govern[s] the question or subject listed with your problem number. (a) Cite the section[s], and (b) using the Appendix to the 2nd Restatement (Vol. 6), list the "Cross References" to "Digest System Key Numbers" (West) for the section[s]. Do not cite comments or illustrations for your answer.

81 181 281 381 481 581	Effect of the death of the offeree.
82 182 282 382 482 582	Assignment of option contracts.
83 183 283 383 483 583	Enforceability of promises that tortiously interfere with the performance of a contract.
84 184 284 384 484 584	What constitutes an interest in land for purposes of the Statute of Frauds.
85 185 285 385 485 585	Rules governing bidding and acceptance of bids at auctions.
86 186 286 386 486 586	Whether a liquidated damage provision in a contract prevents issuance of an injunction or an order requiring specific performance of a contract.
87 187 287 387 487 587	Ancillary restraints on competition.
88 188 288 388 488 588	Punitive damages for breach of contract.
89 189 289 389 489 589	Revocation of divisible offers.
90 190 290 390 490 590	Acceptance of an offer by silence.

For problems 91-100, 191-200, 291-300, 391-400, 491-500, 591-600, use the Restatement (Second) of Judgments (1980). Using the index in Volume 2, find the section[s] (in Vol. 1 or 2) that answer[s] or govern[s] the question or subject listed with your problem number. (a) Cite the section[s], and (b) using the Appendix (Vol. 3), list the "Cross References" to "Digest System Key Numbers" (West) for the section[s]. Do not cite illustrations or comments to the section.

91 191 291 391 491 591   Effective date of a final judgment for res judicata purposes.
92 192 292 392 492 592   Whether incapacity generally is a sufficient ground to avoid a judgment entered in a contested action.
93 193 293 393 493 593   General rules governing relief from a judgment obtained by fraud or duress.
94 194 294 394 494 594   Does irregularity in the content of the notice of an action render the notice inadequate if action notice of an action has been given?
95 195 295 395 495 595   Whether a subsequent action by a bailor is precluded by a prior action by the bailee against a third party for interference with ownership or destruction of the property that is the subject of the bailment?
96 196 296 396 496 596   Rules governing arbitration awards.
97 197 297 397 497 597   Effects of a criminal judgment in a subsequent civil action.
98 198 298 398 498 598   When a default judgment will be excused.
99 199 299 399 499 599   Relief from a judgment based on a mistake of law or fact.
100 200 300 400 500 600   Standing to seek relief.

LIBRARY EXERCISE 35. UNITED STATES CONSTITUTION. Find and cite the federal constitutional provision that governs the subject matter listed with your problem number in proper form. Include the clause in your citation, if appropriate. If the subject matter is governed by more than one provision of the Constitution, you may cite any one of them. Use any available source containing an indexed text or topical division of the U.S. Constitution, such as the United States Code Service or the United States Code Annotated.

```
     Problem #                Subject

 1  177 262 385 498 509    Right to bear arms
 2  178 263 386 499 510    Qualifications of senators
 3  179 264 387 500 511    Quartering soldiers
 4  180 265 388 401 512    President of the Senate
 5  181 266 389 402 513    Full Faith and Credit
 6  182 267 390 403 514    Unreasonable searches
 7  183 268 391 404 515    Runaway slaves
 8  184 269 392 405 516    Cruel punishments
 9  185 270 393 406 517    Admission of new states
10  186 271 394 407 518    Bail
11  187 272 395 408 519    Privileges and immunities
12  188 273 396 409 520    Original jurisdiction of Supreme Court
13  189 274 397 410 521    Punishment of treason
14  190 275 398 411 522    Powers reserved to states
15  191 276 399 412 523    Income tax
16  192 277 400 413 524    Women suffrage
17  193 278 301 414 525    Power of Congress to tax
18  194 279 302 415 526    Post Offices
19  195 280 303 416 527    Patents
20  196 281 304 417 528    Unreasonable seizures
21  197 282 305 418 529    Copyrights
22  198 283 306 419 530    Naturalization
23  199 284 307 420 531    Postal roads
24  200 285 308 421 532    Bankruptcy
25  101 286 309 422 533    Habeas corpus
26  102 287 310 423 534    Congress' power to borrow
27  103 288 311 424 535    Bill of attainder
28  104 289 312 425 536    Repeal of 18th Amendment
29  105 290 313 426 537    Coinage
30  106 291 314 427 538    Ex post facto laws
31  107 292 315 428 539    Commander in Chief
32  108 293 316 429 540    Titles of nobility
33  109 294 317 430 541    Weights and measures
34  110 295 318 431 542    Suits against states - restriction
35  111 296 319 432 543    Slavery prohibited
36  112 297 320 433 544    Counterfeiting
37  113 298 321 434 545    Preference of ports
38  114 299 322 435 546    Amendment of the Constitution
39  115 300 323 436 547    Delivery of fugitives
40  116 201 324 437 548    Just compensation for taking
41  117 202 325 438 549    18-year-old voting
42  118 203 326 439 550    Provision for a Navy
43  119 204 327 440 551    Regulation of commerce with Indians
44  120 205 328 440 552    Letters of Marque and Reprisal
45  121 206 329 442 553    Presents from foreign states
46  122 207 330 443 554    Tax on exports from states
47  123 208 331 444 555    Establishment of religion
48  124 209 332 445 556    Supremacy Clause
49  125 210 333 446 557    Freedom of the press
50  126 211 334 447 558    Pardons
51  127 212 335 448 559    Petitioning for redress
52  128 213 336 449 560    Legislative power vested in Congress
53  129 214 337 450 561    Right to assemble peaceably
54  130 215 338 451 562    Freedom of speech
55  131 216 339 452 563    Probable cause for warrants
56  132 217 340 453 564    Unusual punishments
57  133 218 341 454 565    Trial by jury - $20
```

Problem #						Subject
58	134	219	342	455	566	Speedy and public trial
59	135	220	343	456	567	President - oath of office
60	136	221	344	457	568	Double jeopardy
61	137	222	345	458	569	Excessive fines
62	138	223	346	459	570	Confrontation of witnesses
63	139	224	347	460	571	Equal protection of laws
64	140	225	348	461	572	Involuntary servitude abolished
65	141	226	349	462	573	Free exercise of religion
66	142	227	350	463	574	President's power to make treaties
67	143	228	351	464	575	Right to assistance of counsel
68	144	229	352	465	576	Commerce clause
69	145	230	353	466	577	President's duty to receive ambassadors
70	146	231	354	467	578	Witness against oneself
71	147	232	355	468	579	President - at least 35 years old
72	148	233	356	469	580	Compacts with other states
73	149	234	357	470	581	Executive power vested in the President
74	150	235	358	471	582	President's duty to execute the laws faithfully
75	151	236	359	472	583	Nomination of ambassadors
76	152	237	360	473	584	Guarantee of republican form of government
77	153	238	361	474	585	Debts of the Confederacy not to be paid
78	154	239	362	475	586	Right to vote - race not to disqualify
79	155	240	363	476	587	Death of President (amendment)
80	156	241	364	477	588	Impartial jury in criminal trials
81	157	242	365	478	589	Representatives - at least 25 years old
82	158	243	366	479	590	House of Representatives sole power to impeach
83	159	244	367	480	591	Senators - at least 30 years old
84	160	245	368	481	592	Treason - two witnesses
85	161	246	369	482	593	President's State of the Union address
86	162	247	370	483	594	States prohibited from laying tonnage duties
87	163	248	371	484	595	Revenue bills originate in the House of Representatives
88	164	249	372	485	596	Expulsion of a member from Congress
89	165	250	373	486	597	Senators - must be a citizen for 9 years
90	166	251	374	487	598	Representatives - must be a citizen for 7 years
91	167	252	375	488	599	Senate's sole power to try impeachments
92	168	253	376	489	600	Habeas corpus may be suspended during rebellions
93	169	254	377	490	501	Congress' power to make all "necessary and proper" laws
94	170	255	378	491	502	Two-thirds vote for impeachment
95	171	256	379	492	503	Congress' power to declare war
96	172	257	380	493	504	President limited to two terms
97	173	258	381	494	505	Poll tax prohibited as a qualification of electors
98	174	259	382	495	506	Voting shall not be denied on account of sex
99	175	260	383	496	507	Slavery prohibited
100	176	261	384	497	508	Debts prior to adoption of the Constitution valid

Volume 6 Part 5 1955

LIBRARY EXERCISE 36. UNITED STATES TREATIES AND OTHER INTERNATIONAL AGREEMENTS. Cite the agreement that is printed at the volume and page of United States Treaties and Other International Agreements listed below in proper form.

Problem #	Vol.	Page	Problem #	Vol.	Page
1 112 225 345 470 502	1	760	51 162 275 395 420 552	28	8877
2 113 226 346 471 503	2	13	52 163 276 396 421 553	21	2495
3 114 227 347 472 504	2	1554	53 164 277 397 422 554	28	7259
4 115 228 348 473 505	3	379	54 165 278 398 423 555	2	383
5 116 229 349 474 506	28	437	55 166 279 399 424 556	2	1599
6 117 230 350 475 507	3	3767	56 167 280 400 425 557	3	530
7 118 231 351 476 508	4	939	57 168 281 301 426 558	3	2927
8 119 232 352 477 509	30	757	58 169 282 302 427 559	3	3942
9 120 233 353 478 510	5	453	59 170 283 303 428 560	4	116
10 121 234 354 479 511	5	2010	60 171 284 304 429 561	4	1563
11 122 235 355 480 512	5	2143	61 172 285 305 430 562	5	317
12 123 236 356 481 513	6	507	62 173 286 306 431 563	5	1387
13 124 237 357 482 514	6	2023	63 174 287 307 432 564	5	2263
14 125 238 358 483 515	6	2843	64 175 288 308 433 565	28	5471
15 126 239 359 484 516	6	5715	65 176 289 309 434 566	6	2721
16 127 240 360 485 517	7	161	66 177 290 310 435 567	6	2897
17 128 241 361 486 518	7	2234	67 178 291 311 436 568	6	5739
18 129 242 362 487 519	7	2383	68 179 292 312 437 569	28	3694
19 130 243 363 488 520	8	33	69 180 293 313 438 570	7	2047
20 131 244 364 489 521	8	2447	70 181 294 314 439 571	7	3467
21 132 245 365 490 522	9	131	71 182 295 315 440 572	8	26
22 133 246 366 491 523	10	1	72 183 296 316 441 573	8	2343
23 134 247 367 492 524	10	2087	73 184 297 317 442 574	9	601
24 135 248 368 493 525	10	3014	74 185 298 318 443 575	10	13
25 136 249 369 494 526	29	4183	75 186 299 319 444 576	10	1237
26 137 250 370 495 527	11	1330	76 187 300 320 445 577	25	3090
27 138 251 371 496 528	29	2975	77 188 201 321 446 578	27	4039
28 139 252 372 497 529	12	1390	78 189 202 322 447 579	11	1401
29 140 253 373 498 530	12	3181	79 190 203 323 448 580	12	1127
30 141 254 374 499 531	27	2019	80 191 204 324 449 581	12	1703
31 142 255 375 500 532	13	1227	81 192 205 325 450 582	12	3081
32 143 256 376 401 533	13	2711	82 193 206 326 451 583	13	97
33 144 257 377 402 534	14	251	83 194 207 327 452 584	13	2452
34 145 258 378 403 535	14	1547	84 195 208 328 453 585	27	2353
35 146 259 379 404 536	26	687	85 196 209 329 454 586	14	397
36 147 260 380 405 537	15	1982	86 197 210 330 455 587	14	2222
37 148 261 381 406 538	29	501	87 198 211 331 456 588	15	153
38 149 262 382 407 539	16	1183	88 199 212 332 457 589	15	1439
39 150 263 383 408 540	17	570	89 200 213 333 458 590	27	975
40 151 264 384 409 541	17	1412	90 101 214 334 459 591	26	2905
41 152 265 385 410 542	18	384	91 102 215 335 460 592	26	1674
42 153 266 386 411 543	18	1257	92 103 216 336 461 593	17	2171
43 154 267 387 412 544	18	2503	93 104 217 337 462 594	18	558
44 155 268 388 413 545	19	4568	94 105 218 338 463 595	18	1268
45 156 269 389 414 546	19	5836	95 106 219 339 464 596	18	2510
46 157 270 390 415 547	19	7809	96 107 220 340 465 597	19	5211
47 158 271 391 416 548	20	334	97 108 221 341 466 598	19	5900
48 159 272 392 417 549	28	2167	98 109 222 342 467 599	23	3501
49 160 273 393 418 550	20	3017	99 110 223 343 468 600	26	800
50 161 274 394 419 551	21	403	100 111 224 344 469 501	20	2720

[6 UST] ISRAEL

Surplus Agricultural Commodities

Signed at Washington November 10, 1955
Entered into force November 10, 1955
TIAS 3429

LIBRARY EXERCISE 37. UNITED STATES STATUTES AT LARGE. Using the identifying information given for your problem number, find the statute in United States Statutes at Large. Cite the statute to Statutes at Large in proper form. No reference should be made to the United States Code nor should the subsequent history of the statute (e.g., amendment, repeal, etc.) be noted for this exercise.

Problem #					Identifying Information
1	128	210	322	411	590	86 Stat. 117, Pub. L. No. 92-269
2	129	211	323	412	591	85 Stat. 391, Pub. L. No. 92-140
3	130	212	324	413	592	84 Stat. 1660, Pub. L. No. 91-600
4	131	213	325	414	593	84 Stat. 450, Pub. L. No. 91-351
5	132	214	326	415	594	90 Stat. 2407, Pub. L. No. 94-503
6	133	215	327	416	595	82 Stat. 1345, Pub. L. No. 90-634
7	134	216	328	417	596	90 Stat. 529, Pub. L. No. 94-294
8	135	217	329	418	597	80 Stat. 268, Pub. L. No. 89-495
9	136	218	330	419	598	79 Stat. 653, Pub. L. No. 89-171
10	137	219	331	420	599	78 Stat. 437, Pub. L. No. 88-428
11	138	220	332	421	600	77 Stat. 56, Pub. L. No. 88-38
12	139	221	333	422	501	89 Stat. 679, Pub. L. No. 94-126
13	140	222	334	423	502	75 Stat. 146, Pub. L. No. 87-66
14	141	223	335	424	503	74 Stat. 197, Pub. L. No. 86-503
15	142	224	336	425	504	73 Stat. 470, Pub. L. No. 86-234
16	143	225	337	426	505	72 Stat. 89, Pub. L. No. 85-381
17	144	226	338	427	506	71 Stat. 441, Pub. L. No. 85-172
18	145	227	339	428	507	72 Stat. 614, Pub. L. No. 85-660
19	146	228	340	429	508	69 Stat. 183, ch. 190
20	147	229	341	430	509	68 Stat. 177, ch. 269
21	148	230	342	431	510	67 Stat. 581, ch. 485
22	149	231	343	432	511	66 Stat. 163, ch. 477
23	150	232	344	433	512	65 Stat. 175, ch. 298
24	151	233	345	434	513	91 Stat. 445, Pub. L. No. 95-87
25	152	234	346	435	514	63 Stat. 377, ch. 288
26	153	235	347	436	515	62 Stat. 286, ch. 373
27	154	236	348	437	516	61 Stat. 419, ch. 316
28	155	237	349	438	517	60 Stat. 427, ch. 540
29	156	238	350	439	518	59 Stat. 10, ch. 19
30	157	239	351	440	519	88 Stat. 1978, Pub. L. No. 93-618
31	158	240	352	441	520	58 Stat. 671, ch. 359
32	159	241	353	442	521	56 Stat. 351, ch. 404
33	160	242	354	443	522	55 Stat. 255, ch. 214
34	161	243	355	444	523	54 Stat. 897, ch. 721
35	162	244	356	445	524	53 Stat. 812, ch. 191
36	163	245	357	446	525	52 Stat. 447, ch. 289
37	164	246	358	447	526	50 Stat. 487, ch. 472
38	165	247	359	448	527	51 Stat. 4, ch. 3
39	166	248	360	449	528	49 Stat. 891, ch. 748
40	167	249	361	450	529	48 Stat. 451, ch. 71
41	168	250	362	451	530	47 Stat. 448, ch. 324
42	169	251	363	452	531	46 Stat. 19, ch. 26
43	170	252	364	453	532	45 Stat. 444, ch. 407
44	171	253	365	454	533	44 Stat. 1059, ch. 75
45	172	254	366	455	534	43 Stat. 965, ch. 302
46	173	255	367	456	535	42 Stat. 847, ch. 323
47	174	256	368	457	536	41 Stat. 759, ch. 227
48	175	257	369	458	537	40 Stat. 101, ch. 23
49	176	258	370	459	538	39 Stat. 900, ch. 34
50	177	259	371	460	539	38 Stat. 384, ch. 103
51	178	260	372	461	540	37 Stat. 81, ch. 75
52	179	261	373	462	541	36 Stat. 898, ch. 43
53	180	262	374	463	542	35 Stat. 40, ch. 76
54	181	263	375	464	543	34 Stat. 70, ch. 957
55	182	264	376	465	544	33 Stat. 451, ch. 1761
56	183	265	377	466	545	32 Stat. 786, ch. 338
57	184	266	378	467	546	31 Stat. 3, ch. 7
58	185	267	379	468	547	30 Stat. 416, ch. 339

Problem #						Identifying Information	
59	186	268	380	469	548	29	Stat. 621, ch. 372
60	187	269	381	470	549	28	Stat. 704, ch. 162
61	188	270	382	471	550	27	Stat. 557, ch. 202
62	189	271	383	472	551	26	Stat. 209, ch. 647
63	190	272	384	473	552	25	Stat. 672, ch. 171
64	191	273	385	474	553	24	Stat. 20, ch. 81
65	192	274	386	475	554	23	Stat. 34, ch. 63
66	193	275	387	476	555	22	Stat. 566, ch. 133
67	194	276	388	477	556	21	Stat. 5, ch. 11
68	195	277	389	478	557	20	Stat. 87, ch. 146
69	196	278	390	479	558	19	Stat. 219, ch. 1
70	197	279	391	480	559	18	Stat. 291, ch. 1
71	198	280	392	481	560	90	Stat. 729, Pub. L. No. 94-329
72	199	281	393	482	561	16	Stat. 188, ch. 207 (CCVII)
73	200	282	394	483	562	15	Stat. 125, ch. 186 (CLXXXVI)
74	101	283	395	484	563	14	Stat. 3, ch. 8 (VIII)
75	102	284	396	485	564	91	Stat. 685, Pub. L. No. 95-95
76	103	285	397	486	565	84	Stat. 794, Pub. L. No. 91-378
77	104	286	398	487	566	77	Stat. 473, Pub. L. No. 88-234
78	105	287	399	488	567	76	Stat. 556, Pub. L. No. 87-669
79	106	288	400	489	568	75	Stat. 401, Pub. L. No. 87-164
80	107	289	301	490	569	74	Stat. 397, Pub. L. No. 86-618
81	108	290	302	491	570	73	Stat. 420, Pub. L. No. 86-192
82	109	291	303	492	571	72	Stat. 957, Pub. L. No. 85-793
83	110	292	304	493	572	71	Stat. 607, Pub. L. No. 85-282
84	111	293	305	494	573	71	Stat. 81, Pub. L. No. 85-53
85	112	294	306	495	574	70	Stat. 411, ch. 476
86	113	295	307	496	575	69	Stat. 264, ch. 279
87	114	296	308	497	576	68	Stat. 961, ch. 1074
88	115	297	309	498	577	66	Stat. 579, ch. 669
89	116	298	310	499	578	65	Stat. 189, ch. 303
90	117	299	311	500	579	64	Stat. 773, ch. 906
91	118	300	312	401	580	63	Stat. 621, ch. 486
92	119	201	313	402	581	63	Stat. 157, ch. 176
93	120	202	314	403	582	64	Stat. 832, ch. 946
94	121	203	315	404	583	65	Stat. 131, ch. 275
95	122	204	316	405	584	66	Stat. 634, ch. 755
96	123	205	317	406	585	68	Stat. 495, ch. 553
97	124	206	318	407	586	69	Stat. 533, ch. 572
98	125	207	319	408	587	70	Stat. 668, ch. 742
99	126	208	320	409	588	71	Stat. 45, Pub. L. No. 85-45
100	127	209	321	410	589	73	Stat. 61, Pub. L. No. 86-32

LIBRARY EXERCISE 38. UNITED STATES CODE ANNOTATED. Find the title and section given with your problem number below in West's United States Code Annotated. Using the "Notes of Decisions" in the main part of the volume, (a) answer the question asked and (b) cite the case on which your answer is based in proper form. Do not rely on the form used in the case squib for your citation. Do not indicate the subsequent history of the case in your citation. Cite U.S. Supreme Court decisions to United States Reports only, and do not abbreviate any words in the Memo/Brief form except as specifically provided in Rule 10.2.1(c). Find any needed additional information for the citation by consulting the case in the relevant reporter. If the provision is no longer included in the Code, have another problem assigned.

1 191 207 387 454 514   Under 5 U.S.C. § 553, does a court decision holding that a Board of Parole's rules were invalid on the ground that they were adopted improperly have the effect of retroactively invalidating past Board determinations upon the merits of particular parole cases?
2 192 208 388 455 515   Under 5 U.S.C. § 705, is it an abuse of discretion for a district court to suspend a private antitrust action pending a determination by the Federal Communications Commission of the propriety of a defendant television network's acquisition of a station when the principal issue in the action is whether the acquisition would violate the antitrust laws and the same facts will be reviewed in the administrative proceeding?
3 193 209 389 456 516   Under 5 U.S.C. § 8332, is work with the Civil Works Administration and the Work Projects Administration during the Depression creditable toward retirement from civil service employment?
4 194 210 390 457 517   Under 7 U.S.C. § 1366, when a producer challenges a decision of a review committee upholding the action of a county committee, who has the burden of proof as to fact issues raised by the producer?
5 195 211 391 458 518   Under 8 U.S.C. § 1182, were American Indians excluded by the immigration laws?
6 196 212 392 459 519   Under 8 U.S.C. § 1284, is an alien seaman seeking shore leave from his vessel entitled to an administrative hearing on the determination that he is a mala fide seaman?
7 197 213 393 460 520   Under 8 U.S.C. § 1445, is an alien wife of a citizen of the United States required to make a declaration of intention to become a citizen in connection with her application for citizenship?
8 198 214 394 461 521   Under 10 U.S.C. § 802, can a person accused of a public offense select the tribunal by which he is tried when he is subject to concurrent jurisdiction of military and civil courts?
9 199 215 395 462 522   Under 10 U.S.C. § 1552, are military officers entitled to back pay when their original discharge is illegal?
10 200 216 396 463 523   Under 12 U.S.C. § 86, which establishes a penalty for charging usurious interest, is it a valid defense to the action if it is shown that the defendant sold and assigned the note before maturity in good faith and that it was acting merely as the assignee's agent in collecting it?
11 101 217 397 464 524   Under 12 U.S.C. § 1713, is it within the province of the district court to decide whether a moratorium on a FHA mortgage is in the best interests of the government which is seeking to foreclose the mortgage?
12 102 218 398 465 525   Under 15 U.S.C. § 1, does the fact that the defendant unethically enticed away plaintiff's employees and sought to oppress its own employees whom it presumed had bought stock in its business rival, the plaintiff, in and of itself constitute a violation [of Section 1 of the Sherman Act]?
13 103 219 399 466 526   Under 15 U.S.C. § 2, will a court sanction as lawful block buying under a motion picture license agreement when the pictures were separately priced and each picture was to be sold to the highest duly qualified bidder on a theatre by theatre basis without other conditions?
14 104 220 400 467 527   Under 15 U.S.C. § 13, are retail price fluctuations changing market conditions within the meaning of subsection (c) of Section 13?
15 105 221 301 468 528   Under 15 U.S.C. § 15, is it proper for a Court of Appeals to review the excessiveness or inadequacy of a damage verdict in an antitrust case?
16 106 222 302 469 529   Under 15 U.S.C. § 45, can a court properly review an advisory opinion of the Federal Trade Commission when the same course of action which was the subject of the advisory opinion is also the subject of a cease and desist order issued by the Commission?

17 107 223 303 470 530   Under 15 U.S.C. § 22, are venue and personal jurisdiction virtually congruent?
18 108 224 304 471 531   Under 15 U.S.C. § 77q, is it a violation of the securities fraud provisions for a corporation to lend its credit to another corporation to enable that corporation to make purchases of stock?
19 109 225 305 472 532   Under 15 U.S.C. § 78j, does a showing of plaintiff's contributory negligence justify dismissal of a complaint when the complaint is based on fraud rather than negligence?
20 110 226 306 473 533   Under 15 U.S.C. § 78p, should the "first in, first out rule" be applied to short-swing speculation in corporate securities?
21 111 227 307 474 534   Under 15 U.S.C. § 79k, must a reorganization plan have a provision providing a means of bringing about a fair and equitable distribution of voting power?
22 112 228 308 475 535   Under 15 U.S.C. § 714b, does the Commodity Credit Corporation have the power to subject its property to a warehouseman's lien for storage?
23 113 229 309 476 536   Under 15 U.S.C. § 1052, is "Travelers' insurance" a generic term?
24 114 230 310 477 537   Under 15 U.S.C. § 1114, is the name, "Telicon," a colorable imitation of the name, "Telechron," for trademark infringement purposes?
25 115 231 311 478 538   Is § 1125 of Title 15 of the United States Code intended to prevent the mere act of copying another's label?
26 116 232 312 479 539   Under 16 U.S.C. § 803, what is the primary purpose of subsection (d) of this section (which requires the licensee to establish an amortization reserve account to reflect excess earnings of a hydroelectric project)?
27 117 233 313 480 540   Under 17 U.S.C. § 106, can owners of a number of copyrighted works combine their copyrights through an agreement which would otherwise violate the antitrust laws in order to preserve their property rights under this section?
28 118 234 314 481 541   Under 17 U.S.C. § 107, is the use of citations copied from a previously copyrighted work in support of a new text on the same subject a "fair use" under the copyright laws when the new text is in no part copied from the earlier work and is supplemented with other citations?
29 119 235 315 482 542   Under 18 U.S.C. § 113, is a person a principal for purposes of this section if he is present and encourages the assault and battery?
30 120 236 316 483 543   Under 18 U.S.C. § 203, must the prosecution prove a specific criminal intent, in terms of a conscious purpose of wrongdoing or evil motive?
31 121 237 317 484 544   Under 18 U.S.C. § 371, in order to sustain a conviction for violation of the conspiracy and white slavery statute, is it necessary that the victim of the transportation be innocent of prior sexual misconduct?
32 122 238 318 485 545   Under 18 U.S.C. § 474, would a trial court be abusing its discretion in a counterfeiting prosecution if it refused to grant a mistrial when the prosecutor referred to the defendant's arrest for counterfeiting title certificates and driver's licenses in his opening statement?
33 123 239 319 486 546   Under 18 U.S.C. § 494, is the forgery of a note for the purpose of deceiving a national bank examiner a violation of this section?
34 124 240 320 487 547   Under 18 U.S.C. § 1001, does the entry of a plea of nolo contendre to a charge of receiving money from a federal savings and loan association with the intent to defraud justify disbarment of an attorney?
35 125 241 321 488 548   Under 18 U.S.C. § 1005, is the offense of making false entries in bank officer's reports separate and distinct from the offense of making earlier false entries in the books of the bank for purposes of the (statute of) limitations period?
36 126 242 322 489 549   Under 18 U.S.C. § 1341, does the fact that the defendants proceeded in good faith under the advice of a lawyer constitute an impregnable wall of defense against a charge of mail fraud?
37 127 243 323 490 550   Under 18 U.S.C. § 1461, is a defendant entitled to an acquittal in a prosecution for mailing obscene matter when he does not know that the matter might be characterized as obscene?

38 128 244 324 491 551   Under 18 U.S.C. § 1709, is the issue of whether disclosure of stolen mail by a postal employee was voluntary or forcible a question to be decided by the court or for the jury?
39 129 245 325 492 552   Under 18 U.S.C. § 2113, would evidence showing that the defendant was arrested near the scene of the burglary at 4 a.m. and was wearing clothing containing particles of debris similar to that in the bank that had been burglarized be sufficient to sustain a conviction of aiding and abetting a burglary of a bank?
40 130 246 326 493 553   Under 18 U.S.C. § 2312, will a court of appeals order that a transcript of a closing argument be furnished at government expense when the defendant asserts possible error based upon an alleged prejudicial comment by the prosecutor in that argument?
41 131 247 327 494 554   Under 18 U.S.C. § 2388, formerly section 33 of Title 50, can a person be criminally prosecuted and convicted for his failure to subscribe for liberty bonds?
42 132 248 328 495 555   Under 18 U.S.C. § 3182, is the choice of the method by which extradition proceedings are commenced optional in the demanding state?
43 133 249 329 496 556   Under 18 U.S.C. § 3231, do state courts have jurisdiction over the crime of receiving stolen property belonging to the United States?
44 134 250 330 497 557   Under 18 U.S.C. § 4161, is a prisoner entitled to "good time" credit for the time he was at liberty (without incident) under an erroneous discharge on a writ of habeas corpus procured by him?
45 135 251 331 498 558   Under 19 U.S.C. § 482, do custom authorities waive the right to search persons crossing the border by not searching every person who crosses the border?
46 136 252 332 499 559   Under 19 U.S.C. § 1202, can the uncontradicted testimony of a single, competent, and credible witness be sufficient to discharge the plaintiff's burden of proof in a customs classification case?
47 137 253 333 500 560   Under 46 U.S.C. § 1304, is a "Himalaya" clause void if it attempts to exempt completely noncarriers from liability for negligence?
48 138 254 334 401 561   Does 46 U.S.C. § 682 provide the exclusive remedy (payment of wages) when a seaman is discharged?
49 139 255 335 402 562   Under 21 U.S.C. § 333, is the taxing of costs in a criminal case discretionary with the district court?
50 140 256 336 403 563   Under 21 U.S.C. § 844, is the question whether in a prosecution for illegal possession of narcotics the defendant was insane one to be decided by the court or the jury?
51 141 257 337 404 564   Under 21 U.S.C. § 960, when a search of the defendant at the border is permissible, does the fact that warnings as to the defendant's constitutional rights are not given until after a controlled substance is found require a reversal of a conviction of illegal importation?
52 142 258 338 405 565   Under 21 U.S.C. § 374, are inspectors required to give Miranda warnings advising managers of food warehouses of their rights prior to conducting an administrative inspection when the managers are not in custody?
53 143 259 339 406 566   Under 28 U.S.C. § 1291, is an order denying a motion for a default judgment an appealable order?
54 144 260 340 407 567   Under 28 U.S.C. § 1291, to what is a court of appeals limited in reviewing a Public Utilities Commission's administrative orders?
55 145 261 341 408 568   Under 28 U.S.C. § 1331, do foreign corporations have the right to bring actions against U.S. citizens in federal district courts for causes of action arising under the laws of the United States?
56 146 262 342 409 569   Under 28 U.S.C. § 1331, what is the test for jurisdiction of an action challenging a condemnation proceeding where there are no personal rights involved and an injunction is not sought?
57 147 263 343 410 570   Under 28 U.S.C. § 1332, has it been held that the determination of citizenship is a mixed question of law and fact?
58 148 264 344 411 571   Under 28 U.S.C. § 1332, does a federal court necessarily have jurisdiction to award attorney fees when it has jurisdiction over a minority stockholder's derivative action?
59 149 265 345 412 572   For purposes of 28 U.S.C. § 1335, is the United States considered a citizen of all states when it is a party?
60 150 266 346 413 573   Under 28 U.S.C. § 1341, is it proper for a federal court to enjoin the collection of an illegal state tax when that tax has

clearly punitive qualities and presents such a heavy burden that to decline equitable relief would be to deny judicial review altogether?
61 151 267 347 414 574   Under 28 U.S.C. § 1346, is the United States liable for negligence of its agents if it were to fail to warn herders in an area of anticipated radioactive fallout of planned atomic detonations known to involve substantial danger?
62 152 268 348 415 575   Under 28 U.S.C. § 1346, when a person and his team of mules are in plain view in an open pasture, would it be actionable negligence for a member of the U.S. military to fly a helicopter, which was making a loud noise, directly at and over the person and animals at a height of thirty-five feet?
63 153 269 349 416 576   Under 28 U.S.C. § 1391, in a tenant's action against a landlord for treble damages for rent overcharges pursuant to the Housing and Rent Act, would a district court have venue jurisdiction over the parties if the landlord was a resident of the district in which the federal district court was sitting?
64 154 270 350 417 577   Under 28 U.S.C. § 1391, do the norms prescribed for determining venue for commercial corporations apply with equal validity to charitable corporations?
65 155 271 351 418 578   Under 28 U.S.C. § 1441, is an action to determine ownership of land and federal tax liens properly removable from a state to a federal court when the plaintiff claims payment under the Soil Bank Act and names the Department of Agriculture as a party?
66 156 272 352 419 579   Under 28 U.S.C. § 1441, is there a presumption against jurisdiction in federal court upon removal from a state court?
67 157 273 353 420 580   Under 28 U.S.C. § 1447, does a federal court have the power, on removal of a case from state court, to discharge a testamentary trustee?
68 158 274 354 421 581   Under 28 U.S.C. § 1447, is the issue whether causes of action have been improperly joined a matter for decision by a federal court after the case has been removed from state court?
69 159 275 355 422 582   Under 28 U.S.C. § 1652, in a federal court, does the law of the state where an auctioneer's sale and contract of sale were consummated determine the legal consequences of the auction sale?
70 160 276 356 423 583   Under 49 U.S.C. § 782, does the right to intervene extend to a lienholder of a vehicle when that vehicle may be subject to forfeiture as a result of its use in narcotics violations?
71 161 277 357 424 584   Under 28 U.S.C. § 2111, would an erroneous denial of a motion to quash process be a ground for reversal when the defendant appears and is not prejudiced by the alleged defect in the process?
72 162 278 358 425 585   Under 28 U.S.C. § 2201, was the existence of a cause of action always essential to a bill for declaratory judgment?
73 163 279 359 426 586   Using the notes to 28 U.S.C. § 2243, determine whether at common law a prisoner could traverse the return of a writ of habeas corpus and demand an issue on the legality of his commitment?
74 164 280 360 427 587   Under 28 U.S.C. § 2243, should notice be given to the prosecuting officer when a prisoner is discharged on a habeas corpus writ for an invalid sentence?
75 165 281 361 428 588   Under 28 U.S.C. § 2254, must a state defendant exhaust his remedies on a claim concerning pretrial publicity before seeking federal habeas corpus by either seeking a state habeas corpus proceeding or assigning it as error on appeal?
76 166 282 362 429 589   Under 46 U.S.C. § 971, does an ordinary ship mortgage constitute a maritime lien?
77 167 283 363 430 590   Under 28 U.S.C. § 2255, should the United States be a respondent in a proceeding on a motion in the nature of a writ of error coram nobis attacking a federal conviction?
78 168 284 364 431 591   Under 28 U.S.C. § 2255, does the fact that the petitioner is not represented by nor informed of his right to counsel at the time a juvenile court waives jurisdiction over him entitle him to post-conviction relief?
79 169 285 365 432 592   Does § 2283 of Title 28 of the United States Code preclude the issuance of an injunction in an action to restrain a state court prosecution for the unauthorized practice of law when the United States intervenes on behalf of the plaintiffs because it considers such relief vital to the national interest?

80 170 286 366 433 593   Under 28 U.S.C. § 2284, is there an issue of sovereign immunity when a suit is brought to enjoin the enforcement of state legislative apportionment statutes?
81 171 287 367 434 594   Under 28 U.S.C. § 2674, is the burden of proof upon the defendant in New York if the defense is assumption of risk?
82 172 288 368 435 595   Under 28 U.S.C. § 2674, is the alleged lightening of mink by mutation as a result of disturbance by military aircraft too conjectural and speculative damage to support an award?
83 173 289 369 436 596   Under 29 U.S.C. § 158, is an employer's rule of dress prohibiting the wearing of multiple union badges an unfair labor practice?
84 174 290 370 437 597   Under 29 U.S.C. § 158, is it illegal for an employer, engaged in collective bargaining, to offer a unilateral draft of the contemplated agreement, though such action results in shaping the terms finally agreed upon by the parties?
85 175 291 371 438 598   Under 49 U.S.C. § 1486, may improper venue for review of the Board's orders be waived if an objection is not seasonably asserted?
86 176 292 372 439 599   Under 29 U.S.C. § 160, must the Board conduct a de novo hearing into every unfair labor practice case involving a refusal to bargain?
87 177 293 373 440 600   Under 49 U.S.C. § 1653, is the decision of the Secretary of Transportation authorizing use of federal funds for the construction of an expressway through a public park entitled to a presumption of regularity?
88 178 294 374 441 501   Under 45 U.S.C. § 2, is it the duty of a rail carrier to establish reasonable repair points along its line?
89 179 295 375 442 502   Under 29 U.S.C. § 186, can an employer be a beneficiary of an employee benefit pension trust established under this section?
90 180 296 376 443 503   Under 29 U.S.C. § 203, are telegraph lines that extend through several states instruments of "commerce" for purposes of this section?
91 181 297 377 444 504   Under 29 U.S.C. § 203, is actual physical contact with goods produced for interstate commerce essential to bring a laborer within coverage of this section?
92 182 298 378 445 505   In an action for overtime compensation under 29 U.S.C. § 216, does the fact that the employees participated in making a false record by working before and after they punched their time cards reflect on their credibility as witnesses?
93 183 299 379 446 506   Under 29 U.S.C. § 464, has the legality of union trusteeships been largely a question for the court to determine?
94 184 300 380 447 507   Under 30 U.S.C. § 28, must a prospector take some precaution to protect his location notice from destruction?
95 185 201 381 448 508   Under 31 U.S.C. § 191, are receiver's fees and payment of administration expenses entitled to priority over a debt due the United States in the distribution of an insolvent estate?
96 186 202 382 449 509   Under 33 U.S.C. § 191, must a barge in tow give fog signals?
97 187 203 383 450 510   Under 33 U.S.C. § 409, is a wharfinger's duty to remove a sunken vessel or reasonably warn vessels thereof limited to vessels sunk in the area of land under water actually owned by him?
98 188 204 384 451 511   Under 33 U.S.C. § 905, where neither the owner of the vessel nor demise charterer are personally liable to a longshoreman for unseaworthiness, is a longshoreman entitled to bring a libel proceeding in rem against the vessel?
99 189 205 385 452 512   Under 41 U.S.C. § 16, is the government entitled to recover freight charges paid on goods sold to it under a contract calling for "delivery f.o.b. supply office"?
100 190 206 386 453 513   Under 45 U.S.C. § 56, do state courts have jurisdiction over actions for injuries sustained on board vessels on the high seas?

LIBRARY EXERCISE 39. STATE STATUTES. Using the unofficial or official statutes of the state listed below (unless provided otherwise), find the statutory provision that sets the time period after which the action listed below cannot be brought (limitation of actions). Cite the provision to the statutory compilation you used to find the relevant provision. Check the supplement to the index volume if you have difficulty locating the provision. If you find that the relevant provision has been repealed, have a new problem assigned. Use a pen to write in the section sign in the citation when you are giving typewritten answers and a section sign is not included on the key board.

```
 Problem #                        State/Subject of Action

 1 101 201 301 401 501    Alabama    Equity of redemption (mortgages)
 2 102 202 303 402 502    Alaska    Libel
 3 103 203 303 403 503    Arizona    Foreclosure of a mechanic's lien
 4 104 204 304 404 504    Arkansas    False imprisonment
 5 105 205 305 405 505    California    Libel
 6 106 206 306 406 506    Colorado    Foreclosure of mortgage after taking
                              possession
 7 107 207 307 407 507    Connecticut    Libel
 8 108 208 308 408 508    Delaware    Wrongful death
 9 109 209 309 409 509    Florida    Trespass on real property
10 110 210 310 410 510    Georgia    Breach of covenant restricting land use
11 111 211 311 411 511    Hawaii    Slander
12 112 212 312 412 512    Idaho    Trover
13 113 213 313 413 513    Illinois  Action to enforce contract to make a will
                              (For purposes of this exercise, do not cite the name
                              of the act nor the original section number.)
14 114 214 314 414 514    Indiana    Injury to real property
15 115 215 315 415 515    Iowa    Paternity actions
16 116 216 316 416 516    Kansas    Forcible entry and detention
17 117 217 317 417 517    Kentucky    Breach of contract for sale of goods
18 118 218 318 418 518    Louisana    Land patents ("prescriptive period")
19 119 219 319 419 519    Maine    Contract for sale of goods
20 120 220 320 420 520    Maryland    Libel
21 121 221 321 421 521    Massachusetts    Action by creditor against executor of
                              an estate
22 122 222 322 422 522    Michigan    Malicious prosecution
23 123 223 323 423 523    Minnesota    Libel
24 124 224 324 424 524    Mississippi    Action on unwritten contracts
25 125 225 325 425 525    Missouri    Libel
26 126 226 326 426 526    Montana    False imprisonment
27 127 227 327 427 527    Nebraska    Libel
28 128 228 328 428 528    Nevada    Slander
29 129 229 329 429 529    New Hampshire    Willful trespass
30 130 230 330 430 530    New Jersey    Contracts not under seal
31 131 231 331 431 531    New Mexico    Injury to a person's reputation
32 132 232 332 432 532    New York    Redemption from a mortgage
33 133 233 333 433 533    North Carolina    False imprisonment
34 134 234 334 434 534    North Dakota    Questioning validity of municipal bonds
35 135 235 335 435 535    Ohio    Recovery of personal property
36 136 236 336 436 536    Oklahoma    Oral contract
37 137 237 337 437 537    Oregon    Waste
38 138 238 338 438 538    Connecticut    Action on oral contract
39 139 239 339 439 539    Rhode Island    Wrongful death action brought by
                              beneficiaries
40 140 240 340 440 540    South Carolina    False imprisonment
41 141 241 341 441 541    South Dakota  Recovery of gambling losses (Use S.D.
                              Compiled Laws Annotated)
42 142 242 342 442 542    Tennessee    Libel
43 143 243 343 443 543    Wisconsin    Seduction
44 144 244 344 444 544    Utah    Civil action for seduction
45 145 245 345 445 545    Vermont    Injuries sustained in skiing 46 146 246 346
446 546    Virginia    Suit to avoid a gift
47 147 247 347 447 547    Washington    Slander
48 148 248 348 448 548    West Virginia    Action to recover on a sealed contract
```

Problem #						State/Subject of Action
49	149	249	349	449	549	Wisconsin Assault
50	150	250	350	450	550	Wyoming Trespass on real property
51	151	251	351	451	551	Alabama Libel
52	152	252	352	452	552	Alaska Battery
53	153	253	353	453	553	Arizona Libel
54	154	254	354	454	554	Arkansas Assault
55	155	255	355	455	555	California False imprisonment
56	156	256	356	456	556	Colorado Restraint of trade and commerce involving void contracts
57	157	257	357	457	557	Connecticut Action on a tort
58	158	258	358	458	558	Delaware Waste
59	159	259	359	459	559	Florida Slander
60	160	260	360	460	560	Georgia Action on a promissory note
61	161	261	361	461	561	Hawaii Libel
62	162	262	362	462	562	Idaho Recovery of possession of personal property (Replevin)
63	163	263	363	463	563	Illinois Seduction (For purposes of this exercise, do not cite the name of the act nor the original section number.)
64	164	264	364	464	564	Indiana Contracts not in writing
65	165	265	365	465	565	Iowa Paternity actions
66	166	266	366	466	566	Kansas Contract in writing
67	167	267	367	467	567	Kentucky Malicious prosecution
68	168	268	368	468	568	Louisiana Actions for arrearages of alimony ("prescriptive period")
69	169	269	369	469	569	Maine Assault and battery
70	170	270	370	470	570	Maryland Contracts under seal
71	171	271	371	471	571	Massachusetts Contracts under seal
72	172	272	372	472	572	Michigan Libel
73	173	273	373	473	573	Minnesota False imprisonment
74	174	274	374	474	574	Mississippi Libel
75	175	275	375	475	575	Missouri False imprisonment
76	176	276	376	476	576	Montana Libel
77	177	277	377	477	577	Nebraska Malicious prosecution
78	178	278	378	478	578	Nevada Waste
79	179	279	379	479	579	New Hampshire Trespass to the person
80	180	280	380	480	580	New Jersey Tortious injury to real property
81	181	281	381	481	581	New Mexico Unwritten contracts
82	182	282	382	482	582	New York Wrongful death
83	183	283	383	483	583	North Carolina Libel
84	184	284	384	484	584	North Dakota Action for no-fault insurance benefits
85	185	285	385	485	585	Ohio Trespass to real property
86	186	286	386	486	586	Oklahoma Libel
87	187	287	387	487	587	Oregon Action to cancel a land patent
88	188	288	388	488	588	Wisconsin Replevin (wrongful taking or detention of personal property)
89	189	289	389	489	589	Rhode Island Slander
90	190	290	390	490	590	South Carolina Assault
91	191	291	391	491	591	South Dakota Action on a real property contract (Use S.D. Compiled Laws Annotated)
92	192	292	392	492	592	Tennessee Personal tort actions
93	193	293	393	493	593	Texas Paternity suits
94	194	294	394	494	594	Utah Action for mesne profits of real estate
95	195	295	395	495	595	Vermont False imprisonment
96	196	296	396	496	596	Virginia Distress for rent
97	197	297	397	497	597	Washington Breach of contract for sale under the Washington Uniform Commercial Code
98	198	298	398	498	598	West Virginia Recognizance of bail
99	199	299	399	499	599	Wisconsin False imprisonment
100	200	300	400	500	600	Wyoming Recovery of real estate

JK 416.A3

LIBRARY EXERCISE 40. CODE OF FEDERAL REGULATIONS. Find the provision listed below in the Code of Federal Regulations. Cite the provision in proper form. If the provision no longer appears in the current edition of the Code, complete a different problem for this exercise.

Problem #	Title	Section	Problem #	Title	Section
1 138 258 319 432 512	4	332.30	51 188 208 369 482 562	28	16.203
2 139 259 320 433 513	7	10.2	52 189 209 370 483 563	29	92.50
3 140 260 321 434 514	7	111.42	53 190 210 371 484 564	29	1910.184
4 141 261 322 435 515	7	250.2	54 191 211 372 485 565	29	1951.10
5 142 262 323 436 516	7	724.100	55 192 212 373 486 566	30	77.1300
6 143 263 324 437 517	7	795.3	56 193 213 374 487 567	31	52.61
7 144 264 325 438 518	7	922.27	57 194 214 375 488 568	32	159.4
8 145 265 326 439 519	7	966.14	58 195 215 376 489 569	33	90.3
9 146 266 327 440 520	7	989.210	59 196 216 377 490 570	34	5.61
10 147 267 328 441 521	7	1004.71	60 197 217 378 491 571	32	751.17
11 148 268 329 442 522	7	1098.2	61 198 218 379 492 572	32	852.1
12 149 269 330 443 523	7	1108.8	62 199 219 380 493 573	32	1285.8
13 150 270 331 444 524	7	1464.2	63 200 220 381 494 574	32	1900.11
14 151 271 332 445 525	7	2620.2	64 101 221 382 495 575	32	1600.3
15 152 272 333 446 526	7	2710.5	65 102 222 383 496 576	33	117.561
16 153 273 334 447 527	7	2900.4	66 103 223 384 497 577	33	207.460
17 154 274 335 448 528	9	322.5	67 104 224 385 498 578	33	279.7
18 155 275 336 449 529	9	113.88	68 105 225 386 499 579	35	111.41
19 156 276 337 450 530	10	50.4	69 106 226 387 500 580	36	4.4
20 157 277 338 451 531	10	212.127	70 107 227 388 401 581	37	1.351
21 158 278 339 452 532	13	303.20	71 108 228 389 402 582	38	3.958
22 159 279 340 453 533	14	25.1207	72 109 229 390 403 583	38	21.1021
23 160 280 341 454 534	14	99.3	73 110 230 391 404 584	39	3001.39
24 161 281 342 455 535	14	311.1	74 111 231 392 405 585	40	33.115
25 162 282 343 456 536	14	1213.104	75 112 232 393 406 586	40	52.628
26 163 283 344 457 537	15	371.15	76 113 233 394 407 587	40	86.614
27 164 284 345 458 538	16	5.24	77 114 234 395 408 588	40	141.26
28 165 285 346 459 539	16	303.36	78 115 235 396 409 589	40	416.203
29 166 286 347 460 540	16	1105.9	79 116 236 397 410 590	42	67.115
30 167 287 348 461 541	17	201.2	80 117 237 398 411 591	42	435.1003
31 168 288 349 462 542	18	4.31	81 118 238 399 412 592	43	4.1153
32 169 289 350 463 543	18	159.4	82 119 239 400 413 593	43	2531.1
33 170 290 351 464 544	19	113.38	83 120 240 301 414 594	45	46.107
34 171 291 352 465 545	20	703.304	84 121 241 302 415 595	45	101.133
35 172 292 353 466 546	20	404.1027	85 122 242 303 416 596	45	95.513
36 173 293 354 467 547	20	676.89	86 123 243 304 417 597	45	225.3
37 174 294 355 468 548	21	15.45	87 124 244 305 418 598	45	801.202
38 175 295 356 469 549	21	166.110	88 125 245 306 419 599	47	1.971
39 176 296 357 470 550	21	207.35	89 126 246 307 420 600	47	31.511
40 177 297 358 471 551	21	320.22	90 127 247 308 421 501	47	83.184
41 178 298 359 472 552	21	522.844	91 128 248 309 422 502	49	10.25
42 179 299 360 473 553	21	650.12	92 129 249 310 423 503	49	1084.9
43 180 300 361 474 554	21	1305.09	93 130 250 311 424 504	49	173.306
44 181 201 362 475 555	22	53.2	94 131 251 312 425 505	49	230.0
45 182 202 363 476 556	23	652.5	95 132 252 313 426 506	49	1302.43
46 183 203 364 477 557	24	221.548	96 133 253 314 427 507	50	216.76
47 184 204 365 478 558	24	203.4	97 134 254 315 428 508	15	400.1009
48 185 205 366 479 559	24	800.203	98 135 255 316 429 509	9	381.141
49 186 206 367 480 560	25	160.4	99 136 256 317 430 510	4	332.51
50 187 207 368 481 561	27	211.177	100 137 257 318 431 511	21	1305.08

Pamphlet form next iss. order from the USCA & USCO.

ISLE 33

88

LIBRARY EXERCISE 41. FEDERAL ADMINISTRATIVE DECISIONS. Cite the decision that begins on the page listed below in the designated volume of <u>Federal Trade Commission Decisions</u> in proper form. Cite only the F.T.C. volume.

Problem #	F.T.C. Vol.	Page	Problem #	F.T.C. Vol.	Page
1 168 224 342 437 586	91	751	51 118 274 392 487 536	51	734
2 169 225 343 438 587	2	202	52 119 275 393 488 537	52	619
3 170 226 344 439 588	3	345	53 120 276 394 489 538	53	466
4 171 227 345 440 589	89	531	54 121 277 395 490 539	54	769
5 172 228 346 441 590	5	257	55 122 278 396 491 540	55	1337
6 173 229 347 442 591	6	267	56 123 279 397 492 541	56	862
7 174 230 348 443 592	7	426	57 124 280 398 493 542	57	841
8 175 231 349 444 593	8	400	58 125 281 399 494 543	58	576
9 176 232 350 445 594	9	391	59 126 282 400 495 544	59	780
10 177 233 351 446 595	10	265	60 127 283 301 496 545	60	694
11 178 234 352 447 596	11	181	61 128 284 302 497 546	61	534
12 179 235 353 448 597	12	303	62 129 285 303 498 547	62	1215
13 180 236 354 449 598	89	255	63 130 286 304 499 548	63	1164
14 181 237 355 450 599	14	361	64 131 287 305 500 549	64	629
15 182 238 356 451 600	15	385	65 132 288 306 401 550	65	225
16 183 239 357 452 501	16	393	66 133 289 307 402 551	66	655
17 184 240 358 453 502	17	101	67 134 290 308 403 552	67	744
18 185 241 359 454 503	18	151	68 135 291 309 404 553	68	281
19 186 242 360 455 504	19	187	69 136 292 310 405 554	69	667
20 187 243 361 456 505	20	468	70 137 293 311 406 555	90	406
21 188 244 362 457 506	21	637	71 138 294 312 407 556	71	817
22 189 245 363 458 507	90	328	72 139 295 313 408 557	72	875
23 190 246 364 459 508	23	849	73 140 296 314 409 558	73	835
24 191 247 365 460 509	24	697	74 141 297 315 410 559	74	324
25 192 248 366 461 510	25	1019	75 142 298 316 411 560	75	803
26 193 249 367 462 511	26	852	76 143 299 317 412 561	76	502
27 194 250 368 463 512	27	994	77 144 300 318 413 562	76	464
28 195 251 369 464 513	28	1176	78 145 201 319 414 563	77	906
29 196 252 370 465 514	29	590	79 146 202 320 415 564	77	456
30 197 253 371 466 515	30	647	80 147 203 321 416 565	78	1428
31 198 254 372 467 516	31	742	81 148 204 322 417 566	91	869
32 199 255 373 468 517	32	686	82 149 205 323 418 567	79	518
33 200 256 374 469 518	33	1234	83 150 206 324 419 568	79	667
34 101 257 375 470 519	34	921	84 151 207 325 420 569	80	653
35 102 258 376 471 520	35	569	85 152 208 326 421 570	94	236
36 103 259 377 472 521	36	577	86 153 209 327 422 571	81	567
37 104 260 378 473 522	37	440	87 154 210 328 423 572	81	344
38 105 261 379 474 523	38	279	88 155 211 329 424 573	82	391
39 106 262 380 475 524	39	425	89 156 212 330 425 574	82	1025
40 107 263 381 476 525	40	484	90 157 213 331 426 575	83	696
41 108 264 382 477 526	41	177	91 158 214 332 427 576	84	748
42 109 265 383 478 527	42	165	92 159 215 333 428 577	84	547
43 110 266 384 479 528	43	623	93 160 216 334 429 578	85	237
44 111 267 385 480 529	44	878	94 161 217 335 430 579	85	207
45 112 268 386 481 530	45	502	95 162 218 336 431 580	86	860
46 113 269 387 482 531	46	755	96 163 219 337 432 581	86	425
47 114 270 388 483 532	47	449	97 164 220 338 433 582	87	68
48 115 271 389 484 533	48	999	98 165 221 339 434 583	87	299
49 116 272 390 485 534	49	1284	99 166 222 340 435 584	88	279
50 117 273 391 486 535	50	555	100 167 223 341 436 585	88	546

89

LIBRARY EXERCISE 42. FEDERAL RULES OF CIVIL PROCEDURE. Using the current Federal Rules of Civil Procedure, cite the current rule provision[s] that govern[s] or answer[s] the subject or question listed with your problem number. Note that you are not required to answer the question itself as part of your answer. Current rules can be found in West's Federal Rules pamphlet, Moore's Federal Rules pamphlet, and numerous other sources. Include the relevant subdivision of the rule in your answer, when appropriate.

1 126 292 348 459 513   General rule stating that opposing affidavits may be served not later than one day before a hearing unless the court permits otherwise.
2 127 293 349 460 514   Number of days within which a responsive pleading must be filed after service of an amended pleading.
3 128 294 350 461 515   Must a motion for a more definite pleading be made before a responsive pleading is filed?
4 129 295 351 462 516   Number of days service by mail adds to the period computed from time of service.
5 130 296 352 463 517   Requirement that if a party intends to raise an issue concerning the law of a foreign country, he must include a such notice in his pleading.
6 131 297 353 464 518   Time when requests for jury instructions may be made to the court.
7 132 298 354 465 519   Do the rules allow for the submission of special verdicts to the jury?
8 133 299 355 466 520   May alternate jurors replace disqualified jurors after the jury retires to deliberate?
9 134 300 356 467 521   Is there a time limit on the correction of clerical mistakes in a judgment or order?
10 135 201 357 468 522   Must the complaint be filed at the commencement of a civil action?
11 136 202 358 469 523   Time period after the entry of a judgment or order a motion for relief from that judgment or order may be filed when the basis of the motion is fraud?
12 137 203 359 470 524   When a supersedeas bond becomes effective.
13 138 204 360 471 525   When requests for admissions may be served on the plaintiff and the defendant.
14 139 205 361 472 526   Must the complaint be served with the summons?
15 140 206 362 473 527   Time period within which motions for a new trial must be served after entry of a judgment.
16 141 207 363 474 528   Are averments of time in pleadings considered to be material?
17 142 208 364 475 529   Time when objections to jury instructions must be made.
18 143 209 365 476 530   Time period an answer to a cross-claim must be filed.
19 144 210 366 477 531   Number of days notice that must be given before taxation of costs.
20 145 211 367 478 532   Time when motions to strike from pleadings may be filed.
21 146 212 368 479 533   Upon the death of a public officer who is a party to a pending action, is his successor automatically substituted?
22 147 213 369 480 534   Rules are to be construed to secure just, speedy, and inexpensive determination of every action.
23 148 214 370 481 535   Number of forms of action under the Federal Rules of Civil Procedure.
24 149 215 371 482 536   When does the clerk issue the summons?
25 150 216 372 483 537   When the period of time prescribed or allowed under the Rules is less than seven days, are Saturdays and Sundays counted in the computation?
26 151 217 373 484 538   May the court strike a pleading if a party fails to furnish a more definite statement as required by the court?
27 152 218 374 485 539   Is service required on parties in default for failure to appear in the suit?
28 153 219 375 486 540   Time period within which a motion for relief from a judgment or order must be made when the motion is based on newly discovered evidence.

Civ. R. 59(B)

29 154 220 376 487 541   Time when a judgment or order becomes effective according to the Rules.
30 155 221 377 488 542   Number of times a pleading may be amended, if any, as a matter of course before a responsive pleading is served.
31 156 222 378 489 543   Time period within which an answer to a notice of condemnation must be filed.
32 157 223 379 490 544   May a party amend a pleading at any time with the written consent of the adverse party or by leave of court?
33 158 224 380 491 545   Manner for service of the complaint and summons upon an infant or an incompetent person under the Rules.
34 159 225 381 492 546   Time period within which a response to requested admissions must be made.
35 160 226 382 493 547   Are U.S. marshals authorized by the Rules to serve process?
36 161 227 383 494 548   Must the summons be signed by the clerk before it is served?
37 162 228 384 495 549   Number of days within which an objection must be served after a subpoena duces tecum calling for the inspection and copying of documents has been served.
38 163 229 385 496 550   Number of days notice that must be given before a motion to dissolve or modify a temporary restraining order.
39 164 230 386 497 551   Must a reply to an answer to be filed under the Rules?
40 165 231 387 498 552   When does a temporary restraining order granted without notice automatically expire?
41 166 232 388 499 553   Is a new demand for a jury trial necessary when an action has been removed from a state court to a federal court if such a demand has been made in the state court prior to removal?
42 167 233 389 500 554   Is Columbus Day considered a "holiday" for purposes of the Rules?
43 168 234 390 401 555   Should the time of inspection be included in a request for production and inspection of documents?
44 169 235 391 402 556   How soon after the commencement of an action may interrogatories (to parties) be served on the plaintiff?
45 170 236 392 403 557   Number of days within which answers to interrogatories to parties must be furnished.
46 171 237 393 404 558   Is handing a document to the attorney of a party sufficient service when the Rules permit service to be made upon a party's attorney?
47 172 238 394 405 559   Items that a summons must contain.
48 173 239 395 406 560   May a party amend his pleadings during trial or after judgment to conform with the proof?
49 174 240 396 407 561   In an action against the United States or an officer or agent thereof, number of days a United States Attorney has to file an answer after service of the complaint upon him.
50 175 241 397 408 562   Time period within which a motion to review the taxation of costs must be made.
51 176 242 398 409 563   Do the Rules apply to civil suits in admiralty cases?
52 177 243 399 410 564   Service of a summons, notice, or order on a party who is not an inhabitant of the state or who cannot be found within the state.
53 178 244 400 411 565   Service of summons and complaint upon the United States.
54 179 245 301 412 566   Does failure to make proof of service affect the validity of service under the Rules?
55 180 246 302 413 567   Are "demurrers" for insufficiency of pleading permitted?
56 181 247 303 414 568   Are averments in a pleading (to which a responsive pleading is required) admitted if they are not denied in the responsive pleading?
57 182 248 304 415 569   What a pleading which sets forth a claim for relief should contain.
58 183 249 305 416 570   May a party set forth two or more statements of a claim or defense alternatively or hypothetically in one count or defense?
59 184 250 306 417 571   Is a specific negative averment in a pleading necessary to raise the issue of capacity of a party to be sued?
60 185 251 307 418 572   Must every pleading have a caption?

61 186 252 308 419 573   Must every pleading of a party be signed by at least one attorney of record representing that party?
62 187 253 309 420 574   Rule providing for interpleader.
63 188 254 310 421 575   Is misjoinder of a party a ground for dismissal of an action?
64 189 255 311 422 576   When an applicant will be permitted to intervene as a matter of right.
65 190 256 312 423 577   When a defense of lack of jurisdiction over the person is waived.
66 191 257 313 424 578   Provision permitting the court to strike scandalous matter from a pleading.
67 192 258 314 425 579   Rule provision permitting the filing of a supplemental pleading setting forth transactions which have happened since the date of the pleading sought to be supplemented.
68 193 259 315 426 580   Rule permitting class actions.
69 194 260 316 427 581   Principal rule regulating third-party practice.
70 195 261 317 428 582   Requirement of a short and plain statement of the claim showing that the pleader is entitled to relief.
71 196 262 318 429 583   Rule governing summary judgment.
72 197 263 319 430 584   Must notice be given to the adverse party before a preliminary injunction is issued?
73 198 264 320 431 585   Relation back of amendments.
74 199 265 321 432 586   Allegations to be included in the complaint based upon a derivative action by a shareholder.
75 200 266 322 433 587   Substitution of a party's representative when a party becomes incompetent.
76 101 267 323 434 588   Disability of a judge.
77 102 268 324 435 589   Penalties for filing affidavits in bad faith in conjunction with a summary judgment motion.
78 103 269 325 436 590   Pleading the occurrence of conditions precedent.
79 104 270 326 437 591   Motions for judgment on the pleadings after the pleadings are closed.
80 105 271 327 438 592   Requirement that special damages be pleaded specifically.
81 106 272 328 439 593   Notice of a proposed dismissal of a class action must be given to all members of the class.
82 107 273 329 440 594   Examination of prospective jurors by the court or the parties (or their attorneys).
83 108 274 330 441 595   The circumstances constituting fraud must be pleaded with particularity.
84 109 275 331 442 596   Expenses to be paid by a party improperly failing to admit the genuineness of any document as requested under Rule 36.
85 110 276 332 443 597   Actions brought by or against the members of an unincorporated association.
86 111 277 333 444 598   Malice may be pleaded generally.
87 112 278 334 445 599   Requirement that a pleading setting forth a claim for relief include a short and plain statement of the grounds upon which the court's jurisdiction is based.
88 113 279 335 446 600   In pleading in response to a preceding pleading, a party must set forth affirmatively the defense of an injury by a fellow servant.
89 114 280 336 447 501   Pleadings should be so construed as to do substantial justice.
90 115 281 337 448 502   Existence of another adequate remedy does not preclude a declaratory judgment in cases where it is appropriate.
91 116 282 338 449 503   Motion for a judgment notwithstanding the verdict.
92 117 283 339 450 504   By whom service of process may be made.
93 118 284 340 451 505   Harmless errors not inconsistent with substantial justice.
94 119 285 341 452 506   Parties may stipulate that the jury will consist of less than twelve members.
95 120 286 342 453 507   By whom subpoenas may be served.
96 121 287 343 454 508   When actions pending before the court involve a common question of law, the court may order all the actions consolidated.
97 122 288 344 455 509   In pleading in response to a preceding pleading, a party must set forth affirmatively the defense of laches.

98 123 289 345 456 510   Court may appoint an interpreter for the taking of testimony.
99 124 290 346 457 511   When a motion for directed verdict may be made.
100 125 291 347 458 512   Discovery of the existence of insurance agreements which may satisfy part or all of a judgment entered in the action permitted.

LIBRARY EXERCISE 43. LEGISLATIVE HISTORY OF FEDERAL STATUTES. Using the appropriate volume of West's United States Code Congressional and Administrative News, find the statute described below by consulting the index or popular name table. The date indicated parenthetically is the approximate year of enactment. (a) Cite the statute to the Statutes at Large using the USOC proper form. No reference, however, should be made to the United States Code nor should the subsequent history of the statute be noted for this exercise. (b) State the bill or resolution number of the enacted legislation (e.g., H.R. 9564). No special form is required for your answer to this part. (c) Cite the committee report relating to the legislation listed with your problem number below in proper form. If that report has been reprinted in U.S. Code Congressional and Administrative News, include a parallel reference to the U.S. Code Congressional and Aministrative News in your citation. Indicate missing page numbers for purposes of this exercise by a "___". Note that the first session of Congress occurs in odd-numbered years and the second session occurs in even-numbered years.

Problem #	Statute
1 158 255 328 453 572	Housing Act of 1964 H.R. Rep. No. 1265
2 159 256 329 454 573	Oil Pollution of the Sea (1966) S. Rep. No. 1479
3 160 257 330 455 574	Age Discrimination in Employment (1967) H.R. Rep. No. 805
4 161 258 331 456 575	Wilderness Act (1964) H.R. Rep. No. 1538
5 162 259 332 457 576	Committee on Opportunities for Spanish Speaking People (1969) H.R. Rep. No. 699
6 163 260 333 458 577	Merchant Marine Act of 1970 S. Rep. No. 1080
7 164 261 334 459 578	Revenue Act of 1971 S. Rep. No 437
8 165 262 335 460 579	Ocean Shipping Act of 1978 S. Rep. No. 1260
9 166 263 336 461 580	Vietnam Era Veterans' Readjustment Assistance Act of 1972 S. Rep. No 988
10 167 264 337 462 581	Comprehensive Employment and Training Act of 1973 H.R. Rep. No. 659
11 168 265 338 463 582	Foreign Assistance Act of 1966 H.R. Rep. No. 1651
12 169 266 339 464 583	Employee Retirement Income Security Act of 1974 S. Rep. No. 127
13 170 267 340 465 584	Handicapped Childrens' Education (1975) S. Rep. No. 168
14 171 268 341 466 585	Postal Revenue and Federal Salary Act of 1967 S. Rep. No. 801
15 172 269 342 467 586	Copyrights Act (1976) H.R. Rep. No. 1476
16 173 270 343 468 587	Housing and Urban Development Act of 1968 H.R. Rep. No. 1585
17 174 271 344 469 588	International Development and Food Assistance (1977) H.R. Rep. No. 240
18 175 272 345 470 589	Middle Income Student Assistance Act (1978) H.R. Rep. No. 951
19 176 273 346 571 590	Federal Contested Election Act (1969) S. Rep. No. 546
20 177 274 347 472 591	Bankruptcy - Student Loans (1979) S. Rep. No. 230
21 178 275 348 473 592	Lotteries Transportation of Materials to Foreign Countries (1979) H.R. Rep. No. 230
22 179 276 349 474 593	Newspaper Preservation Act (1970) H.R. Rep. No. 1193
23 180 277 350 475 594	Disqualification of Former Government Employees and Officers (1979) H.R. Rep. No. 115
24 181 278 351 476 595	Suspension of Duties on Metal Waste and Scrap (1978) S. Rep. No. 1243
25 182 279 352 477 596	Emergency Loan Guarantee Act (1971) H.R. Rep. No. 379
26 183 280 353 478 597	Small Business Act (1977) H.R. Rep. No. 1
27 184 281 354 479 598	Federal Rules of Criminal Procedure Amendments (1977) S. Rep. No. 354
28 185 282 355 480 599	Ports and Waterways Safety Act of 1972 S. Rep. No. 724
29 186 283 356 481 600	Voting Rights Act of 1965 H.R. Rep. No. 439

Problem #	Statute
30 187 284 357 482 501	Emergency Medical Services Systems Amendments of 1979 S. Rep. No. 102
31 188 285 358 483 502	Consumer Product Safety Act (1972) S. Rep. No. 835
32 189 286 359 484 503	Social Security Act - Disability Determination (1957) H.R. Rep. No. 277
33 190 287 360 485 504	Vessels - Construction Subsidy (1960) H.R. Rep. No. 1715
34 191 288 361 486 505	Health Programs Extension Act of 1973 H.R. Rep. No. 227
35 192 289 362 487 506	National Banking Laws - Clarification (1959) S. Rep. No. 730
36 193 290 363 488 507	Temporary Unemployment Compensation (1958) S. Rep. No. 1625
37 194 291 364 489 508	Colorado River Basin Salinity Control Act (1974) S. Rep. No. 906
38 195 292 365 490 509	Public Debt Limit Act (1962) S. Rep. No. 1221
39 196 293 366 491 510	Lead-Zinc Producers (1963) S. Rep. No. 239
40 197 294 367 492 511	Energy Policy and Conservation Act (1975) H.R. Rep. No. 340
41 198 295 368 493 512	Energy Policy and Conservation Act (Amendment) (1979) H.R. Rep. No. 510
42 199 296 369 494 513	Pipeline Safety Act of 1979 S. Rep. No. 182
43 200 297 370 495 514	Electric and Hybrid Vehicle Research (1976) H.R. Rep. No. 439
44 101 298 371 496 515	Export Administration Act of 1979 S. Rep. No. 169
45 102 299 372 497 516	Speedy Trial Act Amendments Act of 1979 S. Rep. No. 212
46 103 300 373 498 517	State Veterans' Home Assistance (1977) S. Rep. No. 166
47 104 201 374 499 518	National Consumer Cooperative Bank Act (1978) S. Rep. No. 1211
48 105 202 375 500 519	Airline Deregulation Act of 1978 H.R. Rep. No. 1211
49 106 203 376 401 520	Tribally Controlled Community College Assistance (1978) H.R. Rep. No. 1211
50 107 204 377 402 521	Cigarettes Distribution Racketeering (1978) S. Rep. No. 962
51 108 205 378 403 522	St. Lawrence Seaway Development Corp. (1957) H.R. Rep. No. 473
52 109 206 379 404 523	Diplomatic Relations Act (1978) S. Rep. No. 1108
53 110 207 380 405 524	Federal Hazardous Substances Labeling (1960) H.R. Rep. No. 1961
54 111 208 381 406 525	Labor-Management Reporting Act of 1959 H.R. Rep. No. 741
55 112 209 382 407 526	Nurse Training Act of 1964 S. Rep. No. 1378
56 113 210 383 408 527	District Courts - Jurisdiction (1958) S. Rep. No. 1830
57 114 211 384 409 528	Manpower Development and Training Act of 1962 S. Rep. No. 651
58 114 212 385 410 529	National Foundation on the Arts and Humanities (1965) H.R. Rep. No. 618
59 115 213 386 411 530	Interstate Commerce - Seat Belts (1963) S. Rep. No. 665
60 117 214 387 412 531	Tax Treatment Extension Act of 1977 S. Rep. No. 746
61 118 215 388 413 532	Communication Act Amendments of 1978 S. Rep. No. 580
62 119 216 389 414 533	Airports - Federal Grants (1964) H.R. Rep. No. 1002
63 120 217 390 415 534	Federal Reserve Banks - Gold Reserves (1965) S. Rep. No. 65
64 121 218 391 416 535	Appalachian Regional Development Act of 1965 H.R. Rep. No. 51
65 122 219 392 417 536	Elementary and Secondary Education Act of 1965 S. Rep. No. 146

Problem #	Statute
66 123 220 393 418 537	Excise Tax Reduction Act of 1965 S. Rep. No. 324
67 124 221 394 419 538	Back Pay Act of 1966 S. Rep. No. 1062
68 125 222 395 420 539	Uniform Time Act of 1966 H.R. Rep. No. 1315
69 126 223 396 421 540	Small Business Act - Revolving Funds (1966) H.R. Rep. No. 1348
70 127 224 397 422 541	Marine Resources and Engineering Development Act of 1966 H.R. Rep. No. 1025
71 128 225 398 423 542	Bail Reform Act of 1966 H.R. Rep. No. 1541
72 129 226 399 424 543	Saline Water Conversion Program (1967) S. Rep. No. 219
73 130 227 400 425 544	Military Selective Service Act of 1967 H.R. Rep. No. 267
74 131 228 301 426 545	Mental Health Amendments of 1967 S. Rep. No. 294
75 132 229 302 427 546	Interest Equalization Tax Extension Act of 1967. H.R. Rep. No. 68
76 133 230 303 428 547	Omnibus Crime Control and Safe Streets Act of 1968 S. Rep. No. 1317
77 134 231 304 429 548	Postal Employees - Embezzlement (1968) S. Rep. No. 1317
78 135 232 305 430 549	Aircraft Noise Abatement (1968) S. Rep. No. 1353
79 136 233 306 431 550	Air Carriers - Ownership & Control (1969) S. Rep. No. 185
80 137 234 307 432 551	Securities - Institutional Investors Study (1969) H.R. Rep. No. 501
81 138 235 308 433 552	Educational Television and Radio Amendments of 1969 H.R. Rep. No. 466
82 139 236 309 434 553	Naturalization - Waiting Period (1969) S. Rep. No. 534
83 140 237 310 435 554	Egg Products Inspection Act (1970) H.R. Rep. No. 1670
84 141 238 311 436 555	Seamen's Service Act (1970) S. Rep. No. 1424
85 142 239 312 437 556	Clean Air Amendments of 1970 H.R. Rep. No. 1146
86 143 240 313 438 557	Federal-Aid Highway Act of 1970 H.R. Rep. No. 1554
87 144 241 314 439 558	Emergency Energy Conservation Act of 1979 H.R. Rep. No. 373
88 145 242 315 440 559	Railroad Retirement - Annuities (1971) S. Rep. No. 206
89 146 243 316 441 560	Health Care Benefits - Dependents (1971) H.R. Rep. No. 351
90 147 244 317 442 561	Emergency Loan Guarantee Act (1971) H.R. Rep. No. 379
91 148 245 318 443 562	Atomic Energy Commission - Licenses (1972) H.R. Rep. No. 1027
92 149 246 319 444 563	Education Amendments of 1972 H.R. Rep. No. 554
93 150 247 320 445 564	Civil Defense - Extension (1972) S. Rep. No. 941
94 151 248 321 446 565	Juvenile Delinquency Prevention Act (1972) S. Rep. No. 1003
95 152 249 322 447 566	Economic Stabilization Amendments of 1973 S. Rep. No. 63
96 153 250 323 448 567	Interest Equalization Tax Extension Act of 1973 S. Rep. No. 84
97 154 251 324 449 568	Older Americans Comprehensive Services Amendments of 1973 H.R. Rep. No. 43
98 155 252 325 450 569	Crime Control Act of 1973 H.R. Rep. No. 249
99 156 253 326 451 570	Federal Prisoners - Extension of Confinement Limits (1973) S. Rep. No. 418
100 157 254 327 452 571	Federal Water Pollution Control Act Amendments (1973) H.R. Rep. No. 680

LIBRARY EXERCISE 44. UNITED STATES ATTORNEY GENERAL OPINIONS. Cite the United States Attorney General opinion that begins on the volume and page listed below in proper form.

Problem #	Vol.	Page	Problem #	Vol.	Page
1 168 224 342 417 586	1	368	51 118 274 392 467 536	12	97
2 169 225 343 418 587	2	414	52 119 275 393 468 537	13	135
3 170 226 344 419 588	3	631	53 120 276 394 469 538	14	164
4 171 227 345 420 589	4	523	54 121 277 395 470 539	15	175
5 172 228 346 421 590	5	663	55 122 278 396 471 540	16	271
6 173 229 347 422 591	6	577	56 123 279 397 472 541	17	268
7 174 230 348 423 592	7	652	57 124 280 398 473 542	18	207
8 175 231 349 424 593	8	333	58 125 281 399 474 543	19	181
9 176 232 350 425 594	9	334	59 126 282 400 475 544	20	517
10 177 233 351 426 595	10	382	60 127 283 301 476 545	21	483
11 178 234 352 427 596	11	349	61 128 284 302 477 546	22	383
12 179 235 353 428 597	12	332	62 129 285 303 478 547	23	232
13 180 236 354 429 598	13	481	63 130 286 304 479 548	24	127
14 181 237 355 430 599	14	456	64 131 287 305 480 549	25	89
15 182 238 356 431 600	15	629	65 132 288 306 481 550	26	289
16 183 239 357 432 501	16	489	66 133 289 307 482 551	27	150
17 184 240 358 433 502	17	599	67 134 290 308 483 552	28	201
18 185 241 359 434 503	18	111	68 135 291 309 484 553	29	149
19 186 242 360 435 504	19	676	69 136 292 310 485 554	30	194
20 187 243 361 436 505	20	89	70 137 293 311 486 555	31	282
21 188 244 362 437 506	21	115	71 138 294 312 487 556	32	359
22 189 245 363 438 507	22	589	72 139 295 313 488 557	33	257
23 190 246 364 439 508	23	442	73 140 296 314 489 558	34	376
24 191 247 365 440 509	24	78	74 141 297 315 490 559	35	426
25 192 248 366 441 510	25	59	75 142 298 316 491 560	36	302
26 193 249 367 442 511	26	171	76 143 299 317 492 561	37	435
27 194 250 368 443 512	27	358	77 144 300 318 493 562	38	332
28 195 251 369 444 513	28	366	78 145 201 319 494 563	39	442
29 196 252 370 445 514	29	437	79 146 202 320 495 564	1	473
30 197 253 371 446 515	30	462	80 147 203 321 496 565	2	331
31 198 254 372 447 516	31	216	81 148 204 322 497 566	3	561
32 199 255 373 448 517	32	435	82 149 205 323 498 567	4	415
33 200 256 374 449 518	33	160	83 150 206 324 499 568	5	521
34 101 257 375 450 519	34	162	84 151 207 325 500 569	6	285
35 102 258 376 451 520	35	265	85 152 208 326 401 570	7	523
36 103 259 377 452 521	36	186	86 153 209 327 402 571	8	219
37 104 260 378 453 522	37	204	87 154 210 328 403 572	9	403
38 105 261 379 454 523	38	149	88 155 211 329 404 573	10	261
39 106 262 380 455 524	39	136	89 156 212 330 405 574	11	189
40 107 263 381 456 525	1	302	90 157 213 331 406 575	12	229
41 108 264 382 457 526	2	223	91 158 214 332 407 576	13	336
42 109 265 383 458 527	3	411	92 159 215 333 408 577	14	278
43 110 266 384 459 528	4	378	93 160 216 334 409 578	15	359
44 111 267 385 460 529	5	399	94 161 217 335 410 579	16	269
45 112 268 386 461 530	6	199	95 162 218 336 411 580	17	476
46 113 269 387 462 531	7	338	96 163 219 337 412 581	18	383
47 114 270 388 463 532	8	198	97 164 220 338 413 582	19	477
48 115 271 389 464 533	9	313	98 165 221 339 414 583	20	383
49 116 272 390 465 534	10	171	99 166 222 340 415 584	21	338
50 117 273 391 466 535	11	114	100 167 223 341 416 585	22	531

LIBRARY EXERCISE 45. FORMULATING WESTLAW SEARCH REQUESTS. Assume that (1) you have entered your password, (2) that you have entered your internal file or client identification, and (3) that you have pressed the ENTER key to see a list of the available databases in the WESTLAW service. Assume further that the databases stored in the WESTLAW computer are sufficient to meet the requirements of this exercise. The search queries formulated below should not actually be executed on the WESTLAW terminal. Refer to the discussion and the relevant figures in the Programmed Text in formulating your answers.

(a) Which database would you select to begin a WESTLAW search for the case listed with your problem number in Exercise 32? Give your answer exactly as you would type the database identifier at the terminal. Assume that cases appearing in the first series of a West reporter will be retrieved by West's database identifiers (e.g., assume ATL will retrieve cases appearing in the Atlantic Reporter and the Atlantic Reporter Second).

(b) Assume that you have typed the correct database identifier in part (a) of this exercise and have pressed the ENTER key. After pressing the ENTER key, WESTLAW will display "ENTER QUERY" screen. Formulate a search query using the title field that would retrieve the case listed for your problem number in Exercise 32. Remember to utilize only the appropriate parts of the names of the parties. Note that you want to examine this case only, not cases that cite it.

(c) What would be an easier way to find the case listed for your problem number in Exercise 32? What would you type and enter to do. Remember to give your answer exactly as you would type it.

(d) Formulate a search query that would retrieve cases in which digest paragraphs contain the word authority and the word or phrase listed with your problem number in Exercise 25. Note that you want to search the digest field (containing the case headnotes, topic, title, court, year, citation, key number, and key line of a case) only. Disregard the case name reference in Exercise 25.

(e) Assume that you are searching the CTA (U.S. Courts of Appeals) database. Formulate a search query that would retrieve cases which contain any variant of the basic root of either of the word waiver or the word estoppel and which have been decided after the date listed for your problem number in Exercise 20. Disregard the other references in Exercise 20.

(f) Assume that you are searching the SCT (U.S. Supreme Court) database. Formulate a search query that would retrieve all opinions written by Justice Hugo L. Black that have a digest paragraph classified under the topic and key number listed for your problem number in Exercise 20. Disregard the other references in Exercise 20.

(g) Formulate a search query that would retrieve cases which contain the word or phrase listed with your problem number in Exercise 25 when that word or phrase occurs in the same paragraph with either the word authority or the word influence. Disregard the case name reference in Exercise 25.

(h) Formulate a search request that would retrieve all cases which cite the title and section of the United States Code cited in the question accompanying your problem number in Exercise 38. For purposes of preparing your search request, use a proximity connector for the title and section number. Also include a subject matter word to help insure retrieval of relevant cases only. If an adequate subject matter word is not given in Exercise 38, consult the Code to find such a word.

(i) Assume that you want to "insta-cite" the case listed for your problem number in Exercise 7(b). Assume that you are not currently viewing that case. How would you "insta-cite" the case? How would you do so?

(j) Assume that you are currently viewing the case listed for your problem number in Exercise 7(b). How would you "shepardize" that case?

LIBRARY EXERCISE 46. FORMULATING LEXIS SEARCH REQUESTS. Assume that you have turned on the LEXIS terminal, transmitted your personal identification number, that you have identified the client or the matter, and the list of available LEXIS libraries has appeared on the display screen. Assume further that the libraries stored in the LEXIS computer are sufficient to meet the requirements of this exercise. Give your answers exactly as you would type them at the terminal. The search requests formulated below should not actually be executed on the LEXIS terminal.

(a) Assuming that you have selected the proper library and file, formulate a search request that would retrieve the case listed for your problem number in Exercise 32. Limit your search to the NAME segment, and include only the appropriate parts of the names of the parties. Note that you want to examine this case only, not cases that have cited it.

(b) Assume that you have found a reference to the <u>Federal Reporter</u> citation listed with your problem number in part (a) of Exercise 7. Assume that you have selected the GENFED (General Federal) Library and are searching the USAPP File. Formulate a search request that would retrieve this case (assuming it is a United States Court of Appeals decision). Note that you want to examine this case only, not cases that have cited it. Limit your search to the CITE segment.

(c) What is a faster and more efficient way to retrieve the case listed with your problem number in part (a) of Exercise 7? Describe what you would do or type?

(d) Assume that you have selected the GENFED (General Federal) Library and are searching the DIST (District Courts) file. Formulate one search request that would retrieve cases which contain any variant of the basic root of either the word <u>waiver</u> or the word <u>estoppel</u>, which have been decided by a federal district court sitting in the state listed for your problem number in Exercise 20, and which have been decided after the year listed for your problem number in Exercise 20. Note that your search request should retrieve only cases that satisfy all of the above criteria.

(e) Assume that you have selected the GENFED (General Federal) Library and are searching the US (U.S. Rpts.) file. Formulate a search request that would retrieve all opinions written by either former Chief Justice Harlan F. Stone or former Justice Hugo L. Black on the topic or phrase listed for your problem number in Exercise 28. Disregard the section reference in Exercise 28.

(f) Formulate a search request that would retrieve all cases that cite the title and section of the <u>United States Code</u> noted for your problem number in Exercise 38. For purposes of preparing your search request, use a proximity connector and do not omit the title number. Also include a subject matter word to help insure retrieval of relevant cases only. If an adequate subject matter word is not given in Exercise 38, consult the <u>Code</u> to find such a word.

(g) Assume that you want to find the parallel citations for the citation listed with your problem number in Exercise 3 as well as the citation of any case that directly affects its validity as a precedent. Describe exactly how you could do so using the "Auto-Cite" service.

(h) Describe exactly what you would do to "shepardize" the case listed for your problem number in Exercise 7(b). Assume that you want to limit the Shepard's display to those cases that have explained headnote 1 or 2 of that case.

(i) Assume that you want to modify your search request after the computer has displayed the number of cases found through Level 1 to require that the cases retrieved in Level 2 not contain the words <u>mandamus</u> or <u>prohibition</u>.

Notes

Notes

Notes

Notes

Notes

Notes

Notes

Notes

Notes